BECOMING WORLD WISE

BECOMING WORLD WISE

A GUIDE TO GLOBAL LEARNING

Richard Slimbach

Sty/us

STERLING, VIRGINIA

Sty/us

COPYRIGHT © 2010 BY STYLUS
PUBLISHING, LLC.

Published by Stylus Publishing, LLC
22883 Quicksilver Drive
Sterling, Virginia 20166-2102

Library of Congress Cataloging-in-Publication Data
Slimbach, Richard, 1952–
    Becoming world wise : a guide to global learning /
Richard Slimbach.
        p.   cm.
    Includes index.
    ISBN 978-1-57922-346-5 (cloth : alk. paper)
    ISBN 978-1-57922-347-2 (pbk. : alk. paper)
1. International education.   2. Foreign study.
3. Tourism.   I. Title.
lc1090.S59   2010
370.116—dc22   2009042337

13-digit ISBN: 978-1-57922-346-5 (cloth)
13-digit ISBN: 978-1-57922-347-2 (paper)

Printed in the United States of America

All first editions printed on acid-free paper
that meets the American National Standards Institute
Z39-48 Standard.

Bulk Purchases

Quantity discounts are available for use in workshops
and for staff development.
Call 1-800-232-0223

First Edition, 2010

DEDICATED TO

Donald D. Dorr
1935–2009
colleague—confidant—cosmopolitan
In gratitude for his love of
beauty and truth and justice
and me

CONTENTS

ACKNOWLEDGMENTS

Becoming World Wise weaves together the many strands of my unfinished journey in world learning. I'm deeply grateful for the many people who touched my life in ways that have influenced the reflections shared in the pages of this book.

To pioneers in the fields of social anthropology, international education, global studies, cultural studies, and missiology who taught me to cherish the life of the world. Although their names are too numerous to list, their life example, and published work have guided my own thinking for almost three decades.

To the innumerable people, in far-flung areas of the world, who took the time to befriend and tutor me. Through their generosity of spirit I came to understand a way of being in the world where knowledge and experience, learning and living, become one and the same thing. Their imprint remains on me, and this book.

To the professional "tribes" who contributed ideas and inspiration—especially The Forum on Education Abroad, the Council for International Education Exchange (CIEE), and the Section on U.S. Students Abroad (SECUSSA) of NAFSA Association of International Educators. They continue to open up to a new generation the special kind of wisdom offered through educational travel.

To Leslie Ann Slimbach, life partner for nearly 30 years, whose example of being present with people, in both their pain and their joy, continues to reveal to me the heart and soul of world learning.

To John von Knorring, president of Stylus Publishing, for endorsing the project and lending expert guidance on structure and ideas. To Rachel Jendrzejewski for editing and reacting to chapters while making a life in

Poland. To political cartoonist extraordinaire Polyp (alias Paul Fitz) for the cartoon, and to the United Nations Environment Programme (UNEP) for the diagram—both in chapter 3. To Rebecca Pratt for working her magic on the cover.

Finally, to the hundreds of intrepid global studies students at Azusa Pacific University. Their spirit of discovery and humble respect for that which transcends them continues to inspire hope in the task of "mending" our world. Many of their voices are heard in this text as they attempted to describe intercultural learning experiences that have taken place in over 50 nations since 1995. This book honors them, along with the thousands of other "lordly ones" scattered across the globe.

> There are people everywhere who form a Fourth World, or a diaspora of their own. They are the lordly ones! They come in all colours. They can be Christians or Hindus or Muslims or Jews or pagans or atheists. They can be young or old, men or women, soldiers or pacifists, rich or poor. They may be patriots, but they are never chauvinists. They share with each other, across all the nations, common values of human understanding. When you are among them you know you will not be mocked or resented because they will not care about your race, your faith, your sex or your nationality, and they suffer fools if not gladly, at least sympathetically. They laugh easily. They are easily grateful. They are never mean. They are not inhibited by fashion, public opinion, or political correctness. They are exiles in their own communities, because they are always in a minority, but they form a mighty nation, if they only knew it. It is the nation of nowhere.

> —JAN MORRIS, *Trieste and the Meaning of Nowhere*

INTRODUCTION

AFTER ONLY THREE DAYS in Ho Chi Minh City, Vietnam, I am starting to get antsy. "I want to see the Vietnamese countryside," I explain to my companion as I straddle a rented motorbike and begin a daylong excursion to points north. Because Vietnam has recently opened its doors to outsiders after decades of isolation, I anticipate a rare opportunity to witness a land and its peoples in their pre-commercialized innocence. I'm not disappointed. The shimmering green rice paddies, the coconut palms, the pristine, white-sand beaches, the turquoise waters, and the small food stalls and cafes dotting the sides of the two-lane national highway—the scenery is truly spectacular.

Before reaching the fledgling resort city of Nha Trang, I slow the motorbike and turn off the highway onto a narrow dirt lane. For 10 or 15 minutes the trail leads me past rice fields, house clusters, and the curious gazes of farmers. I catch myself thinking that, just maybe, I'm the first Westerner to be seen by these villagers. Within a few minutes a large thatched hut comes into view, with a mob of locals stuffed inside.

I dismount the bike and shyly approach the hut for a closer look. Being several inches taller than the others, I stoop down to peer inside, curious as to what all the excitement is about. Tables and chairs are filled with young men (only) sipping noodle soup, drinking *Bia Hoi* (a popular Vietnamese beer), and smoking cigarettes. But their attention is singularly focused on one thing: an enormous full-color TV propped up on an old table. My immediate reaction is to wonder how a big-screen happened to wash up on the unspoiled Vietnamese countryside. Is nothing sacred? If that weren't enough, I notice that it's tuned to CNN, broadcasting the daily news—in English!

1

The news continues to run for several minutes before being interrupted by one of the older viewers. He signals to the store owner to switch channels. For the next 15 minutes the hut is filled with MTV, serving up a string of hits by Madonna, Springsteen, and Snoop Dogg. The younger viewers move into orchestrated head and hip movements synchronized to the beat. Their unison lip-synching betrays a common fluency in a universal language—music—with no respect for boundaries. I just stand there, a bit awestruck. Here is a crowd of perhaps 30 monolingual (in Vietnamese) villagers, hardly aware of my presence, fastened on a dream world that got there way before I did.

A World in Motion

This scene helps to illustrate the fact that we live in a world that increasingly escapes our grasp. Rural teenagers in Vietnam are now connected to the people, products, images, and values generated by modern urbanites on the other side of the globe. Cable TV and fiber-optic technologies enable cultural flows that defy the borders of space and culture. Chances are, at least some of those village Vietnamese will eventually find themselves leading a transnational life that stretches across different cities, if not nations. More than likely they will experience a weakening attachment to family and place and gradually branch out, like their counterparts in the West, to create and control their own lives. In a global age, one's life is more nomadic than sedentary. It's spent not behind a plow on a plot of land but in cars and trains, on a cell phone or the Internet, and within cities that house all the nation's peoples, each one discarding old identities and fashioning new ones.

This kind of cultural convergence has led some to question what relevance educational travel might have when the rest of the world appears to be just a reflection of ourselves. In his book *The Naked Tourist*, Lawrence Osborne (2006) laments that there's "nowhere left to go" because "tourism has made the world into a uniform spectacle" with "everyone wandering through an imitation of an imitation" (p. 4). Even prior to the advent of mass tourism, Claude Lévi-Strauss (1955) observed that civilization ceased to be "that delicate flower which was preserved and painstakingly cultivated in one or two sheltered areas of a soil rich in wild species" (p. 38). He pessimistically predicted a monocultural world depleted of authentic peoples and pristine places and, thus, of truly educative experiences.

On the surface, Osborne and Lévi-Strauss appear to be right. Western music, movies, fashions, and technologies are literally *everywhere*, influencing the tastes and aspirations of virtually *everyone* on earth. In fact, there are precious few places on the planet where U.S. culture has not spread, and done so promiscuously. Bangkok and Jakarta now contain new housing developments with names like Orange County and Manhattan Gardens. Pepsi and Coca-Cola ads line the streets of every major city in China. MTV, Macintosh, and McDonald's serve up fast music, fast computers, and fast food to an ever-expanding swath of humanity. Hollywood blockbusters dominate the global movie market. In fact, U.S. corporate culture is so ubiquitous that if you or I were parachuted into a shopping mall after hours in the air, it would take some investigation to know whether we were in Manila or Manhattan, Bangkok or Berlin. Everything from the architectural design and interior décor to store names and shopper "look" would bear such a generic sameness that the mall could literally be anywhere.

Fortunately, the spread of U.S. consumer culture does not tell the whole story. There's abundant evidence to suggest that societies don't uniformly submit to foreign goods and ideas. Those who view Westernization as either a dangerous embrace of corrupting values or a U.S. strategy for world domination will actively *resist* its local reach and influence. Islamicists, for example, ban satellite television in order to restrict global information flows. Others, such as the Arab-language Al Jazeera, Britain's BBC, and the Pacifica radio network in the United States, use new communications technologies to present a view of the world that one doesn't get from Time Warner and Rupert Murdoch. Smaller states and peoples find ingenious ways to defend themselves against the new economic and cultural juggernaut.

Yes, some will actively resist or reject elements of a globalized culture. More often, however, they will fashion new fusions. At the height of the Iraq War, a newspaper photo showed Taliban fighters in Afghanistan toting Kalashnikovs on one arm and a sports bag with a Nike swoosh on the other. Some Europeans may view every Big Mac as an ominous sign of U.S. cultural imperialism, but an institution even as homogenizing as

McDonald's regularly improvises to suit the local context, serving up McFalafels in Egypt and "seaweed burgers" in Japan. In China, instead of leading to the Americanization of tastes, McDonald's set off a boom of local fast-food variations. Beijing's Fastfood Company now has over 1,000 outlets serving Chinese favorites like roasted duck and dumplings. Local consumers don't doubt that they can drink Coke, eat at McDonald's, and sport Nike accessories without "becoming American" in any real sense. The entertainment, food, and fashion industries are becoming more standardized, but without dissolving inherited tastes and traditions. The new combines with and coexists alongside the old.

This is actually good news for those of us still hoping to learn something from journeys abroad. The globalization process appears to be reorganizing and homogenizing 21st-century world cultures without abolishing their distinctiveness. They still are different, but in uniform ways. They have more choices but are often choosing similar things. This is what causes the world's peoples and places to appear, in Pico Iyer's words, "half strange and half strangely familiar." Instead of indulging a sentimental longing for an irrecoverable past, we should treat the complexity of our contemporary situation as offering a "teachable moment" that is truly extraordinary.

No doubt there are areas of the world where a modern worldview has so penetrated the fabric of local society that one rarely seems to encounter cultural strangeness. We should also expect to navigate a "blowback" of resistance produced by the excesses of U.S. popular culture in many traditional areas of Asia and Africa. But risks like these shouldn't discourage us from experiencing peoples and places that exhibit new and unexpected combinations of ideas, identities, and lifestyles. The visual dominance of global chains, Internet cafes, and brand names may seem to be creating a global village whose central shrine is a placeless shopping arcade. But we know better. The Thai or Tibetan teenager listening to hip-hop on an iPod also inhabits a lively and persistent local culture that is full of available wonder for intrepid culture learners. What matters most is not that there are virgin lands awaiting original discovery. What's important is that we should discover things that are new to us and feel the same wonder and elation as if they were new to everyone else.

Pathways to Global Learning

At its best, global learning takes us away from our usual habitat in order to explore the realities of a wider world and our responses to it. Although global learning is often associated with college-level study-abroad programs, there are as many forms of educational travel as there are proverbial roads to Rome.

High-school graduates take a break from the academic grind in order to explore the world and redefine themselves during an adventure-filled "gap" or "bridge" year. Colleges and universities sponsor a dizzying array of education-abroad programs. Short-term religious workers perform sacred service as they build houses, care for orphans, dispense medicines, do peacemaking, and share their faith. Each year Oxfam and the Peace Corps mobilize thousands of volunteers to work in areas ranging from education and the environment to youth outreach and community development. Thousands of others pound nails with Habitat for Humanity, join scientific field expeditions with Earthwatch Institute, and complete English-teaching gigs in far-flung places like Bolivia and Mongolia. Not to mention the thousands of soft-core "volun-tourists," both young and old, who combine the hedonism of tourism with the altruism of service along roads less traveled. In each case, participants can be expected, albeit to different degrees, to apply their unique skills and empathetic ability to enrich human lives and ecosystems.

One of the great joys of educational travel, in whatever form, is to experience familiar things within an unfamiliar context. The very act of moving from one place to another helps create a space where we can bump up against strangeness and reexamine some of the settled assumptions we hold regarding the world—and ourselves. The world becomes a living classroom—a place to watch and wonder, to enter into the experiences and perspectives of others, to communicate across differences, and to use knowledge on behalf of the common good. To be thus "liberated" from the constraints of ignorance and myopia has long been heralded as the aim of a truly liberal education.

Yet, intellectual and ethical development rarely happens by merely learning *about* other peoples and places, through either reading the pages of a book or the viewing of a Blockbuster DVD. It seems to take up-close-and-personal encounters with those of other social worlds to instruct us about our common humanity and our deepest differences, all the while inducing us to live beyond narrow identities and allegiances. When we *do* something with others—live with them, work or study alongside them—we *become* something together. We construct a self that can bridge the chasms that divide us and contribute something of enduring value to others.

Becoming World Wise supports us in the task of rebuilding a common "home," metaphorically speaking, with distant others. Although we may inhabit different geographies, cultures, families, and political systems, we are increasingly bound together by a single fate and shared identity. In a world that is smaller and yet more complex than ever before, our educational challenge is to understand and to value both our differences and our commonalities, our separateness and our togetherness.

This text will assist anyone who is intent on having his or her whole being—body, mind, and heart—stretched through the intercultural experience but who perhaps is unsure about how to prepare for it or fully benefit from it. Special attention, though, is given to the scholarly traveler. Academic study abroad has traditionally attracted undergraduate students eager to learn another culture, another language, and another set of disciplinary perspectives. More recently, international internships and joint work projects have helped students to develop an ethic of care and justice, along with rare insight, into cultural habits and life circumstances radically different from their own.

Education abroad has gradually evolved from the 18th-century Grand Tour–type undertaking, which was restricted to Europe—and elite Europeans—and was more about social credentialing than cultural immersion. Today it features a wild mix of program types and participants, extending to different locations and virtually every academic field. It's possible to study—in English—international business in China, international relations in Brussels, international law in South Africa, public health in Kenya, renewable energy in Iceland, film in India, and art in Florence. Many of these programs are winter (J-term) and summer short courses, making them accessible to nontraditional and working students. Some feature intensive language courses that immerse you in the places where the language is spoken every day—Chinese in Hong Kong, Spanish in Mexico, Arabic in Egypt, Hindi in India, or Swahili in Kenya. Others include international internships, allowing you to work elbow to elbow with indigenous leaders and to obtain an insider's perspective on local realities.

Raising the Bar

Although the *potential* for acquiring a truly global education has never been greater, actually achieving it requires more than simply "being there." Much depends on whether our field experiences are structured in ways that promote meaningful intellectual and intercultural learning. Pressure to satisfy student demand can easily lead to hastily constructed programs that lack focus and clear definition. In such cases, any preparatory training that would help us to interact effectively in our overseas setting tends to drop out. This deficiency has fairly predictable consequences. Without the requisite understandings and skills to learn with and from those in our field setting, we will tend to accumulate novel experiences but without stepping much outside our comfort zones. When this "cocooning" occurs, we can't expect much deep learning to take place.

But the stakes are even higher when we consider the largely untapped potential that global learning has to contribute to the development or "subjective well-being" of local communities. By 2025, the world's population is expected to swell to 8 billion people, with 95 percent of the growth occurring in the southern hemisphere, and mostly in its burgeoning cities. These are the places where economic fortunes are rising but where the gap between the rich and the poor is widening. This is also where environmental health and political security are most threatened.

Not surprising, more and more Western students are choosing to conduct their global-learning terms in this "emerging world." Not only does it host some of the most fascinating cultures and lively economies on earth, but it is also a cultural sphere where persistent local elements are overlaid with outside influences, as my journey into the Vietnamese countryside revealed.

This helps to explain why China has become one of the most desirable learning destinations, hosting over 10,000 U.S. students annually. If the trend continues, it will surpass Britain, Italy, France, Spain, and Australia in popularity. Students sense that places like China, India, and Brazil, no less than England and France, are part of a mixed global future that they need to get their heads and hearts around.

Along with this more eclectic mix of program locations, we find the goals and mission of study abroad also to be "under construction." Students and educators alike are searching for deeper, more meaningful intercultural experiences that respond to the world's novel fusions, as well as its persistent confusions. On one hand, the world's unprecedented level of economic, cultural, and political integration offers dramatic new opportunities for wealth creation, cultural exchange, and cross-national cooperation. On the other hand, our "globalized" world, fueled by notions of limitless progress and prosperity, is becoming more economically divided, more socially isolated, and more culturally commodified, even as the earth rapidly approaches its carrying capacity. Converging tastes and cross-border migrations may give the world an "it's a small world after all" feel, but that small world is also vulnerable like never before to political nationalism and identity-based violence.

The goal of educational travel is to help us navigate this complex and contradictory world while challenging the limits of our intellectual and intercultural abilities. *Becoming World Wise* serves this goal by casting a vision of global learning that is small enough, immersed enough, ecologically "soft" enough, long enough, connected enough, structured enough, cheap enough, and hope filled enough to support deep changes in our lives, and in the lives of others.

The Common Good

As mentioned previously, one of the central assumptions of this text is that merely learning *about* the world is not enough. Global learning must be not only *in* the world but also *for* it. Educational travel should leave the world a saner, stronger, and more sustainable place. Encouraging signs in this direction can be seen in the explosion of philanthropic travelers, "voluntourists," and service learners. Numbering in the tens of millions, they are contributing time, talent, and treasure to local communities all over the world. This is just one indication of a fundamental shift in education abroad—away from being exclusively a private benefit toward being also a public good.

The opening chapter of *Becoming World Wise* tries to interpret the drive to travel with a conscience. Implicit in this global movement, however, is an issue that strikes to the heart of global learning: how best to balance our educational and self-improvement needs with the developmental needs of destination communities. Without a doubt, short-term study and service abroad carries deep personal satisfactions. But it also runs the risk of unleashing well-meaning but untrained individuals on unsuspecting communities. A flash-in-the-pan, three-weeks-for-humanity approach to education abroad raises serious concerns about the depth and quality of learning, as well as the integrity of any assistance provided. We're left with a defining question: Having generated all this energy to understand and potentially mend the world, how can we actually harness it to protect and positively impact the cultures and environments we visit?

This question circulates throughout the chapters that follow, focusing our attention on how our travel, study, and service abroad can promote the "common good." I use this phrase as a beacon that points us in a particular direction, toward seeing the ultimate goal of our global learning as the healing of a broken world. The idea of the common good, originally articulated by Aristotle and St. Thomas Aquinas, perhaps finds its fullest articulation in the 1948 Universal Declaration of Human Rights. In the Declaration we find a shared moral vision that has stimulated over 60 treaties to protect human rights and countless discussions over global ethics. It offers some of our best grounding to understand the world and address its greatest challenges.

Tenzin Gyatso, the 14th Dalai Lama, reminds us that "humanity is one, and this small planet is our only home" (n.d.). Healing actions can grow only from a humble awareness of being deeply connected with and responsible to the rest of the human and nonhuman universe. Intellectual learning alone rarely fosters this type of solidarity. It seems to require direct, embodied contact that allows us to hear the cries of a distressed creation, to find ways to create local friendships, and to work, side by side, to provide local, modest, but intensely human lifelines. Ultimately, that is why we cross the boundaries of nation, culture, language, religion, and social class: to create what Harvard political scientist Robert Putnam calls "bridging capital"—acts of friendship and solidarity rooted in a common reverence for human dignity, local knowledge, and the moral good. Such acts express the firm hope that our shared humanity, beyond our real differences, provides the necessary foundation for finding common solutions to the threats facing the world today.

How might our global learning be shaped to promote the common good? Much depends on *why* and *how* we leave, and also how we return. Again, that's what makes predeparture training and postsojourn analysis so important. Done well, both processes help us to realize the transformative potential of our journeys. Prefield preparations move us beyond discussions of packing lists and assorted "dos and don'ts" to consider the ultimate purposes and practical learning strategies needed for us to enter deeply into our host culture. The postsojourn process should help us to integrate the experiences and insights from the field into our ongoing academic and personal lives. Both are indispensable points in a single continuum of global learning (Hanratty, 2001; LaBrack, 1993; Summerfield, Sibley, & Stellmaker, 1997).

The need to prepare ourselves, both logistically and intellectually, for our in-field learning becomes all the more critical in light of the trend toward shorter and shorter programs, with more and more of them being conducted in "nontraditional" locations. Developing a nuanced understanding of our host culture, and grasping our potential to either benefit or damage it, takes time and intentionality. Even those with the best intentions can unwittingly impact a society negatively if we are unfamiliar with it. It's up to us, along with the programs that send or sponsor us, to ensure that we "do no harm" abroad. The growing number of campus-based, online, and in-country orientation courses is encouraging evidence that many education-abroad professionals are seeking to do just that (LaBrack, 2003; Paige, Cohen, Lassegard, Chi, & Kappler, 2002; Rhodes, 2008).

Mapping the Journey

The structure of the book intentionally links cross-cultural orientation to reentry concerns. Each of the eight chapters marks a different "leg" of an ever-expanding journey of involving ourselves with the world in order to understand it; to interpret it; and, in whatever ways possible, to mend it.

Chapter 1, "Wise for the World," portrays a divided world, encouraging us to conceive of global learning as an opportunity to form an intercultural bridge between ourselves and distant others.

Chapter 2, "The Story We Need" is more introspective. It asks us to reflect upon the related questions of purpose and meaning—the "why" behind our cross-cultural journeys. It calls for global learning to be grounded in a defining story that imbues it with ultimate intention and transformative potential.

Chapter 3, "The Mindful Traveler," continues the inward journey by examining the motivations, expectations, and cultural habits that frame *how* we travel and affect the places and peoples we visit. We're asked to imagine a traveling style that maximizes the benefits and minimizes the harm to our host communities.

Chapter 4, "Making Preparations," and **Chapter 5**, "Carrying Knowledge," structure a series of practical-planning and informational-research tasks designed to enhance the experience of living and learning within a foreign culture. These tasks include Internet-based travel planning and place- and problem-specific information searches, along with the use of various electronic databases, to compile a set of academic materials to support our field study and service.

Chapter 6, "Living With Paradox," surveys the road of disorienting trials and paradoxes that so often attend our journey. Instead of seeing them as foes to either fight or flee, we're encouraged to use them to amplify our consciousness and call forth new cultural insight.

Chapter 7, "Getting Oriented," offers a basic strategy for acclimating ourselves to a new community. It features a set of information-gathering exercises to become practiced in the basic "arts" of meeting people and discovering their social world.

Chapter 8, "The Journey Home," returns us to the world of the regular day. It explores the highly individualized and often turbulent experience of readjusting to one's home culture after months abroad. This final chapter brings us full circle, from our predeparture preparation to postexperience applications that bestow a boon of world wisdom to others.

Taken together, the chapters that follow offer an integrated design for cross-cultural learning aimed at transforming our consciousness while also contributing to the flourishing of the communities that host us. Although they primarily reference foreign study and service situations, the ideas are just as relevant to intercultural learning within domestic settings. In a "globalized" world, diverse cultures intermingle near and far, at home and abroad.

One final note: Throughout the text, various terms are used to mark distinctions among social norms, political cultures, economic realities, and ethical values. Our use of the terms *West* or *western*, for instance, is meant to refer more to mental borders than to geographic. Being *western* describes a particular *mindset*—one derived from early Greco-Roman and Judeo-Christian culture, and the influence of political and economic institutions that emerged through Enlightenment thought, the scientific and technological "revolutions," and imperial conquest. Compared to other countries and peoples, those that are *western* tend to favor market capitalism, liberal democracy, rationalism, innovation, principles of justice, gender equality, and strong political and military ties to Western Europe and the United States. Though using *western* and *non-western* helps to make sense of hugely complicated realities of culture and power, we do so fully realizing that today's world cannot be neatly divided into sealed-off and completely uniform cultures. All societies are increasingly fragmented between Westernizers and non-Westernizers, rendering the real clash of civilizations, to borrow Samuel Huntington's (1993) famous phrase, more *within* civilizations than between them.

Analogous to the labels *western* and *non-western* are the ideas of *First World* and *Third World*. The notion of a *Third World* gained popularity during the Cold War to distinguish those nations that were neither aligned with the West ("First World") nor with the Soviet Union ("Second World"). With the gradual demise of communism, the term *Second World* fell out of use. However, many practitioners continue to employ the term *Third World* to signify the poverty, marginality, and economic dependency of peoples, nations, regions, and continents in profound contrast to the financial and political power of the First World. More recently, less pejorative-sounding terms have been substituted for *Third World*, including "developing countries," "global South," or "majority world," leaving us with terminological chaos. All of these expressions are used interchangeably in the text, helping us to appreciate the fact that, again, in a globalized world, geographic location is far less important than economic and political relationships, along with real-life conditions. We find that the Third World can just as easily include parts of Los Angeles and rural Korea as it does the Sahel and Karachi.

References

Gyatso, T. (n.d.). *Compassion and the individual.* Retrieved April 2, 2010, from http://www.dalailama.com/messages/compassion

Hanratty, K. (2001). Full circle learning in study abroad. *International Educator,* *10*(3), 28–34.

Huntington, S. (1993). The clash of civilizations? In *Foreign Affairs,* 72(3), 22–49.

LaBrack, B. (1993). The missing linkage: The process of integrating orientation and re-entry. In R. M. Paige (Ed.), *Education for the intercultural experience* (pp. 241–280). Yarmouth, ME: Intercultural Press.

LaBrack, B. (Ed.). (2003). *What's up with culture?* School of International Studies, University of the Pacific. Retrieved December 5, 2009, from http://www.pacific.edu/sis/culture/

Lévi-Strauss, C. (1955). *Tristes tropiques.* New York: Penguin.

Osborne, L. (2006). *The naked tourist.* New York: North Point Press.

Paige, R. M., Cohen, A. D., Lassegard, J., Chi, J. C., & Kappler, B. (2002). *Maximizing study abroad: A students' guide to strategies for language and culture learning and use.* Minneapolis: Center for Advanced Research on Language Acquisition (CARLA), University of Minnesota.

Rhodes, G. (2008). *Global scholar online courses.* The Project for Learning Abroad, Training, and Outreach (PLATO). Retrieved September 15, 2008, from http://globalscholar.us/

Summerfield, E., Sibley, R., & Stellmaker, H. (1997). Predeparture orientation and re-entry programming. In W. Hoffa & J. Person (Eds.), *NAFSA's guide to education abroad for advisers and administrators* (2nd ed., pp. 233–253). Washington, DC: NAFSA Association of International Educators.

WISE FOR THE WORLD

*Wisdom lies in the awakening of the entire soul from the
slumber of its private wants and opinions to awareness
of the common world order.*

—HERACLITUS

I N A N A T T E M P T to help college students think about their responsibility toward others, Princeton ethicist Peter Singer (1997) asks them to imagine that their route to school takes them past a shallow pond.

I say to them, you notice a child has fallen in and appears to be drowning. To wade in and pull the child out would be easy but it will mean that you get your clothes wet and muddy, and by the time you go home and change you will have missed your first class.

I then ask the students: Do you have any obligation to rescue the child? Unanimously, the students say they do. The importance of saving a child so far outweighs the cost of getting one's clothes muddy and missing a class that they refuse to consider it any kind of excuse for not saving the child. Does it make a difference, I ask, that there are other people walking past the pond who would equally be able to rescue the child but are not doing so? No, the students reply, the fact that others are not doing what they ought to do is no reason why I should not do what I ought to do.

Once we are all clear about our obligations to rescue the drowning child in front of us, I ask: Would it make any difference if the child were far away, in another country perhaps, but similarly in danger of death, and equally within your means to save, at no great cost—and absolutely no danger—to yourself? Virtually all agree that distance and nationality make no moral difference to the situation.

At that point Singer points out to his students that we're all very much like that person passing the shallow pond. It's within our power to save lives or reduce great suffering at minimal cost to ourselves. For the cost of a new CD, a week of lattes, or a concert ticket, we can make a life-or-death difference for someone, somewhere in the world.

There may once have been a time when a desire to aid others on the other side of the world could not easily be translated into action. Our sense of involvement with the fate of others was in inverse proportion to the physical distance that separated us. Not anymore. The Internet and television have brought images of suffering in distant lands into our immediate consciousness. Jet transport and the on-the-ground presence of citizens associations and official aid agencies now make it possible to deliver and distribute emergency help within a matter of days. In many cases, all we have to do is pull out a credit card and phone in a donation to Tearfund or the International Red Cross, who will fly in everything from emergency food and medicines to leguminous trees.

If we were students in that class, our initial response to Singer's challenge might be to sound off numerous objections: How can we be certain that our donation will actually get to the people who need it most? Doesn't most aid get distributed on political grounds, not according to need, and then get swallowed up in administrative waste and corruption? In any case, aren't the effects of charity less than a drop in the ocean of humanity? How can it hope to offset geographic handicaps, exploding populations, and unfair terms of trade as the primary drivers of poverty? What point is there in trying to save lives until these root problems are solved? In fact, what assurance do we have that our giving of money, and even voluntary service, won't *worsen* the situation, making the victims more dependent on outside handouts instead of helping them to help themselves?

There are undoubtedly many good reasons why, given all the available talent and treasure, we have yet to make poverty history. But even if a substantial percentage of our donation were wasted by irresponsible bureaucrats or crooked governments, the cost to us is so slight and the potential benefits so great that we would seem to be obliged to give it.

A Drowning Creation

Our awareness of humanity's "shallow ponds" has never been greater, nor has the challenge to our moral intuitions. In part, we have global media networks to thank. A constant flow of information on a drowning creation reaches those of us securely placed on the "high ground" of the global economy. This is a world of walled and gated subdivisions, information highways, corporate careers, and almost endless opportunity to roam a world of difference in a cocoon of sameness 30,000 feet above the ground. Outside are the "other" nomads—the *poor* nomads—who cross borders as economic or environmental refugees. Living as they do in villages or shantytowns, their attempts to rise out of poverty are doomed by an absence of viable livelihoods, cultivatable soil, clean water, and legitimate government.

In 1976 Mahbub ul Haq, a Pakistani official with the World Bank, detailed the cruel divide splitting an affluent North from an impoverished South. "A poverty curtain has descended right across the face of our world," he said, "dividing it materially and philosophically into two different worlds, two separate planets, two unequal humanities—one embarrassingly rich and the other desperately poor" (p. xv). Thankfully, much has changed since ul Haq penned these words. The curtain has been steadily lifting. Virtually all so-called developing countries have adopted market-oriented policies and, in varying degrees, benefited from advancements in telecommunications, information technology, health, and infrastructure. By 2006, the global poverty rate had been cut by nearly 75 percent from 1970 levels (even though, because of population growth over this same period, the actual numbers of the absolutely poor grew). Meanwhile, the offshoring and outsourcing of business functions to manufacturers and service providers abroad has served, in author Thomas Friedman's words, to "flatten" the competitive playing fields between Northern and Southern countries (Friedman, 2006).

But what happens if you are the kind of person, culture, or nation that doesn't "flatten" so easily? Instead of being swift and agile, you move slowly. Instead of networking electronically across borders you live your life largely unplugged. Instead of staying continuously updated with strategic information in order to compete and innovate, you can barely read or find a decent-paying job. For about two billion of humanity, information security, job security, food security, and political security are distant dreams.

In a winner-take-all world, the "losers" get stuck in history. Robert Kaplan (1994), in his prescient *The Atlantic* essay "The Coming Anarchy," quotes Thomas Fraser Homer-Dixon, a global security expert. "Think of a stretch limo in the potholed streets of New York City, where homeless beggars live," writes Dixon. "Inside the limo are the air-conditioned post-industrial regions of North America, Europe, the emerging Pacific Rim, and a few other isolated places, with their trade summitry and computer-information highways. Outside is the rest of mankind, going in a completely different direction." In travels at home and abroad, we traverse this radically bifurcated world—one part well off, well fed, and pampered by technology; the other, larger part condemned to a life that Thomas Hobbes described as "poor, nasty, brutish, and short."

Economic inequality. So, the good news is that the third world has shrunk. Four of the six billion people on the planet live in countries that are developing—some, like China and Brazil, at amazing speed. The bad news is that the gap between the global rich and the global poor continues to widen, both between and within countries. In 1960, the average income in the 10 richest countries was 30 times the average income in the 10 poorest countries. By 1990, it had doubled to 60 times, and by 2000 it was 80 times. The capital income differential is not only increasing but increasingly increasing. Our world has reached the point where, according to the *World Development Report 2007*, "There are around 1 billion people living at the margins of survival on less than US$1 a day, with 2.6 billion—40 percent of the world's population—living on less than US$2 a day" (World Bank, 2006, p. 25). That's half the world living on less than the price of a Starbucks Frappuccino.

Life expectancy. Radical differences in quality of life among the world's peoples are nowhere more shockingly revealed than in life expectancy. Here is where health, job security, income, and environmental risks are all weighed in the balance. What we find is that in the 10 richest countries people live to be, on average, about 80 years old. But in the 10 poorest countries, people can expect to live only about 45 years. And in the most hungry and AIDS-afflicted areas of Africa, the divide is even wider. While the average person born today in Japan and Sweden will live 82 years or more, those born today in Malawi, Botswana, and Swaziland will live fewer than 40 years. Is it right that some children are able to live twice as long as others simply because of an accident of birth?[1]

Nutrition. Or consider levels of nutrition. While 1.6 million people—mostly in advanced industrialized nations—constantly worry about eating too much, over one billion people worry about whether they will be able to eat at all (Food and Agriculture Organization of the United Nations, 2009). This is more than the population of the United States, Canada, and the European Union combined. Contrary to what one might expect, this is not because of food shortages. The problem is one of *access*, not only to food, due to uneven distribution and reduced incomes, but also to nonfood benefits like education, health care, and a healthy living environment. For instance, diarrhea, one of the leading causes of death among the developing world's children, is usually the result of an unclean water supply. A child with diarrhea will be unable to absorb available nutrients and unable to learn well in school. A poor education will ultimately mean poor job prospects and low income, which in turn, predicts poor nutrition.

By contrast, the West has long been associated with the so-called diseases of *affluence*—obesity, diabetes, and cardiovascular disease. In the United States alone, over 65 percent of adults are overweight by international standards, and 26 percent are considered obese. But because of mass urbanization and the globalization of modern food processing and marketing techniques, high-calorie diets and sedentary lifestyles are sweeping the developing world. Fresh (open-air) markets, once the major source of food, are disappearing. In their place are large supermarkets peddling foods high in fat and sugar. Developing nations must now confront not only growing numbers of hungry people, but also epidemic rates of obesity.

Gender inequality. Similarly, gender inequality extends across the globe and often takes wanton and brutal forms. Forced marriage and bride burning are still prevalent throughout the Asian subcontinent. In India, where boys are often considered more valuable than girls, genetic testing of unborn children results in the abortion of an estimated half-million female fetuses each year. Similarly, throughout rural China millions of female infants go unregistered and remain "missing." The resulting imbalance between the sexes has become so severe that over 100 million Chinese men are not able to find a wife. This has spurred the kidnapping and slave trading of poor, mostly young, women for forced "marriages." In fact, the U.S. State Department estimates that upward of 600,000 women are trafficked across national borders worldwide, 70 percent of them for sexual exploitation. And this number doesn't account for the millions of women, some as young as five years old, who are part of the ever-expanding commercial sex trade.

Education. Educationally, the North–South divide only widens. Being able to read, think critically, and make informed choices is not only a key part of mental development; it is also a prerequisite for participating in democratic life. The top billion benefit in both ways as a result of high rates of secondary school graduation and college enrolment. By contrast, the bottom billion entered the 21st century unable to read a book or sign their names. Additionally, upwards of 100 million children throughout the developing world do not regularly attend primary school, the majority of these girls. In a world of enormous wealth, these children are locked out of a basic education by an inherited cycle of disadvantage. Some of the children are needed by their families to fetch water, farm, or care for younger siblings. Others are bonded to labor in some local industry to pay off a family debt. Still others live or make a living on the streets of third world cities, and have little or no access to the formal education system.

Technology. Cell phone and wireless networks may offer some "technological leapfrogging" opportunities for overcoming handicaps in landline infrastructure and reducing the digital divide. But the rapid growth of telecommunications throughout the world masks large regional disparities. Many developing countries have computer and Internet penetration rates that are one hundredth of the rates found in North America and Europe. Although 6 out of 10 people in the United States own a computer, there are fewer than 6 personal computers per 1,000 people in India and only 18 per 100 people in Europe and Central Asia. In sub-Saharan Africa, the divide only widens: U.S. computer use is 550 times that of Ethiopia, for example.

A similar pattern is evident in Internet use. Whereas roughly half of the North American population uses the Internet, only about *one half of 1 percent* of those living in South Asia and sub-Saharan Africa do so

(Chin & Fairlie, 2004). It takes money to buy, use, and repair communications technologies, making per capita income differences an important factor in explaining the global digital divide. But so too are factors like telephone-line density, access to electricity, years of schooling, and illiteracy rates.

Environment. In addition to the human toll, conditions of poverty exact a terrible cost to the environment. Poor people are forced to exploit their natural resources beyond the point of long-term sustainability just to survive in the present. This results in the destruction of millions of acres of forests, grasslands, and wetlands each year, along with the life that moves within them. According to the National Research Council (2008), an average of 100 animal and plant species are driven extinct every 24 hours. Steven Sanderson (2002) of the Wildlife Conservation Society predicts that "within a few decades, orangutans, Asian elephants, Sumatran tigers, Chilean flamingos, Amur leopards, and many other well-known species will likely disappear." However humble, each of these species is a masterpiece of biology, uniquely fitted to its environment. Their loss, along with native habitats, not only will impoverish the entire creation; it will make the world a much more dangerous place. Experts like Homer-Dixon predict that environmental scarcity will be *the* national-security issue of the early 21st century. Unless it is checked and reversed, we can expect to see diseases spread and group conflicts intensify, prompting mass migrations (Homer-Dixon, 2001).

Urban shelter. Under the pressure of urbanization, habitats lost for species of plants and animals become habitats occupied by millions of new city dwellers. By 2025 the earth's population will swell to 8 billion. Some 95 percent of this increase will occur in the poorest regions of the world (Africa and South Asia), and overwhelmingly in their cities. The locus of poverty has irreversibly moved from the countryside to the cities.

Though we've been slow to acknowledge this new demographic fact, the 2003 U.N. Habitat report *The Challenge of Slums* provided something of a wake-up call. In the world it describes, masses of poor people are packing their meagre belongings, abandoning their ancestral lands, and moving to the cities—over 70 million people every year, 1.5 million people per week, 130 people every minute. Already one billion persons—one out of every six—live in slum communities. That figure is expected to mushroom to two billion by 2030, making one out of every four people on the planet a squatter citizen.

Unfortunately, with the supply of unoccupied land largely exhausted, there is no more room to squat. In today's third world slums, would-be squatters are forced to become renters, paying high prices for small, subdivided spaces on properties originally occupied, for free, by other poor migrants. And if searching out adequate shelter wasn't challenge enough, most urban poor must also improvise livelihoods in the "informal sector," as street vendors, cycle taxi drivers, day laborers, and domestics. The result is an entire global social class fundamentally and permanently disconnected from a decent existence, much less the formal world economy.

A Distant World Only?

Our tendency might be to file realities like these under the mental category of a distant "developing world." But media images of stranded, largely Black survivors of the 2005 flooding in New Orleans served to remind us that, even in the nations of the North, the chasm between the places-of-privilege and the places-of-poverty continues to deepen. The signs are both familiar and increasingly widespread:

◊ Communities of affluence contiguous with communities of poverty and crime
◊ Little access to quality schools and affordable health care
◊ Decline of low-skill jobs and devaluation of wage labor
◊ Unaffordable housing and rising homelessness
◊ Pathologically high levels of family breakdown and criminal activity
◊ Minority communities alienated from the dominant English-speaking culture
◊ Spatial concentration and stigmatization of the poor
◊ Deteriorated physical environments
◊ Overburdened infrastructure of water, power, and transportation
◊ Loss of shared hope and transcendent meaning

This "new poverty" coexists with unprecedented affluence in modernizing megacities the world over. The divide is not primarily geographic—

between North America and South Asia, for example. It has to do with basic political and economic relationships that split the "winners" from the "losers" *within* every place. Virtually all of the world's major metropolitan areas host two distinct socioeconomic realities in almost surreal juxtaposition. The one most of us know—designed for privileged forms of human life—features supermalls, luxury condominiums, gated subdivisions (replicas of Los Angeles suburbs), high-rise office towers, trendy restaurants, and wide boulevards lined with exclusive retailers like Ralph Lauren and Tiffany & Co. The "other city," completely off the tourist maps, is marked by substandard or makeshift housing, narrow lanes, piled trash, and corner markets. As the social mixing between the classes occupying these two spheres has declined, so has that hard-to-define social bond known as "trust."

The North–South divide illustrated by these "dual cities" is, according to Columbia University economist Jeff Sachs (2006), *the* central drama of our time, and bridging it, "the homework of our generation." Is Sachs right? Do we, the global rich, owe anything to suffering strangers and ecosystems? Why *should* we feel morally implicated in the problems of gross income inequality, malnutrition, women's education, deforestation, and AIDS—especially when they are affecting people we have never met, with whom we have little in common, and whose consequences will touch us only tangentially, if at all? The aspiration toward "global citizenship" may be valid up to a point, but few of us expect distant "outsiders" to have the same grip on our sympathies and commitments as our nearest and dearest. It's hard to love something as amorphous as "humanity" in the abstract, or to be intimate with billions. Are we left to conclude, then, that we have *no* obligations toward them?

Indeed we do, if only because of the covenant of human solidarity. John Donne memorably expressed it long ago: "No man is an island, entire of itself. . . any man's death diminishes me, because I am involved in mankind; and therefore never send to know for whom the bell tolls; it tolls for thee." There is a common ground for the common good. This explains why most moral philosophers agree that people—all people— have a moral claim to basic human needs, to a life compatible with human freedom and dignity. Conditions that deny people even minimal food, shelter, work, education, and representation deny them the basic resources for a life worth living. Corrective actions on behalf of the "losers" in the new world economy become acts of justice, a global public good.

Like the provision of all such goods, it's difficult to know just who is responsible for making it happen. Many nation-states in the regions of greatest need are, for numerous reasons, failing miserably. And no world government is on the horizon. Decades of top-down "solutions" by development assistance specialists have precious little to show. Even the lending programs of international financial institutions like the International Monetary Fund and World Bank have had only mixed success. Sobering realities like these have led development economists like William Easterly (2007) and Dambisa Moyo (2009) to conclude that what the poor need most are not more grandiose schemes but grassroots opportunities to take charge of their own development.

A central contention in this book is that educational travel has a limited, though profoundly important, contribution to make to peoples' own development. As study-abroad students, international service-learners, missioners, or other outside agents of humanitarian care, we have the rare opportunity to support and strengthen a community-driven process of change. But any participatory role must emerge out of a dynamic learning process. It must be framed by an empathetic grasp of how people in a given setting think—how they make sense of their lives in relation to the complex forces and choices that face them. And it must be rooted in a basic trust in the ability of people, no matter how disadvantaged, to improve their lives. Only then are we on sustainable footing. Only then are we in a position to discover how our skills and knowledge might be utilized in side-by-side solidarity with our community hosts.

The first step in this journey is to venture outside our comfort zones and get involved directly and personally in the lives of others, especially those occupying the margins of society. Our educational goal in these situations is to create respectful and mutually beneficial relationships through which we can hope to better understand a complex and oftentimes heartbreaking global reality. This is the necessary basis for narrowing the distance—both physical and moral—between "us" and "them," thus encouraging a more connected and responsive humanity.

Our journey outward into these unfamiliar social worlds is simultaneously a journey inward. While our experiences may tend to disturb our socially conditioned ways of living and thinking, we also discover new sources of emotional support and world understanding, both through others and within ourselves. High-dissonance experience within a safe, supportive social environment becomes a powerful catalyst for re-examining our identities and loyalties in light of new realities, and from vantage points previously inaccessible to us. Upon returning home, our challenge is to then transform our new consciousness into responsible actions within nearby communities.

Competing Purposes

Of course, we each have intensely personal reasons for traversing new social worlds, and it's not always to assist social change. That's not to say that we aspire to be nothing more than a common-grade tourist or self-indulgent drifter. Like the wandering scholars of medieval times, some of us traverse national and cultural borders with the simple expectation that rubbing up against new places and peoples and ideas will generate a more *global consciousness*. Part pilgrim, part explorer, and part visiting scholar, we may journey abroad to challenge our complacencies and question our assumptions about life elsewhere. In the process, we're invited to transcend the natural impulse to define our selves exclusively in terms of our national and cultural heritage.

Others of us hope a term of global study and service abroad will enhance our *economic competitiveness*. Reports of U.S. college students lagging behind their international counterparts in foreign-language ability and geographic literacy have some of us worried. Likewise do stories of Western corporations "outsourcing" to foreign nationals who are already bilingual, technically adept, and knowledgeable in their fields. A globalized education promises us an enriched resume and a competitive "edge" on potential collaborators and rivals in other parts of the world.

These twin drivers often coexist with an intensely personal agenda of *self-discovery*. Travel allows us to distance ourselves from our homespun social standing and experiment with new identities and life directions. Who do I want to be in this place? What kind of lifestyle do I want to adopt? Within fluid circumstances where our sense of self in relation to the world is much more "up for grabs," we have the opportunity to discover a person we hardly knew at home. Freedom from normal roles is not, however, without its own hazards—one of the most common being the temptation to regress into a childlike fantasy world, what one author describes as "playing queen/king for a day." Instead of earnestly searching for a wider reality, we use travel as a temporary escape *from* reality. For our outward journeys to achieve their transformative potential, we must learn to exercise some vigilance and self-discipline in maintaining a cultural and moral "center."

These are just a few of the many and overlapping reasons to journey abroad. The deeply personal or reward-focused motivations confront us, however, with a basic dilemma: how to study and serve in ways that benefit those in our destination communities when our focus is on what the experience will do for *us*. Upon returning home, we expect our friends and family members to ask us immediately, "How was your trip?" Our somewhat reflexive response might be to emphasize how "forever changed" we are by the amazing places we visited and people we met.

Preserved in our memories of experiences abroad are often some important life lessons, not the least of which is a profound sense of gratitude. The problem is that an exclusive focus on satisfying personal needs tends to eclipse a concern for *why* certain realities exist, *how* our lives may be implicated in those realities, and *what* our basic obligations are. When this happens, the foreign setting easily becomes a pleasant backdrop for an individualistic episode that simply reinforces the already familiar. "Students return from study-abroad programs having seen the world," writes Ben Feinberg (2002), "but the world they return to tell tales about is more often than not the world they already knew, the imaginary world of globalized, postmodern capitalism where everything is already known, everyone speaks the same language, and the outside world keeps its eyes on those of us who come from the center." Feinberg ends with a question aimed at sojourners and educators alike: "Can our programs challenge that perception of the world, instead of allowing it to sink in more deeply?" His answer: "Probably not."

Millennials Rising

That's the bad news. The good news is that many "new generation" travelers are looking for something beyond the pursuit of peak experiences and the satisfaction of personal needs. More and more are venturing off the beaten path of study-abroad-as-usual with a passion to discover meaning in their life by helping to mend the brokenness of the world.

In 2007, author and celebrated *New York Times* journalist Thomas Friedman (2007) criticized young adults as being members of Generation Q, meaning "quiet" and "less radical and politically involved as they need to be" on important social questions. Friedman must have been working off the dominant stereotype of millennials as self-absorbed, entitlement oriented, and commitment averse. The reality, at least from my perspective, is quite different. Far from being silent and disengaged, many of this generation *are* making noise. They're just doing it in small, practical, and intensely local ways.

Every generation is defined by the global events that surround it. The Civil Rights movement, the Cold War, the women's movement, the threat of nuclear weapons, Vietnam—all of these struggles shaped earlier generations. Those born after 1981 have come of age in the shadow of 9/11 and the Iraq War. The burning towers and the growing death toll of war are etched on the generation's collective consciousness. They are also well aware of the cruel divide between the "winners" and the "losers" in the global economy, even if most haven't carefully explored the causes. What they do know, almost intuitively, is that they face an insecure future—one marked by pandemic disease, economic depression, peak oil, proliferating slums, guerilla warfare, and the destructive effects of global warming.

For the rising generation, "global engagement" is less about mass rallies, sit-ins, and social movements aimed at broad social reforms and more about seeing incremental changes in relation to specific issues that they care deeply about. Through international service-learning programs and faith-based mission trips, hundreds of thousands have been exposed to the "other side": malnourished child-scavengers in Mexico, AIDS and tuberculosis sufferers in Africa, girls rescued out of Southeast Asia's sex industry, and homeless women living off the streets in U.S. inner cities. Female millennials seem particularly passionate about the conditions facing third world women and at-risk children. They are moved to action for causes as diverse as human trafficking and environmental education, AIDS orphans and micro-enterprise development. Their activism is

grounded in the fervent belief that they *can* help, consciously and deliber-
ately, to save the world—one donation, one purchase, and one service
project at a time.

This fresh sense of hope and opportunity is spilling over into education
abroad. In 2004, two college students named Michael and Tyler traveled
to the western highlands of Guatemala as part of a field-study program
sponsored by Azusa Pacific University. They spent five months in the
coffee-farming community of Santa Anita, documenting the personal stories of those caught up in corruption, racism, and the terror of Guatemala's 36-year civil war. After returning to campus, they turned these stories
into a video documentary titled *Voice of a Mountain,* which they sell at
screenings held at schools and churches (http://voiceofamountain.com).
Fifty percent of their profits go toward scholarships for the children of
the Santa Anita community.

A year earlier, three young filmmakers from San Diego, fresh out of
college, set out to expose the effects of a 20-year-long war on the children
of northern Uganda. The film *Invisible Children: Rough Cut* was released
shortly after, followed by the founding of Invisible Children, a nonprofit
organization dedicated to raising awareness, funds, and volunteers
through student clubs to build schools in northern Uganda. Their website
(www.invisiblechildren.com) describes them in a way that reflects many
millennials: "We are storytellers. We are visionaries, humanitarians, artists and entrepreneurs. We are individuals—part of a generation eager for
change and willing to pursue it."

As I write this, a cohort of 25 "road scholars" is teamed up with local
citizens in a variety of international service and study projects aimed at
improving community life. Sean is working with traditional healers and
community health workers in Cape Town townships to strengthen the
role of music in raising awareness of HIV/AIDS prevention strategies.
Stevie has joined with local environmentalists in Papua New Guinea to
organize village communities against large-scale development and the
erosion of traditional customs. Holly and Heather are partnered with
national teachers in Central America to provide educational opportunities for primary-school children. Jenna is involved in a joint outreach and
research project with a citizen group in Kolkata working for the rights
and rehabilitation of sex workers and their children. Each of these students, as cultural outsiders under the direction of local leaders, is exploring solutions to some of our most vexing human problems. They see the

realities but also the possibilities. For them, the future isn't inevitable—it can be shaped by compassionate action.

Half a century ago, most young adults were anxious to get out of high school, marry, have children, and start a long-term career. Times have changed. A high-tech, knowledge-based, and globally competitive marketplace requires that they approach their careers with broad experience and marketable skills. Marriage itself is seen as a distant event, to be postponed until all degrees are earned and identity and career issues are settled. That leaves footloose millennials with a wide-open decade—extending between high-school graduation day and the eventual settling down with spouse and house—to discover new places, embrace the unknown, and act in ways that hold out hope for the world.

Bridging the World

What we've described thus far are some of the world's major fractures, along with the emerging generation restless to heal them. We are at a unique moment in history, at the intersection of at least four major developments that carry a fresh sense of hope and possibility for bridging the global gap.

1. *The increased movement of students across borders to study, to serve, and to teach.* Students are increasingly choosing to travel in an educational and altruistic mode in hopes of better empathizing with and practically assisting people in need. The Erasmus and other Socrates/Lifelong Learning programs within the European Union have created international learning opportunities for more than 1 million students, a figure expected to increase by 300 percent by 2015. In the United States, the number of undergraduates studying abroad for academic credit grows by double-digit percentages each year. According to *Open Doors 2007* (Chin & Rajika, 2008), an annual survey of student mobility, the number of Americans studying abroad almost tripled in one decade—from 84,000 in 1997 to 220,000 in 2007. And the Paul Simon Study Abroad Foundation Act, once approved by Congress, hopes to increase that number to 1 million. This would involve *half* of all U.S. undergraduates in foreign study each year.

2. *An emerging global "consensus" on the need to act in ways that reduce absolute poverty and its tragic effects.* The 1990s heralded a new approach to "development," the rallying cry of which was poverty reduction. Of particular influence has been the set of eight Millennium Development Goals, a kind of "blueprint" for global action that was adopted by all 191 member states of the United Nations in 2000 (United Nations, 2009). These goals have served to galvanize an unprecedented level of strategic thinking on behalf of the world's most vulnerable populations. Constituents as diverse as anti-globalization protesters, rock bands, rich-country governments, and indigenous nongovernmental organizations (NGOs) have plans in place to halve extreme ("dollar a day") poverty, reduce the child mortality rate by two thirds, achieve universal primary education, and halt the spread of HIV/AIDS, all by the target date of 2015.

3. *The growth in individual giving—of time, talent, and treasure—to improve life quality around the world.* What the UN described as the "grotesque and dangerous polarization" between the global haves and have-nots has actually served to propel charitable giving to its highest levels ever. By 2012, it's expected to top $300 billion. There may be a variety of motives behind giving money: compassion and paternalism, goodwill and White guilt, public interest and tax deductions. But whatever the reason, transferring some of our disposable income to those with little earning power is one way we feel we can help equalize life chances in an unjustly divided world, and without seriously cramping our personal lifestyle.

A veritable revolution in thinking and practice has especially taken hold among the global nonprofit sector and a wide range of wealthy business leaders, technology entrepreneurs, private equity investors, and political figures. Warren Buffett, Google's Larry Page, and eBay's Pierre and Pam Omidyar have invested hundreds of millions of dollars in organizations extending access to clean water, affordable houses, primary health services, small-business loans, and clean energy. The most celebrated of these new philanthropists are undoubtedly Melinda and Bill Gates, who in 2005 contributed a cool $443 million to fund their foundation's efforts to improve public education and to fight the AIDS and malaria epidemics in Africa. Joining Gates that same year was Bill Clinton, who, following his presidency, formed the Clinton Global Initiative.

In a matter of months he succeeded in getting assorted heads of state, billionaires, and celebrities to commit $46 billion (yes, *billion*) to fix the world's problems. At a more grassroots level, organizations like the San Francisco–based New Global Citizens seek to mobilize the potential of the nearly 71 million new millennials under the age of 25 who collectively control over $211 billion in annual spending and who may see themselves, through their charitable acts, as agents of positive change in the world.

4. *The extraordinary expansion of global travel and tourism, now the single largest segment of the world economy.* Travel of all types has become the planet's largest industry, generating more than 12 percent of global GNP. During the 12-year period between 1990 and 2002, international tourism arrivals grew by 54 percent (about 700 million), and the World Tourism Organization predicts that demand will *double* by 2020 to an incredible 1.6 billion visitors (UNWTO, 2009). Travel encircles the globe through an astonishing integration of sectors—from resort construction and travel tours to guidebook and suntan lotion production—and employs 1 out of every 15 workers across the planet. In fact, the principal occupation of millions of humans is now transporting, feeding, housing, and indulging the whims of the *billion* people who travel internationally each year.

A significant amount of that travel now takes place in the global South. In fact, international tourism arrivals in developing countries have grown by an average of 9.5 percent per year since 1990, compared to 4.6 percent worldwide. Tourism has become the leading service export sector in 24 of the least-developed countries and the first source of foreign exchange earnings in 7.[2] In 11 of the 12 countries that account for 80 percent of those living on less than one dollar a day, tourism either plays a significant role or is rapidly growing.

These four trends coalesce in ways that help us imagine how the goals of educational travel might be wedded to community well-being. The more adventuresome sojourners are already venturing into the so-called nontraditional regions of Asia, Latin America, Africa, and the Middle East. Many hope to broaden their intellectual and cultural horizons while also "doing good" in ways that reduce the vulnerability of the poor. As just one example, in 2007 the Foundation for Sustainable Development fielded 325 collegiate interns who injected more than 125,000 service hours and $650,000 into community-based organizations in the developing world. Might attempts like these to bridge the global gap be the moral and intellectual frontier of education abroad? (See Figure 1.1.)

Efforts in this direction are variously described in the travel literature as "ecotourism," "responsible travel," "community-based tourism," and "altruistic tourism." Though distinct in emphasis, each aims to organize group travel in ways that sustain or enhance the geographic, social, economic, cultural, or spiritual character of a place. Some are "pro-poor" in the sense that they intentionally seek to extend income-generating and cultural-enrichment opportunities to those who find themselves at the "bottom of the pyramid." At the same time, they are "pro-learning" in the sense that they help the nonpoor to escape the tourist ghetto and to build the kind of relational bridges that can help them better understand the trials *and* the treasures of the peoples and places that host them.

As already noted, poverty has many faces. Poverty is lack of secure shelter. Poverty is being sick and not being able to see a doctor. Poverty is losing a child to illness brought about by unclean water. Poverty is not having access to school and not knowing how to read. Poverty is not having a job. Poverty is living one day at a time. Poverty is powerlessness—the lack of political representation and freedom. In short, poverty is a life situation people want to escape.

Educational travel, even when conducted responsibly, can't be expected to reverse these powerful and entrenched conditions. Alone, it won't make poverty history, remedy massive market failure, or stall global warming. Neither will it stabilize population growth or eradicate infectious disease. Human advantage and disadvantage is rooted in an array of inexorable forces—like geography, climate, and labor market shifts—that lie outside anyone's direct control. The complexity of these realities

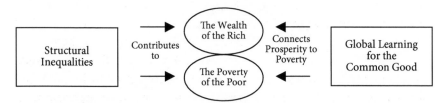

FIGURE 1.1   Bridging the wealth-poverty gap

defies any universal "blueprint" for development or for how we, as global
learners, might best support it. Interventions by outsiders are notoriously
tricky. Our mere presence, much less the funding and building of schools
or health clinics, can easily upset the existing distribution of wealth and
power in host communities. We want to do good, but our actions might
unwittingly generate resentment among some and dependence among
others. Good intentions don't always lead to the desired results.

There's no way around it: tourism, as the world's largest industry, *is*
going to have an impact. The direction of that impact, whether for good
or ill, largely rests with us. As educational travelers, we can choose to
resist the global consumer culture that pervades the travel industry—
distorting our perception of other cultures and the ecosystems that sustain them—and participate in a new culture of sustainability. We can
resolve to craft ventures that minimize the harm and maximize the positive effects on local communities. At this moment of profound economic
and environmental crisis, can we expect to do anything less?

Rethinking "Development"

For a moment, imagine taking up residence in a rural village as part of a
field-research or service-learning project. As yet unfamiliar with the village's internal dynamics, it would be quite natural for us to assume an
easy consensus as to what "development" or "the common good" means
for residents. Stan Burkey (1993) describes this as the "harmony model,"
which outsiders unwittingly project on foreign societies:

> We are received with garlands, smiling faces and friendly handshakes; we
> experience festivals, dancing, weddings, and other occasions where the
> whole community appears to be participating. Wouldn't it be nice to live in
> such lovely harmony with our friends and neighbors instead of the hectic,
> competitive, disassociated urban life to which so many of us are addicted?
> (p. 40)

Within a few short weeks, however, we discover that below the surface
of a homogeneous social structure are power hierarchies, conflicting
interests, and patterns of discrimination and exclusion. Within the single

village community there are peasants and professionals, landless laborers and petty capitalists, government agents and drug mafias. If we were to randomly select 10 people from across these groups and ask them, "What makes for community well-being?" and "What gives meaning to your life together?" we could expect to get 10 different answers. Even if those 10 persons could agree on certain values and interests, they would certainly disagree about their relative priority.

In the final analysis, the individuals or interest groups themselves must judge what a healthy, prosperous, and caring society might look like, but rarely will that judgment be representative of the entire community. At the same time, as foreign students and project volunteers there are ways that we *can* support a process of positive change, especially at the grass-roots level. Much depends on how we position ourselves in relation to the community groups—as listeners more than talkers, learners more than teachers, and facilitators more than leaders.

What we now call "development" has its roots in the verb *to develop*, meaning "to unroll" or "to unfold"—to bring into the open an optimal state of flourishing previously hidden in the folds. A "developing" society was one that progressed from one condition to another, more desirable condition. Traditionally, this idea of positive change was linked to economic growth. A country that moved from underdevelopment to development produced more and more goods and services for national consumption, as well as higher levels of personal savings and international investment. Along with economic change, the national population was expected to undergo a transformation in its underlying worldview and in its core social, economic, and political structures. *Development* thus became synonymous not only with *economic growth* but with Western-style *progress* and *modernization*.

Many assumed that the creation of wealth would easily "make poverty history" wherever it took root. Instead, what emerged was a greater widening of the gap in wealth and power between rich national elites and the rest of society. We witness this growing economic inequality today throughout Europe and North America, but perhaps most starkly in the non-Western world. Here a relatively "advanced" sector geared to the global export market coexists with a relatively "backward" sector oriented toward local needs. These have alternatively been called formal and informal, capitalist and subsistence, modern and traditional. This "dual economy" is most obvious within third world megacities where towering skyscrapers cast dark shadows on teeming shantytowns. Yet, even back in the "developed" West, the remarkable growth in productivity and accumulation of wealth has coincided with record levels of family violence, incarceration, substance addiction, obesity, clinical depression, and income inequality.

What we learn from the experience of non-Western *and* Western societies is that rapid economic growth does not automatically reduce poverty or inequality. Nor does it necessarily increase the participation of the poor in their own development. These defects in the Western way of wealth have led development specialists to redefine "development," "progress," and "the common good" in favor of a broader set of values and relationships between and among virtually all aspects of existence: from the human to the environmental; the psychological to the political; and the spiritual and cultural to the social and economic. It's now common to talk not just about the material assets of a given nation or community but also its "social," "natural," and even "spiritual" forms of wealth (Halpern, 2004; Hawken, 2000; Zohar & Marshall, 2004).

Economic reforms have no doubt helped hundreds of millions of people to build up significant assets, along with the status, honor, and influence that wealth brings. But without strong families and neighborhood associations, healthy ecosystems, and a vibrant spirituality that gives life and ultimate purpose to the entire life system, it is impossible to sustain economic growth or a society that functions for the good of all.

For the third world peasant and slum dweller as much as the average resident of Rome and London, the "common good" is not understood in the abstract. It translates into grounding memories, meaningful work, a livable wage, clean water, food security, a sense of "place" and social connection, access to land or credit, and access to quality schools and life-saving medicines—all with the support of a just public administration. Most important, it emphasizes the *power located within the people themselves* to make decisions that can alter the basic conditions that affect their lives.

The common good does not just happen. It requires the people to decide, and act together, to solve their own problems. As outsiders, we have the opportunity to bridge the global gap by relying on and learning from the expertise, strengths, and collective wisdom of the community. We learn to serve *with* the people without doing things *for* the people.

Acts of solidarity may include investigating the outcomes of delivering sexual and reproductive health education to secondary students, or organizing after-school programs for primary school children. They might involve us in community-wide efforts to provide literacy classes for women, to construct composting toilets, and to get food supplements to malnourished mothers. In each case, we are participants, not principals. We work at the behest of local groups on local projects led by local people addressing local issues with local resources.

Choosing the High Road

The contribution that international study and service can make to bettering the world largely depends on us as individuals, along with the programs that sponsor us. Educational travel, like tourism generally, is ambivalent. Under certain conditions it can enrich the cultural and socioeconomic life of host communities while providing us with unequalled resources for reshaping our world awareness, self-consciousness, and style of life. Under other conditions it can simply be just one more consumer product that we collect with the wealth we've accumulated within a grossly unequal system of "winners" and "losers."

Not surprisingly, prepackaged and consumer-oriented forms of educational travel have steadily come under fire. Almost 50 years ago, Irwin Abrams, a leading authority of the international peace movement, lamented that the "typical study tour" had become "no more than sightseeing with a syllabus." Today, similar concerns surround the pervasive consumerist/entitlement mentality that U.S. students, in particular, export to regions beyond (Engle & Engle, 2003; Ogden, 2008). American students abroad may not have stars-and-stripes patches sewn onto their backpack, or see themselves as having much in common with their "tourist" counterparts on luxury cruises and package tours. But neither are they eager to relinquish many of the comfortable amenities and social networks of home.

A postconsumerist, community-based model of global learning will go far toward dismantling the "Ugly American" or other national caricature that routinely describes foreigners abroad. You know the stereotype: pampered twenty-somethings who leave home with little preparation, arrive at the program site largely clueless, and rarely break away from the exclusive company of other foreigners; who dress and act oblivious to the subtleties of local culture, and judge everything by the standards of home; who hang out in Western-style eateries, party in the international dorms or local clubs, all the while demeaning local ways, which they understand poorly; who use Internet cafes to send dispatches from a "field" they are largely detached from to a "home" that they never really left; who then carry back to campus assorted symbolic reminders of having "been there"—online photo albums, local handicrafts, maybe a Eurail pass— but little of the new cultural knowledge, language ability, and perspective change that marks a well-traveled mind. "Far from experiencing another culture deeply and on its own terms," notes Adam Weinberg (2007) of World Learning, "these students (at best) simply get the American college experience in a different time zone."

"So what?" you might reply. "It's my time and my money. If I want to just enjoy myself, that's my prerogative. After all, what real difference can I make anyway?" We might feel completely justified by the raw facts of life to adopt a "whatever" attitude toward the world, disengaged from caring too much about anything. But within every unfeeling cynic is a closet idealist—one who questions whether there *could* be a higher purpose to life than mere self-indulgence. Rick Blaine is the cynical American expatriate played by Humphrey Bogart in the classic film *Casablanca*. He expresses principled indifference on all issues: "I stick my neck out for nobody" and "The problems of this world are not my account" are his constant refrains. But in the end he acts with moral commitments bigger than himself. He manages, in the words of Martin Luther King, Jr., to "hew out of the mountain of despair a stone of hope."

To rise above a world poisoned by pessimism requires, first off, that we clarify the kind of world we hope for (this will be the subject of chapter 2). The act of creative visioning, in itself, will do much to wean us from what Weinberg (2007) dubs the "low road" approach to global learning. Then, by taking steps to widen our circle of concern, we are free to face the world, not as naive optimists, but as hopeful realists who embrace the triumphs *and* the tribulations of the human experience.

Know that you won't be alone in this quest. The ranks of those looking for a "high road," a way to empathetically navigate the world's complexity, continue to expand. More and more are keen to join the quest for adventure with an instinct for justice, to speak to the world's great challenges with a strong moral voice. Though many are barely adults, they share a conviction voiced by famed playwright-dissident Vaclav Havel as he addressed the joint session of the U.S. Congress in 1990. "We are still incapable of understanding," Havel declared, "that the only genuine backbone of all our actions, if they are to be moral, is responsibility— responsibility to something higher than my family, my country, my company, my success" (quoted in Smith, 1995, p. 108). Is this sense of global responsibility a passing fancy, a mere expression of naive altruism? Or might it be, quite literally, a prime condition of our planet's survival? The answer lies within each of us who venture abroad to make a break with the familiar and discover a wisdom that is distinctively, finally, *for* the world.

FOR REFLECTION AND DISCUSSION

1. Peter Singer suggests that our moral intuitions to assist others are overly influenced by physical proximity, so that we feel much stronger obligations to our families, friends, and fellow citizens than to those thousands of miles away. Do you agree or disagree? What do you think causes us *not* to bring more people into our intimate sphere of concern?
2. Educational travel has typically focused attention on the benefits to the sojourner. Try to imagine your term abroad organized in ways that balance personal benefits with benefits to the host community. What might it look like to travel, not just *to* the world, but also *for* it?

Notes

1. Statistics in this section draw on the following sources: Shaohua Chen and Martin Ravallion, *The Developing World Is Poorer Than We Thought, but No Less Successful in the Fight Against Poverty*, World Bank, Policy Research working paper, no. WPS 4703, August 2008; *The World Health Report 2006: Working Together for Health*, World Health Organization, April 2006; *2007 Human Development Report* (HDR), United Nations Development Program, November 2007;

United Nations Department of Economic and Social Affairs, *Millennium Development Goals Report 2007*, United Nations Publications, August 2007; and *The State of the World's Children 2008: The Women and Children*, UNICEF, January 2008.

2. The list of "least developed countries" includes Afghanistan, Angola, Bangladesh, Benin, Bhutan, Burkina-Faso, Burundi, Cambodia, Cape Verde, Central African Republic, Chad, Comoros, Democratic Republic of the Congo, Djibouti, Equatorial Guinea, Eritrea, Ethiopia, Gambia, Guinea, Guinea-Bissau, Haiti, Kiribati, Lao People's Democratic Republic, Lesotho, Liberia, Madagascar, Malawi, Maldives, Mali, Mauritania, Mozambique, Myanmar, Nepal, Niger, Rwanda, Samoa, São Tomé and Príncipe, Senegal, Sierra Leone, Solomon Islands, Somalia, Sudan, Togo, Tuvalu, Uganda, United Republic of Tanzania, Vanuatu, Yemen, and Zambia.

References

Burkey, S. (1993). *People first: A guide to self-reliant participatory rural development*. London: Zed Books.

Chin, H., & Rajika, B. (2008). *Open doors 2007: Report on international educational exchange*. New York: Institute of International Education.

Chin, M., & Fairlie, R. (2004). *The determinants of the global digital divide: A cross-country analysis of computer and Internet penetration*. Economic Growth Center, Yale University. Retrieved March 29, 2010, from http://www.econ.yale.edu/growth_pdf/cdp881.pdf

Easterly, W. (2007). *The white man's burden: Why the West's efforts to aid the rest have done so much ill and so little good*. New York: Penguin.

Engle, J., & Engle, L. (2003). Neither international nor educative: Study abroad in a time of globalization. In W. Grunzweig & N. Rinehart (Eds.), *Rockin' in Red Square: Critical approaches to international education in the age of cyberculture* (pp. 25–39). London: Lit Verlag.

Feinberg, B. (2002, May 3). Point of view: What students don't learn abroad. *The Chronicle of Higher Education*, B20.

Food and Agriculture Organization of the United Nations. (2009). *1.02 billion people hungry*. Retrieved March 22, 2010, from http://www.fao.org/news/story/en/item/20568/icode/

Friedman, T. (2006). *The world is flat*. New York: Farrar, Straus and Giroux.

Friedman, T. (2007). Generation Q. *The New York Times* (October 10). Retrieved February 9, 2009, from http://www.nytimes.com/2007/10/10/opinion/10friedman.html

Halpern, D. (2004). *Social capital*. Boston: Polity Press.

Hawken, P. (2000). *Natural capitalism*. New York: Back Bay Books.

Homer-Dixon, T. F. (2001). *Environment, scarcity, and violence*. Princeton, NJ: Princeton University Press.

Kaplan, R. (1994, February). The coming anarchy, *The Atlantic*. Retrieved March 20, 2010, from http://www.theatlantic.com/magazine/archive/1994/02/the-coming-anarchy/4670/

Moyo, D. (2009). *Dead aid: Why aid is not working and how there is a better way for Africa*. New York: Farrar, Straus and Giroux.

National Research Council. (2008). *In the light of evolution, volume II: Biodiversity and extinction*. Washington, DC: National Academies Press.

Ogden, A. (2008). The view from the veranda: Understanding today's colonial student. *Frontiers: The Interdisciplinary Journal of Study Abroad, 15*, 35–55.

Sachs, J. (2006, September 14) *The end of poverty—the homework of our generation*." Lecture delivered at the University of Notre Dame, West Bend, IN.

Sanderson, S. (2002). The future of conservation. *Foreign Affairs* (Sept.–Oct.). Retrieved December 10, 2009, from http://www.foreignaffairs.com/articles/58253/steven-sanderson/the-future-of-conservation

Singer, P. (1997, April). The drowning child and the expanding circle. *New Internationalist*. Retrieved January 9, 2010, from http://www.utilitarian.net/singer/by/199704--.htm

Smith, T. (1995). *America's mission*. Princeton, NJ: Princeton University Press.

ul Haq, M. (1976). *The poverty curtain*. New York: Columbia University Press.

United Nations. (2009). *The millennium development goals report 2009*. New York: Author. Retrieved March 15, 2010, from http://www.un.org/millennium goals/

United Nations World Tourism Organization. (2009). *Tourism 2020 vision*. Retrieved January 21, 2010, from http://www.directorytourism.com/articles _28_Tourism-2020-Vision.html

Weinberg, A. (2007, May 8). Quantity or quality in study abroad? *Inside Higher Education*. Retrieved February 2, 2010, from http://www.insidehighered.com/views/2007/05/08/weinberg

World Bank. (2006). *World development report 2007: Development and the next generation*. New York: Author.

Zohar, D., & Marshall, I. (2004). *Spiritual capital: Wealth we can live by*. San Francisco: Berrett-Koehler.

THE STORY WE NEED

*The purpose of education is to show a person how to define
himself authentically and spontaneously in relation to the world.*
—THOMAS MERTON, *Love and Living*

MANY OF US choose to study or serve abroad during a time of intense self-exploration and questioning. Who do I want to be? What do I want to do with my life? What kind of person do I want as a life partner? Where do I want to settle? And why does it even matter?

As life defining as these questions are, only a narrow stratum of global society enjoys the unrestrained time and financial wherewithal to search out answers. For these fortunate few, key transitions like going away to college can offer extended periods to experiment with new living arrangements, new friendships, new majors, new ideas, and new loves. Leaving home for distant locations only intensifies this identity exploration. No longer children but not quite adults, travels abroad can signal something of a "rite of passage"—a profound movement from an adolescent preoccupation with social standing to greater independence and self-sufficiency. It is little wonder so many returnees speak of their sojourns as "life changing," as they often generate vital reconnections with oneself and the outside world.

Misadventures Abroad

But this change is far from automatic. In fact, there seems to be a rising chorus of international educators complaining of how *little* serious exploration beyond the self there is among those choosing to study abroad.

40

While program leaders appreciate the hip and outdoorsy style of many participants, it doesn't take much, they say, for casualness to turn to self-containment, curiosity to conservatism, and a sense of world discovery to intellectual timidity.

It comes as no surprise that emerging adults raised in a hyperindividualistic society are generally focused on personal enjoyment and self-expression. In his best-selling novel *I Am Charlotte Simmons* (2004), Tom Wolfe graphically portrays the subtle ways college environments can influence young women and men to seek relief from their numbness and boredom through an endless stream of unencumbered carnivalesque experiences centered on the bottle, the "bowl," and the bed. Conspicuously absent are dreams to follow and life projects to pursue. A refrain from a song by Smashing Pumpkins comes uncomfortably close to describing this loss of definable purpose in life: "There's nothing left to do. There's nothing left to feel."[1]

In a world shorn of fixed referents and a unified center, is it any wonder that student travel is often viewed as just one more consumer attraction in an unending global mall? Never mind bird flu and terrorism; the real threat to the longstanding promise of a truly global education is the temptation to reduce what is a deeply purposeful journey to a self-indulgent spectacle, fatally out of focus. It was Oliver Cromwell who once noted, "A man never goes so far as when he doesn't know where he is going." Without a sense of origins and destinations, and removed from the moorings of family and friends, far too many sojourners exhibit a level of moral recklessness that would shock even their on-campus counterparts. Consider the following three "snapshots" of student misadventures:

The *New York Times* reports:

> There were the Americans in Amsterdam who used their dorm-room windows to dispose of their trash, raining it down on passers-by. Or the ones in Spain who got into a knife-and-stick fight with locals. Then there are the students who trash hotel rooms in their best rendition of a rock band on tour, who get arrested in Central America for carrying drugs and then become indignant about it, or who disappear from classrooms for weeks on end because the party scene elsewhere was more alluring. (Winter, 2004)

Illinois Wesleyan University junior Anna Deters (2005) sends this dispatch from Amsterdam:

> Quite frankly, I'm ashamed of the Americans here. . . . One kid went to jail the first night he was here because the *politie* found him stumbling drunk in the streets, lost, and near to passing out on the sidewalk. Several other people I know have been kicked out of bars and coffee shops for being too loud and rowdy. They run around the city like they own the place, smoking joints while walking to class, disturbing the residents while yelling loudly in quiet neighborhoods, walking in the bike lanes, imbibing to blackout at every opportunity, buying bikes from junkies, frequenting the Red Light District and attending live sex shows, etc. It's unspeakably embarrassing.

New York University's student newspaper rehearses a "fairly typical" story from Clerico, a senior at NYU's Florence campus:

> The first night, my eight roommates and I invited the whole building to our room, and we bought as much alcohol as the nine of us could carry. . . . Take the best, craziest weekend of your life, and then span it out over four months. . . . That's study abroad. (Palsson, 2005)

Study abroad, indeed. An increase in episodes like these certainly challenges the assumption that taking a semester off to study abroad will actually have a net educational benefit for either travelers *or* the community members that host them. If we tend to get out of foreign study what we bring to it, we have to ask ourselves: What do we "see" for our global-learning term? If we view the world as signifying nothing and going nowhere, a place where we simply exert ourselves to secure personal advantage, study abroad will only serve to decorate our resume or satisfy our wanderlust. But if we define our purpose in the world as promoting what is good and just, those same sojourns will be oriented toward comprehending the world in order to remake it. Mere knowledge *about* the world is not sufficient as its own end; it is always situated in particular values and oriented toward ends beyond itself. This is why our overarching objective cannot merely be to become more "globally competent," as important (and difficult) as that might be. The question is, Globally competent *for what purpose?*

No Loom to Learn By

Our principal predicament was expressed years ago in lines from a wonderful sonnet by Edna St. Vincent Millay, "This Gifted Age":

> Upon this gifted age, in its dark hour
> Rains from the sky a meteoric shower
> Of facts . . . they lie unquestioned, uncombined.
> Wisdom enough to leech us to our ill
> Is daily spun; but there exists no loom
> To weave it into fabric . . .
>
> (Gibbons, 1997)

As a generation we are awash with information. All too often, however, we lack a coherent tale, a "loom" to weave all our learning into a fabric of hopeful action in the world. We're left with fragments of information *about* the world without any true wisdom *for* the world.

Think about it: Which of the world's most aggravated problems simply need more or better information to be solved? If the numbers of street children continue to multiply in the cities of the South, inadequate information is not to blame. If rising temperatures are melting the glaciers that feed the rivers that irrigate the rice and wheat fields that feed millions of people in India and China, it's not because of insufficient information. Are we most deficient in information or in a coherent story that envisions a certain kind of future for the world and prescribes the means to achieve it?

One of the great paradoxes of higher education is that intelligent young people invest tens of thousands of dollars to be tutored in academic disciplines that touch virtually all aspects of their lives *except* the critical area of moral purpose. When it comes to this, most universities—and the education-abroad programs they sponsor—leave them alone. The fallout from this deficit is increasingly being born by global educators. Reluctantly they must face the uncomfortable fact that there's one thing worse than *not* sending students abroad: it's sending immature, ill-prepared, and myopic students whose presence in an overseas community affects more harm than good.

Perhaps what we most fundamentally lack is not so much the "right" type of program but a story that can give purpose and passion to our learning. Native American author Thomas King (2008) tells us that "the truth about stories is that that's all we are" (p. 153). We live and learn *by* our stories and *in* our stories. Stories are the mental architecture for the choices we make on everything from our destinations abroad to whom we'll befriend and how we'll use our time. Most of our stories are unconsciously held. For the most part, we simply live the stories that have been planted in us by parents and peers, and by the powerful images of wealth, power, fun, and beauty that bombard us daily. As ones with the capacity for mindful choice, we also plant stories in ourselves. We construct assumptions and expectations that mark our lives and give certain meaning to our global learning, for better or for worse.

The Great Dream

The upshot is this: To change the world requires that we change our consciousness, the stories we live by. Look at the lives of people like Martin Luther King, Jr., Joan of Arc, or Helen Keller—those who lived from and for something that reached beyond themselves. One quality seems to stand out above all: a steadfast *vision*. Despite opposition and personal limitations, they were able to firmly connect their personal interests to a future expectation of a more just and humane world.

In *How to Change the World*, Daniel Bornstein (2007) makes a similar observation in relation to less legendary champions of social change—people like Kailash Satyarthi, of Global March Against Child Labor in New Delhi, and Dina Abdel Wahab of The Baby Academy in Cairo. "On a daily basis," says Bornstein, "they manage to align interests, abilities and beliefs, while acting to produce changes that accord with their deepest convictions" (p. 288). They care for abandoned children and vulnerable women, provide jobs and develop businesses, plant trees and rehab dilapidated houses. The creative energies they marshal to improve the world, though focused in different directions, share a common impetus—a compelling vision of a preferred future that is humane, just, safe, and abundant.

Vision is an act of seeing, an imaginative perception of what *should* and *could* be. It begins with dissatisfaction—even indignation—over the status quo, and it grows into an earnest quest for an alternative. Global learning that serves the common good faces the world as it is and declares, "This is unacceptable—the despair, the dispossession, the exploitation, the contempt for human dignity—there must be another way." Then it dares to dream. "Nothing much happens without a dream," declares Robert Greenleaf. "And for something great to happen, there must be a great dream. Behind every great achievement is a dreamer of great dreams" (2002, p. 16).

Is there a great dream or story, then, that is capable of energizing our global learning? If there is, how might we internalize that vision in such a way to better grasp it and struggle for its realization through the choices and tasks that are within our reach?

Questions like these tend to elicit a strange silence from our academic disciplines. Most choose to either ignore or devalue regions of experience penetrable only through faith, consciousness, and spirit. That leaves us to draw on the rich symbols and beliefs within the world's wisdom traditions for the story power we need.

Mahayana, one of the two major strains of Buddhism, emphasizes noninjury and *ahimsa* (compassion) toward all of life, both human and nonhuman. Ancient Israel spoke of the great dream as *shalom*, and the contemporary Jewish community speaks of *tikkun olam* (healing the world). In Islam, the idea of *maslaha* guides governmental responsibility to promote the public interest or common good. Jesus taught it as the *kingdom of God*. Opting for the more culturally neutral term the *Great Economy*, essayist Wendell Berry (1987) nevertheless draws on religious tradition to define his idea. Each of these expressions captures a vision *of* and *for* a world "made right," a world where all individuals and institutions, families and peoples, the natural world in all its richness, and the divine powers that provide ultimate meaning for existence are knit together and fulfilled in mutual respect and delight. Alienation and exclusion, domination and subjection, oppression and exploitation are finally overcome.

The diagram in Figure 2.1 suggests some primary features of a story—a great dream—that can instill ultimate meaning and direction to our global learning. It considers human persons in intimate and interdependent relationship with the Spirit or Higher Power, that is, the "ground of all being," or source of spiritual intelligence and fulfillment. The whole creation is a manifestation of this Spirit, a seamless and interacting whole

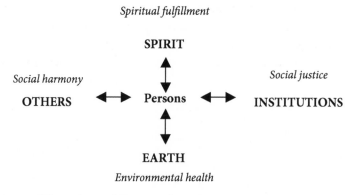

FIGURE 2.1   Dimensions of the great dream

that cannot be fully explained by its constituent parts. The well-being of persons is inseparable from the well-being of *others* (across cultures, classes, and creeds); of the various *institutions* that "fix" social existences; and of the *earth*, the natural world that surrounds and sustains human life. The universe is seen as a dynamic and interacting unity; like a hanging mobile, each part is related to and affected by every other part.

The Lakota people have a beautiful phrase that signifies the inseparability of human life from all other elements of the universe through space and time. When the Lakota leave the sweat lodge they say *mitakuye oyasin* ("all our relations") as a prayer of respect, honor, and love for all of creation. All beings and all things—from the whirling galaxies and timber wolves to the children we give birth to, to their children, and theirs and theirs—are part of an integrated, continuous web of life. One very extended family. Or, in John Donne's discerning words, "Every man is a piece of the continent, a part of the main." Only now are many of us realizing that what we thought was a freestanding and autonomous self is meaningless apart from caring connections to family and friends, community and country, earth, and Spirit.

Redemption Story

Humans are specially graced with reflective consciousness and the capacity to choose among the possibilities of our nature. As such, we have the unique opportunity to connect an inner journey of self-discovery with an outer journey of world discovery. We can choose whether or not to work for a world in which intimacy and mutuality, fairness and freedom, relationships and the common good reign supreme. Much depends on our framing story. Does it give us a foundational understanding of how the world works? Is it a vision *for* life in that it reveals life-giving ways to live? Specifically, does it sufficiently energize us to actually relate to the "other" with a concern for the common good? Does our story enable us, in the words of German philosopher Theodor Adorno (1978), to "contemplate all things as they would present themselves from the standpoint of redemption" (p. 153)?

The story we need is one that envisions a redeemed, fully flourishing world. But that still remains all too abstract unless we have some idea of *what type of flourishing* we are hoping for. The great work of making the world more just and life serving is not, first and foremost, about blockades and boycotts, or even about creating new social and economic structures. Buddhist scholar Joanna Macy (2000) underscores the indispensability of core values in creating positive futures:

> New coalitions and new ways of production are not enough. . . . They will shrivel and die unless they are rooted in *deeply held values*—in our sense of who we are, who we want to be, and how we relate to each other and the living body of Earth. That amounts to a shift in consciousness. . . . It is, at root, a spiritual revolution, awakening perceptions and values that are both very new and very ancient, linking back to rivers of ancestral wisdom.

The most serious challenges facing the world today—malnutrition, infectious disease, climate change, conflicts over land use, and political corruption—are not narrowly economic in nature. Taken together, they signal a fundamental crisis of culture, of the core values needed to reshape a consciousness committed to the well-being of the poor and the planet.

Paul Ray and Sherry Anderson (2000) have documented a growing international movement to evolve a new set of core life-values grounded in the teachings of major religious traditions, in the advocacy of international social movements, and in the body of universal human rights standards. Together, these emerging values summon us to imagine an alternative culture, the kind of world that global learning might help to create and sustain:

◊ *Stable family and community bonds* in which different age groups constantly interact with and genuinely care for each other (versus mobile and temporary ties based on power and economics)

◊ *Diverse cultural values and traditions* (versus a global monoculture rewarding speed, youthfulness, beauty, convenience, power, and competitiveness)

◊ *A healthy natural environment* supporting improved communities for all the earth's citizens (versus the extraction of natural resources for nonessential commodity production and capital accumulation)

◊ *Self-respect and group security* as the fruit of being true to oneself (versus emotional insecurity and alienation underlying a hunger for material status symbols)

◊ *Meaningful work* that enables persons to earn a living wage, and that produces necessary goods and services without harming the environment (versus highly mechanized and depersonalized labor that treats workers as mere "costs" and that is valued solely for enabling more and more consumption)

◊ *Location-specific education* in intimate relationship to the community and ecosystem (versus a "universal" education that trains specialists for a global technological society)

◊ *Human worth and dignity* regardless of one's age, color, sex, social standing, and physical condition (versus one's value calculated in terms of one's capacity to earn money, contribute to the gross national product, or fulfill the fantasies of others)

◊ *The diffusion of economic power* through the broad ownership of land, technology, and capital (versus the concentration of economic power in the hands of a privileged few)

◊ *Responsible technological development* that helps meet the needs of the world population and expresses human creativity (versus technical "advancements" that result in mass unemployment, abuse of nature, and objects of false dependence)

◊ *A communal "soul"* existing in communion with the divine and in personal interdependence (versus the empty, autonomous "self" that seeks to connect with others through the consumption of various products, experiences, and lifestyles)

We might be tempted to dismiss such lofty ideals as utopian and extravagant. But without some sense of ultimate value and purpose, we're left with nothing to orient our study and service, to keep us from losing our way as a redemptive influence in our host communities. Deep values, rooted in our psyche and culture, can either diminish or enlarge our collective sense of human possibility. True, we face some grim realities. Global climate change threatens to produce disastrous flooding that could devastate countless lives and erase scores of villages from the map. And we may yet destroy ourselves with atomic or bacterial weapons. We work, not for a perfect world, but for one a little better. The values that shape our consciousness may not, in themselves, be sufficient to determine specific details of public policy. Nevertheless, they help to clarify *a special kind of desire* that can help direct the course of our living, learning, and service abroad.

Awakening From the False Dream

Our desire to work for a world "set right" and flourishing in the totality of its relationships will inevitably put us at odds with the status quo, and the public narratives that sustain it. Market capitalism, rationalism, technicism, individualism, materialism, and many other *isms*, as ways of seeing, shape the way we experience the world. Each may contain important truths. The problem comes when those truths are inflated and used to exclude other, perhaps more accurate, ways of seeing.

For example, is it true that the relentless pursuit of power and profits is more important than other human and ecological considerations? Is it also true that our current problems can be solved by the simple application of enlightened reason and improved technology? Or that happiness naturally follows unfettered greed and material abundance?

Every society turns around myths that claim the imagination and allegiance of its citizens. When the old stories fail to produce a more satisfying life or humane world, their power and legitimacy begin to fade. At that point we can choose to remain adrift in a meaningless void, and settle for flipping channels from one reality show to another. Or we can break through our indifference and ignorance. We can choose to carry our questions into new social worlds, exploring how other people, living under other life circumstances, offer alternative answers to the "big questions" of human nature, the good life, the nature of power, the persistence of evil, and bettering the human condition.

For a "great dream" to energize a more cosmopolitan education, it must first break through the *false dream* that many of us have learned to accept as indisputable fact. According to this tale, we live in a "closed," purely mechanical, and wasting universe. What we know as "life" is but an accident devoid of intrinsic meaning and ultimate purpose, much less divine destiny. Consciousness and free will are illusions. The world we inhabit is inherently hostile and competitive, a place where "fit" individuals, institutions, and nations survive, and the weaker perish. In such a dog-eat-dog world, the only rational course for intelligent individuals is to survive, reproduce, make money, and seek distraction from their existential loneliness through self-gratifying experience. The global problems that confront us will, over time, be overcome by industrial progress and technological innovation.

This story has, over the last 300 years, deeply shaped what we know as the "modern way of life"—a single, secular, rational, and commercial global civilization. Modern civilization has, without a doubt, registered remarkable achievements. Lewis Mumford, the acclaimed philosopher of modern life, captures in *The Pentagon of Power* (1974) much of its "good" face: "the invention and keeping of the written record, the growth of visual and musical arts, the effort to widen the circle of communication and economic intercourse far beyond the range of any local community: ultimately the purpose to make available to all [people] the discoveries and inventions and creations, the works of art and thought, the values and purposes that any single group has discovered" (p. 331). Which of us would want a world without the opportunity to think the thoughts of Simone de Beauvoir or Rousseau, to benefit from medical advances and technological innovation, to travel to distant lands, and to live under a legal system that safeguards human rights? Can we deny the value of the expanded choice, extended life, and exchange of culture made possible by the modern way of life?

At the same time, features of civilization's very "success" have created unprecedented threats to planetary health. In almost every corner of the globe, we witness the trivialization of tradition, the severing of individual ties to extended family and village, the substitution of machines for human labor, the disregard for environmental limits, and the flooding of unregulated markets with consumer goods and toxic garbage. As moderns, we tend to have less time, less peace of mind, more obesity, more pollution, more crime, more war, and more spiritual barrenness. For the first time in history, we're tempted to reduce the human project to the making and spending of money. Herman Daly and John Cobb (1994) use strong words in their assessment of the modern condition: "We are living by an ideology of death and accordingly we are destroying our own humanity and killing the planet." They conclude, "If we continue on our present paths, future generations, if there are to be any, are condemned to misery" (p. 21).

Naturally, we would like to have it all—to preserve civilization's perceived benefits while restraining its destructiveness. But we haven't found a way to do that yet, even though mass demonstrations from Berlin to Seattle have focused global attention on the predicament, and with a fair amount of success. What might be more significant, however, is how these protests reveal an acute disaffection from a world-story that no longer offers a rising generation ultimate meaning or direction in life. Perhaps this is most visible among the independent traveler set, itinerating from one place to another in search of a radical alternative. Maggie reports from Granada, Nicaragua:

> The longer I stay at this hostel the more fascinated (and less attracted) I am by backpacker culture. There are just so many people completely disinterested in the world that was handed to them in North America or Europe. The whole structure and lifestyle of our developed civilized culture just doesn't appeal to them at all. So they just drift for as long as they can possibly manage to do it, searching for the biggest waves, the greatest dive, the best party, or whatever. I talk about them as if I'm an outsider, but I'm definitely one of them. I'm not sure what I'm searching for . . . knowledge I guess.

Albert Einstein famously observed, "No problem can be solved from the same level of consciousness that created it." Like Maggie, we carry the potential to "leaven" the larger culture with an alternative consciousness, one born of authentic humility, an ever-broadening horizon of global awareness, and the will to act on behalf of the common good. But first we must liberate ourselves from the grip of the myths, institutionalized values, and unconscious needs and status symbols that we've internalized as "normal" and that seem virtually inescapable.

In the R.E.M. music video for "Everybody Hurts," the band gets caught in a Los Angeles traffic jam. The camera moves slowly across rows and rows of cars, compressed bumper to bumper, and then to the desperate faces of commuters stuck in their sweltering cars. Subtitles translate their interior monologues of isolation, pain, and futility. Then, suddenly, a lone man decides he's not going to take it anymore. He steps from his car, closes the door, and just walks away. Others follow suit, one by one, until all of the thousands of cars are left vacant. An unbearable condition is simply abandoned.

The story we need seeks to protect the creative and life-affirming aspects of the modern way of life. But it also calls us to resist and abandon those aspects that undermine human flourishing. For instance, exporting a lifestyle of conspicuous consumption to the rest of the world—complete with 2,500-square-foot homes, gas-guzzling SUVs, and Quarter Pounders—is simply not sustainable. According to the Center for the New American Dream, if each of the planet's 6 billion inhabitants were to consume at the level of the average American, we would need four additional planets' worth of natural resources. Indian feminist Kamla Bhasin recalls the time when a British journalist asked Mahatma Gandhi whether he would like India to enjoy the same standard of living as Britain. Gandhi replied, "To have its standard of living a tiny country like Britain had to exploit half the globe. How many globes will India need to exploit to have the same standard of living?" (in Mies & Shiva, 1993, p. 322).

Healthy, habitable planets are hard to find, and the vital signs of the one planet we have, on both a socioeconomic and ecological level, are not good. Even if it *were* possible to globalize the "American dream," we'd still have to ask ourselves, Why? Although the "haves" of this world have never been better off materially, are we happier than we were 50 years ago? Researchers like Gregg Easterbrook (2004) tell us that, beyond a certain minimum level, more money—and the things money can buy—simply fails to deliver on its promise of dignity, freedom, and happiness.

What most of us need is not more money but more meaningful relationships and life projects.

Grounding our global learning in a liberated imagination enables us to break through cultural illusions and ethical paralysis into a more radical (from the Latin *radix*, meaning "root") understanding of what is going on. In "Redemption Song," Bob Marley sings of freedom in terms of emancipating ourselves from mental slavery. Only as our minds are set free can we see and experience the world as it truly is. At the point of our *overarching purpose* and *underlying passion*, our imagination is released from captivity to a culture of programmed self-gratification into a life committed to the common good.

An Alternative Imagination

What follows are four primary action sequences, or "scenes," of the alternative story we need: finding our true self, embracing the stranger, engaging the powers, and healing the earth. Considered together, they envision a certain way of being in, learning from, and responding to a wounded world. These four operations should be seen as constituting a *broad horizon* rather than a precise formula. A horizon establishes what is both visible and possible in the world here and now. It suggests something "beyond" our current vision for ourselves in relation to other humans and inhabitants of the earth—a state of world flourishing in which justice is the ground and responsible action is the vehicle.

Finding Our True Self

Thomas Merton once remarked, "Our real journey in life is interior." External experience may occupy most of our waking hours, but we ultimately live from the depths of our being—from our intentions, ideas, and impulses. This complex "world within," largely invisible to others, makes possible and profoundly affects the relationships we have to the social and natural worlds that surround us. The health of communities thus finds its primary impetus in the character of persons, in our "true self" or "soul." Not only is it the best gift we can send out to those around us; it is also a gift received through others. This helps to explain why many travelers look to journeys abroad to put the tenuous certainties of self at risk. We intuitively recognize the self to be fluid and malleable, able to be reshaped by our exposure to other selves formed in other places.

If we allow, global learning will not only carry us into the world around us, but also into this world within. The sudden vulnerability we experience as we arrive in an unknown place stripped of familiar surroundings, people, and routines renders us acutely aware of who we are, or at least of who we're *not*. The ideas that helped us understand our world, the rituals and customs that marked our development, the language that connected us to others—these are no longer available to us in the same way. Then compound these mental and emotional displacements with the physical displacements of intense heat or cold, a new diet, and irregular water or electricity. The net result is to feel vulnerable, deprived, lost, and alone.

Under these conditions, who wouldn't wish to escape, either into a parallel world of cultural similars and modern amenities or into intense personal experience induced by mind-altering substances, new travel adventures, or sexual escapades? However expressed, the impulse to seek relief from the natural displacements involved in cross-cultural living is understandable, even predictable.

The problem is that all choices have a trajectory. Over time, choices in a particular direction act to color the way we see ourselves, as well as the world. Each of us already perceives and interprets our new surroundings on the basis of our particular racial, social-class, and gender identities. Now add to this the "coloring" of our personal character, the sort of person we are. Social *and* moral "locations" together inform vision, and vision shapes action.

It follows that the more we find ourselves the product of our own desires, the more we will distance ourselves from the authentic relationships and enduring values that *could* form a true self. "I have met too many people who suffer from an empty self," writes Parker Palmer. "They have a bottomless pit where their identity should be—an inner void they try to fill with . . . anything that might give them the illusion of being better than others" (2009, p. 38).

As educational travelers, our first and perhaps most challenging task is to allow our host culture to become a place where we can struggle against the fictional self that is revealed through our feelings of ignorance, inadequacy, and childlike dependence. Henri Nouwen (2000) used his journal to reflect on this transformative process during a six-month sabbatical in Latin America:

> When we walk around in a strange milieu, speaking the language haltingly, and feeling out of control and like fools, we can come in touch with a part of ourselves that usually remains hidden behind the thick walls of our defenses. . . . When we become aware that our stuttering, failing, vulnerable selves are loved even when we hardly progress, we can let go of our compulsion to prove ourselves and be free to live with others in the fellowship of the weak. That is true healing. (p. 17)

Writing from Bangkok, Thailand, Jaimie similarly notes the hidden sides of self that often get exposed while living in a new culture:

> In my frustrations with other people here I have realized how much of the struggle comes because of my pride and my unwillingness to humbly admit the privilege that I carry in myself—in being American, white, and rich. My privilege carries with it a great deal of pride that desires to be acknowledged, served, and looked up to. How unwilling I am to be hidden!

In both cases, the psychological stress associated with cross-cultural learning actually carries the power to expose us, heal us, and complete us. Instead of trying to numb the pain, we allow ourselves to feel our weakness and vulnerability. This is what ultimately separates the educational traveler from the foreign soldier or proselytizer. Rather than trying to conquer the worlds we visit or convert them to our way of thinking, we surrender to them. The fact that we are strangers in the land quickens our attention and leaves us wide awake to our thoughts and emotional responses. Our journey may be filled with much outward movement, but we are mostly traveling inside ourselves, to destinations never quite arrived at when we're surrounded by sameness.

Therein lies one of the truest, and largely untapped, values of cross-cultural living and learning: its talent for bringing to light what Italian novelist Cesare Pavese (2009) calls "the essential things . . . things tending toward the eternal." Ironically, we tend to discover the things that are fundamental to happiness and meaning not when we seek them directly, but when we are set off balance or otherwise come to an end of ourselves. It's at those times that we are most open to be formed by those virtues that have long been recognized by all cultures and wisdom traditions as the proper goal of existence (Kidder, 1994). Love, truthfulness, fairness, freedom, unity, tolerance, responsibility, and respect for life—together they indicate the soul qualities of those privileged to be purified through the struggles and encounters of the intercultural experience.

Embracing the Stranger

While the story we need begins within us, it cannot be fully realized apart from others. All of us are born and reared with groups, work and play in groups, and develop our sense of who we are (i.e., identity) and what passions we'll pursue (i.e., vocation) in groups. To be is to be in relationship. This is why the story we need must project a distinctly *social* vision—one of understanding, trust, and reciprocity that reaches across our deepest differences. It seeks to answer the interpersonal alienation endemic to world societies through an embrace of those who are "stranger" to us.

Although estrangement and conflict continue to beleaguer those sharing much in common with each other, their most pernicious forms manifest between groups who, though occupying common physical space, exist as the "other" to each other. In 1992, Los Angeles erupted in violent rioting and looting with painful consequences for the city's Koreans, African Americans, and Latinos. Worldview clashes persist between the Catholics and Protestants in Northern Ireland, between Arabs and Israelis in Palestine, between Hindus and Muslims in India, between Sunnis and Shiite Muslims in Iraq. Not to mention the murderous civil wars ravaging entire nations throughout Africa. In each of these hot spots, the capacity of trust has eroded to the point where a shared "good" is a distant dream.

These realities present us, as global learners, with one of our most important tasks: to understand within our destination communities the kind of relations that exist between the powerful and the weak, teachers and students, adults and children, women and men, the healthy and the sick, and so on. And not just on a cognitive level. Our challenge is to welcome local residents into our lives, to know them by name, and to bridge some of the deepest differences. The practical and deeply personal "embrace" that we extend to others does not replace a tough-minded assessment of sociopolitical reality. It simply recognizes the fact that, whatever else might be done to promote just and open human relations, they will not be sustained without a deeply interpersonal process that is capable of turning strangers into friends. This is the poignant lesson revealed through Bishop Desmond Tutu of South Africa. As chair of the Truth and Reconciliation Commission following the horrors of Apartheid, he discovered the power of confession and forgiveness in enabling perpetrator and victim to "hold hands as we realize our common humanity" (Tutu, 2000).

Hospitality is customary in many societies and we will often find ourselves on the receiving end of special kindnesses from local hosts. Such displays of warmth and generosity give expression to the natural human ability to recognize essential sameness beneath and despite real differences. Yet for many of us this kind of "welcome" doesn't come naturally. Our Western way of life doesn't encourage us to stock up on extra food for travelers, much less invite them to live with us. To the contrary, we're taught from childhood to view strangers with suspicion. By the time we're adults we've learned to reject some and to identify with others by projecting stereotypic images and forming alliances. In time the framework of our social interactions comes to resemble a checkerboard where we learn to relate primarily to persons in our own (or nearby) squares.

As we cross into other cultures, we carry this homegrown social checkerboard around in our minds. Those we encounter on the streets of London or Addis Ababa will be lumped almost instinctively into the mental categories that are native to us: White, Black, woman, man, elderly, finely dressed, dirty, factory worker, professional, and so on. Eventually we may collect more information and describe them more fully. But the tragic consequence of "boxing" is that we relate to people on the basis of the label we've put on their box, rather than encountering them as unique individuals.

Is it possible, then, for a Hindu student to "think Muslim" or for an American to "think Cuban"? The answers are found in our willingness to genuinely "welcome" others as a natural extension of a secure and recentered self. Rather than seal ourselves off from local residents, we open ourselves up to give to and receive from those who inhabit different histories, languages, experiences, and perspectives. This might be in the home of a local family, on the seat of a long-distance bus, or in the community organization where we volunteer. In each setting, we learn to sit, to ask questions, and to genuinely listen. The aim is not to debate and convince, but to be shaped by *another* way of life.

This doesn't mean that foreign guests and local hosts will, after exploring each other's worlds, suddenly want to swap places. Relations marked by deep-seated suspicion and separation can have historical roots that resist thin forms of "intercultural understanding." Nevertheless, our willingness to think and feel as the other is an indispensable first step toward forming trusting and reciprocal relationships across cultures. As Miroslav Volf (1996) reminds us, "Within social contexts, truth and justice are unavailable outside the will to embrace."

The embrace of strangers is also the path leading to a more transcultural self. Every culture is a vast treasure chest of languages and lifestyles, arts and achievements, moral energies and spiritual insights. Each also stands in need of radical correction of its self-deceits. Face-to-face exchanges within cross-cultural settings offer rare opportunities for us to complement and correct, enrich and educate each other. The result can be a broader knowledge and fuller truth than either partner could reach apart from the other. Reflecting on his years of living and teaching abroad, Bernard Adeney (1995) concludes:

> Truth is often bigger than any one person's ability to grasp it. By recognizing the particularity of all our knowing, we are free to look for wisdom in opposing opinions without compromising what is valuable in our own. As we begin to love people in another culture, we can begin to identify with them and see the truth they understand. As we make their truth our own, we become new people, formed by the synthesis of two cultures. (p. 65)

Like a plant, then, we attempt to reach down into the cultural soil of our host community to identify and adjust our perspectives to those values and insights that complement or correct our own. This process often confronts us with our national pride, our false attachments, and our personal insecurities. It's a "conversion" of sorts—the process of being *delivered from* self-absorption and being *opened to* a bigger, more complex understanding of the world and, thereby, of ourselves.

Engaging the Powers

The dynamics involved in rediscovering our true self and learning to embrace strangers within our field settings necessarily focuses our attention on the conscious choices that we, as individuals, make to think and act in certain ways. This challenges the all-too-common assumption that deep and enduring change in the world can be realized through institutional reform alone. "A better system will not automatically ensure a better life," remarked Vaclav Havel, one of the few voices of dissent prior to the collapse of communism in Czechoslovakia. "In fact the opposite is true: only by creating a better life can a better system be developed" (1996, p. 173). The most fundamental social entities are persons like you and me.

Nevertheless, we are *socially embedded* persons who live and move and have our being through various social forms or "institutions." Right from birth, families, schools, mass media, and other forms of human organization induct us into a shared set of norms and values, habits and skills. Together, these enable us to survive and flourish within a given society, whether at home or abroad. Families have the potential to shape us into psychologically mature and physically healthy group members. Schools and religious associations can inculcate creative expression and transcendent meaning for life. The modern university offers each new generation access to the riches of the human experience and achievement. Regional industries and businesses supply the essential goods and jobs that support satisfying livelihoods. Each of these interlocking institutions, through its regulative beliefs and practices, is an indispensable protector and channel of life.

But it is also true that, like individual persons, these same powers may suffer deep and dangerous distortion and end up working *against* life. Over time we find that families and schools, customs and corporations all tend to develop basic conventions and commitments that outlive the

people who constitute them. While this social longevity benefits communities by providing stability and continuity, there is also a shadow side.
In time the powers may take on an identity and purpose largely independent of the people who participate in them. At this point they may repudiate their vocation to serve the common good by channeling human
activity into self-serving and life-degrading directions. Examples abound
in the economic exploitation and bureaucratic routine manifested in
third world sweatshops; in entrenched forms of political corruption that
enrich a powerful elite while depriving the poor of basic services; in culturally supported notions of gender or racial superiority that subordinate
one group to another; and in the destruction of civilians and natural
habitats in civil war.

Global sojourns often position us to experience realities like this firsthand and on a daily basis. Over time we come to the sober realization
that personal goodness and enlightened cultural understanding *alone* are
simply unable to alter certain social realities. The story we need refuses
to be caught in false alternatives. Instead, it articulates an indivisible
vision of life, insisting that a "better life" and a "better system" cannot
be realized one apart from the other. Global learning must reach in both
directions—toward persons and toward structures—simultaneously.
Here our individual efforts to be a better person and to befriend the
stranger are complemented by the task of "engaging the powers," that is,
discerning the social and political character of those local institutions in
which we participate.

The "powers" manifest great internal mystery and complexity. To
appreciate how they might, under certain conditions, bolster community
well-being and under other conditions undermine it requires that we
encounter them at the point of their most positive *and* negative manifes-
tations. Typically this involves finding viable roles within the local culture—for example, as a guest within a welcoming rural family or as an
intern at a community school or health clinic. Both settings would afford
us direct experience with the mixed character of each institution. Within
the family we would no doubt witness generosity of spirit mixed with an
unfair, gender-based distribution of power, resources, and responsibilities. The school or health clinic might have facilities equipped with
renewable energy systems and multimedia kiosks, but also teachers and

health workers who are either chronically truant or, when present, emotionally detached from their pupils or patients.

As we inhabit different structures of social life within our destination communities, some roles and practices are bound to elicit feelings of strong discomfort, if not disgust. Consider the many tolerated forms of sexual harassment within male-dominated countries. Erica recounts an incident at her internship involving a 27-year-old Argentine supervisor:

> My office manager . . . is constantly making passes at women that work in the organization, constantly touching them, and can be very condescending when giving orders. The other day I was helping him with his emails when he starts joking around. He puts his hand on my knee and says something like, "You are my secretary. You give me my coffee, a back massage, or anything else I want, when I want it." I'm a bit in shock and don't know how to handle the situation since he's one of my bosses. I get up, laugh it off, and say, "yeah, right."

In every culture there will be certain behaviors that violate deep-seated beliefs and values. After mulling over the incident and ventilating your visceral feelings, perhaps in a journal, try to interpret *why* you feel the way you do. What meaning do you assign to the particular behavior based on *your* cultural "instruction"? Then, how is that behavior defined in *this* cultural context? For instance, how do local women explain the fact that they shoulder almost all the household responsibilities or are routinely objectified by men? What is their subjective experience of it? Do they *necessarily* perceive and define these realities as gender discrimination or harassment? What might these everyday practices "say" about the internal culture of the family or service organization?

Any attempt to "engage" (judge) institutionally embedded powers begins with understanding the reality *in the people's terms*. As culture learners, our primary aim is not to find a perspective to evaluate the others' culture; it is to undertake the deep cultural analysis necessary to first see *our* enculturated selves more clearly. Only then are we rightly positioned to raise the moral and ethical issues involved in *their* behavior. In other words, we take the beam out of our own eyes so that we can begin to see the speck in our neighbor's.

Cases of cultural outsiders using direct action to reform entrenched powers within a host setting are relatively rare. One of the most interesting involves London-born photojournalist Zana Briski, who traveled to Kolkata, India, to live in the notorious red-light district known as Sonagachi. Her award-winning film *Born Into Brothels* (2004) tells the story of eight children of prostitutes who learn, through photography workshops, to document the world that surrounds them. It takes Briski months to gain real access to the place and its residents (a brothel owner finally let her have a room), but in time she establishes rapport with the madams and landladies, the pimps and police, the "line" of sex workers and their children.

Through an unconditional "embrace," a world of understanding is opened to her. In time she comes to see prostitution in Sonagachi as being not so much a choice as a settled way of life bound up within structures of poverty and patriarchy. She then decides to act. Networking with various agencies throughout the city and beyond, Briski attempts to get the children out of the brothel-slum and into boarding schools where an inherited way of life can be broken. In the process she must face unyielding institutional resistance. The Indian bureaucracies endlessly stall the required paperwork. Fatalistic mothers prevent their daughters from leaving for fear of losing a future source of income. Some schools refuse to accept the children of "criminals."

Some of us may chafe at any image of activist Westerners involved in schemes to improve the lives of ill-fated subjects abroad. We're understandably suspicious of the growing number of uninformed and misguided service projects that reflect a patronizing "missionary tendency" (Woolf, 2005). One way to guard against this tendency is to recognize the ways our own lives and institutional behavior are complicit with the harm that we condemn elsewhere. No doubt many of us purchase name-brand clothes manufactured under sweatshop conditions. We drive CO_2-emitting automobiles that contribute to global warming and war making. We drink coffee and eat chocolate produced by underpaid farmers. Not to mention the hundreds of items that we use every day that unwittingly support a complex web of exploitation and profiteering over which we seem to have little, if any, control (Bales, 2000).

At the end of the day we must concede the disturbing fact that we live in this world at each other's expense. Our affluence as world learners is proximately related to, and supported by, the poverty of those who host us. This dilemma is not resolved by indulging feelings of personal guilt, nor by throwing up our hands and concluding that the relations between actions and consequences are just too complex to understand, much less accept any moral responsibility for. "Complexity" easily becomes, in the words of John Holloway, "the great alibi, both scientifically and morally." Instead of blithely surrendering to the system that promises to protect our privilege, our challenge is to redouble our efforts to figure out how to engage the powers in such a way as to help them form, reform, or sustain a responsible role in shaping the common good.

Healing the Earth

A fourth scene in the story we need involves the encounter between humans and the earth that sustains us. One of the momentous changes of the last few decades has been the enlarged public awareness of two fundamental and related problems that continue to threaten the stability of the planet. The first, as discussed in chapter 1, is the world's *growing poverty and inequality*: "a billion people living in dire poverty alongside a billion in widening splendor" (Hobsbawm, 2000, p. 169). The second is the accelerating *impoverishment of the natural environment* brought about by unsustainable levels of resource extraction and commodity consumption.

For those of us raised in urban-industrial societies, our bonds with the natural world tend to be quite fragile. We can go for months without smelling a flower, touching an indigenous tree, breathing clean air, or meeting an animal in the wild. It often takes us being transported into more untreated settings to appreciate that our very existence depends on the products and services of a generous earth. There we come to see how a particular climate system allows productive agriculture to meet basic food needs. How the hydrological cycle provides residents with fresh drinking water. And how the earth's natural ecosystems—its forests and wetlands, mountains and grasslands—provide abundant services that we otherwise take for granted: water purification, decomposition of wastes, climate and disease control, carbon sequestering, spiritual inspiration, and recreation. These products and services are all "gifts" of a sacramental universe, essentially holy but not infinitely available, nor invulnerable to being pushed beyond their limits.

In fact, our current demand for nature's services has far exceeded what it can provide. Although the high-growth global economy has doubtlessly raised millions of poor people into new middle classes, that same economy is based on a mode of production that entails transforming living nature into dead commodities. Driven by high consumption, resources are being used faster than they can regenerate and waste is being created faster than it can be absorbed.

Experts refer to this as "ecological overshoot," a failure to adapt to the limiting conditions of our earthly habitat. And it is this overshoot that lies at the root of our most serious and persistent ecological problems: shrinking forests, depleted or eroded soils, overgrazed grasslands, dwindling fisheries, desertification, water scarcity, disappearing species, polluted air, and increasing numbers of poor people (Halweil, Mastny, Assadourian, & Flavin, 2004). Joined by the newer problems of climate change and ozone depletion, this "quiet crisis" threatens all of the planet's life-forms and perhaps our very survival as a species. Humans have always thought about their relationship to the environment, but the present generation must face a set of dilemmas that is unprecedented in history.

The old story tried to convince us that we are a superior species, segregated from nature and possessed with the unrestricted right to exploit the earth's bountiful resources to meet our needs and fulfill our desires. Such a relationship to the earth not only degrades the intrinsic value of nonhuman creation apart from its utility for humans; it also diminishes our potential as persons to realize our full humanity through right relationship with nature. The words of Catholic theologian Henri Nouwen (2000) ring true:

> As long as we relate to the trees, the rivers, the mountains, the fields, and the oceans as our properties to be manipulated by us according to our real or fabricated needs, nature remains opaque and does not reveal to us its true being. When we relate to a tree as nothing more than a potential chair, it cannot speak much to us about growth. When a river is only a dumping place for our industrial wastes, it no longer informs us about

movement. . . . The dirty rivers, the smog-filled skies, the strip-mined hills, and the ravaged woods are sad signs of our false relationship with nature. (pp. 86–87)

We desperately need a new story, one that helps us to see, with Wendell Berry (1994), that "we are holy creatures living among other holy creatures in a world that is holy" (pp. 98–99). This new "seeing" will insist that the trees, plants, oceans, and mountains are alive and real and holy along with us. I'm reminded of this fact every night at about 10:00 as a family of raccoons emerges from the storm drains to search for food in my backyard. How should I regard them? As an annoyance in my world or subjects in their own world (one long displaced by urban development)? My educational task in relation to these critters is to understand them on their own terms, and not simply as objects of control.

It has taken me nearly half a lifetime to see myself, not just as a sojourner or a citizen, but also as a resident of the earth—an earthling. For years I didn't belong anywhere with a full heart; an itinerant lifestyle rendered me ecologically "homeless," in the sense of having no geographic center and little inability to let the outer world flow into my being. Only gradually, and somewhat reluctantly, did I find real home-making and life grounding in caring for the local ground and nonhuman inhabitants of the places where I live.

The Greek word *oikos*, from which we get the words *eco*nomics and *eco*logy, means "house" or "household." The earth is our home, with boundaries that necessarily extend beyond human populations to encompass the wildlife, soils, waters, and plants of the household. This has implications for the way we conceive of "host community" as well as "intercultural learning." Our host community is a single household of human and nonhuman life. Understanding and caring for that life, though primarily oriented toward empathetic involvement with human strangers, also entails sustained attention to and firsthand encounters with earth others.

How might our intercultural journeys also be ecological journeys? Taking up residence abroad, we can do no better than to follow the lead of sage earth-keepers like Annie Dillard. One of our first tasks, suggests Dillard, is to put down actual roots, to "explore the neighborhood . . . to discover at least *where* it is that we have been so startlingly set down" (1998, p. 14).

This exploration can begin with the immediate area surrounding the town or city in which you settle. In addition to learning the names of streets and localities, set out to learn the natural neighborhood: who and what lives there and why, who's native and who's alien. Expect to discover that an array of interacting life systems "host" you: soils and waters, native trees and blossoming flowers, habitats of wild animals, wind patterns, and seasonal changes. Learn to comprehend this natural community by taking time to walk slowly and observantly throughout the area. Look for examples of living things interacting. Document what you see, hear, smell, and feel in a field journal using words and pictures. Allow your encounters to form bonds of affection between you and the natural world that surrounds you.

A deepened sense of belonging and connectedness to the biotic community will naturally manifest in the lifestyle we adopt within our host communities. Aldo Leopold's call in 1948 for a "land ethic" is echoed today in the push to mitigate the adverse effects of travel. Recommendations by the eco-conscious read like a traveler's "code of conduct": Travel from one destination to another by train or bus, and then use a bicycle to get around. Support conservation-oriented tour operators and guides. Don't disturb plants and animals in their natural habitats. Take only photographs (after first asking permission) and leave only footprints. Buy locally grown foods rather than imports. Resist buying poorly made and disposable souvenirs. Learn to take short showers and to turn off lights and heaters when not in use. Wash clothes by hand.

All sound advice, although it still may not go far enough. It is one thing to "go native" in one's consumption patterns during a relatively short stint abroad. It's quite another to allow temporary deprivations to prompt a deep appraisal of the driving forces behind our lifestyles back home.

Our tendency is to ponder the problems of the global ecosphere in the abstract rather than to relate them to our everyday lifestyle choices. Our ways of thinking about and acting in the world are rooted in socially shaped and shared dispositions and values. As Robert Bellah reminds us, "Most of the threats to the planetary ecosystem are the results of habitual human ways of relating to the physical world, ways of dictating institutional arrangements" (Bellah, Madsen, Tipton, Sullivan, & Swidler, 1992, p. 14).

Global learning can contribute to earth healing, but only as it sets our imaginations free to see and experience the world differently. International field experiences that interrupt and upset the "habitual human ways" that we have come to accept as "normal" and even "natural" can make us newly aware of how those habitual behaviors are tied not only to our psychological desires but also to the institutions that are energized by those habits and desires, and to the global ecosphere that suffers as a result.

The sight of a clear-cut rain forest in Central America can prompt us to consider how our personal demand for mahogany furniture or beef burgers makes it financially worthwhile for others to cut down the rain forests. The physical repulsion we might feel as we're stuck in fume-belching traffic in Manila or Bangkok can drive us to question our own attachment to the private automobile. The observable contrast in the shape and texture of fruits and vegetables sold in street stalls with those sold in the modern supermarket back home can cause us to question why we demand produce without the blemishes of caterpillar teeth and, thus, why it is profitable for farmers to use pesticides. Direct encounters with an unfamiliar reality can act as springboards into considering the habitual ways we seek to aggrandize ourselves at the expense of non-human creation.

This is all part of awakening from the false dream in order to form new, ecologically rooted selves. The more centered and stable our selves become, the more our inner emptiness and conflict can be overcome, and the less we will crave the intense consumerism that fuels the motor of environmental deterioration. This personal transformation begins by connecting the dots between our inner lives and consumption patterns, global institutions, and environmental impacts. In the process we transcend a trendy interest in "going green" to ask the questions that *really* matter: How do these institutions act to continually stimulate my desire (need) for their products? To what extent do I willingly cooperate with these high-prestige structures in order to gain the approval of others? How do I feel about the consequences of this complicity: the global production of even greater profit and stimulation, the strengthening of institutional power and influence over my personal desires, and the further estrangement from my true self and from nature? And what, if anything, am I willing to do about it?

Conclusion

Robert Hutchins stands out as one of the United States' most audacious and innovative educators. As president of the University of Chicago, he saw higher learning as a means to unsettle students' minds and to widen their horizons. At one point in his career, he declared: "Civilization can be saved only by a moral, intellectual, and spiritual revolution. If education can contribute to a moral, intellectual, and spiritual revolution, then it offers a real hope of salvation to suffering humanity everywhere. If it cannot, or will not, contribute to this revolution, then it is irrelevant and its fate is immaterial" (in Smith, 1990, p. 304).

Our conviction is that global learning can contribute to—and even provide the cutting edge for—that revolution. But it must be grounded in a defining story that gives it ultimate meaning, purpose, and direction. Will an alternative narrative serve to awaken a new consciousness among a new generation of budding internationalists? Or will the outcome of our globetrotting be finally judged as irrelevant and immaterial? Much depends on what we ultimately "see" and hope for.

For Reflection and Discussion

1. Someone once told Socrates that a certain man had grown no better by his travels. "I should think not," replied Socrates, "he took himself along with him." What about us? What is the relationship between the psycho-emotional "baggage" we carry abroad and how we affect, and are affected by, our field experiences?
2. How compatible are your motivations and expectations for global learning with the four scenes of the "story we need"? Where do they converge, and at what points do they diverge?

Note

1. Smashing Pumpkins, "Bullet with Butterfly Wings," from the album *Mellon Collie and the Infinite Sadness*, Virgin Records America, 1995. Lyrics by Billy Corgan.

References

Adeney, B. (1995). *Strange virtues.* Downers Grove, IL: InterVarsity Press.

Adorno, T. (1978). *Minima moralia: Reflections on a damaged life* (E. F. N. Jephcott, Trans.). London: Verso.

Bales, K. (2000). *Disposable people: New slavery in the global economy.* Berkeley: University of California Press.

Bellah, R., Madsen, R., Tipton, S., Sullivan, W., & Swidler, A. (1992). *The good society.* New York: Alfred A. Knopf.

Berry, W. (1987). *Home economics.* New York: North Point Press.

Berry, W. (1994). *Sex, economy, freedom and community: Eight essays.* New York: Pantheon.

Bornstein, D. (2007). *How to change the world: Social entrepreneurs and the power of new ideas.* New York: Oxford University Press.

Briski, Z. (Director). (2004). *Born into brothels: Calcutta's red light kids* [Motion picture]. United States: Red Light Films.

Daly, H., & Cobb, J., Jr. (1994). *For the common good.* Boston: Beacon Press.

Deters, A. (2005, May). *Letters from Amsterdam.* Retrieved April 1, 2010, from http://www.iwu.edu/~iwunews/Abroad/abroadlog.html

Dillard, A. (1998). *Pilgrim at Tinker Creek.* New York: Harper Perennial.

Easterbrook, G. (2004). *The progress paradox: How life gets better while people feel worse.* New York: Random House.

Gibbons, J. (1997). *This gifted age: Science and technology at the millennium.* New York: Springer.

Greenleaf, R. (2002). *Servant leadership.* Mahwah, NJ: Paulist Press.

Halweil, B., Mastny, L., Assadourian, E., & Flavin, C. (Eds.). (2004). *State of the world 2004.* New York: W.W. Norton.

Havel, V. (1996). The power of the powerless. In G. Stokes (Ed.), *From Stalinism to pluralism.* New York: Oxford University Press.

Hobsbawm, E. (2000). *The new century.* London: Little, Brown.

Kidder, R. (1994). *Shared values for a troubled world.* Hoboken, NJ: Jossey-Bass.

King, T. (2008). *The truth about stories: A native narration.* Minneapolis: University of Minnesota Press.

Macy, J. (2000, Spring). [Interview with Sarah Ruth van Gelder] The great turning. *YES!* Retrieved April 1, 2010, from http://www.yesmagazine.org/issues/new-stories/333

Mies, M., & Shiva, V. (1993). *Ecofeminism.* London: Zed Books.

Mumford, L. (1974). *The pentagon of power: The myth of the machine, Vol. II.* New York: Mariner Books.

Nouwen, H. (2000). *Clowning in Rome: Reflections on solitude, celibacy, prayer, and contemplation.* New York: Doubleday.

Palmer, P. (2009). *A hidden wholeness.* San Francisco: Jossey-Bass.

Palsson, N. (2005, June 22). Sex, drugs and study abroad: Overseas sites dens of booze, debauchery. *Washington Square News.* Retrieved December 23, 2009, from http://media.www.nyunews.com/media/storage/paper869/news/2003/11/05/UndefinedSection/Sex-Drugs.Study.Abroad-2391007.shtml

Pavese, C. (2009). *This business of living: Diaries 1935–1950.* Piscataway, NJ: Transaction Publishers.

Ray, P., & Anderson, S. (2000). *The cultural creatives: How 50 million people are changing the world.* New York: Harmony Books.

Smith, P. (1990). *Killing the Spirit: Higher education in America.* New York: Penguin Books.

Tutu, D. (2000). *No future without forgiveness.* New York: Image Books.

Volf, M. (1996). *Exclusion and embrace.* Nashville, Abingdon Press.

Winter, G. (2004, August 23). Colleges tell students the overseas party's over. *New York Times.* Retrieved April 1, 2010, from http://query.nytimes.com/gst/fullpage.html?res=9903E2DE143EF930A1575BC0A9629C8B63

Wolfe, T. (2004). *I Am Charlotte Simmons.* New York: Farrar, Straus and Giroux.

Woolf, M. (2005, March/April). Avoiding the missionary tendency. *International Educator.* Retrieved June 5, 2009, from http://www.nafsa.org/_/File/_/InternationalEducator/WoolfMarApr05.pdf

THE MINDFUL TRAVELER

Thou hast made me known to friends whom I knew not,
Given me seats in homes not my own.
Thou hast brought the distant near
And made me a brother of the stranger.
—RABINDRANATH TAGORE, *Gitanjali*

DURING HIS LONG and extraordinary life (1861–1941), Tagore, the beloved Bengali poet and educator, journeyed to 30 countries on 5 continents. What's surprising is that he was ambivalent about travel. He privately confessed, "I am not a born traveler. I have not the energy and strength needed for knowing a strange country." Nevertheless, his exchanges with the intellectuals and common people of the places he visited profoundly shaped his vision of global community. Convinced that borders were folly, his ideal became the world citizen, the Universal Man. "The complete man must never be sacrificed to the patriotic man, or even to the merely moral man," he warned in a letter from New York to a friend (Tagore, 1996). For Tagore, patriotism and nationalism were but passing phases in the evolution of the human community. He believed that in time, and with the increase of cultural exchange, the cosmopolitan ideal would be reached. That humanity is too good for narrow interests and exclusive loyalties.

If he were alive today, Tagore would no doubt smile on an emerging generation of a "new cosmopolitans." They, like he, are attempting to think and live between the local and the universal, the traditional and the modern, the material and the spiritual. And these aren't just old-school

71

revolutionaries trying to overturn the old order, nor technophobic hippies wanting to unplug the system and return humanity to a hunter-gatherer lifestyle. They are hybrid figures that don't fit nicely into *any* of the established categories. Their social vision isn't at home with the religious Right or the secular Left, with the White House (big government) or Wall Street (big business). While not exactly unpatriotic, they've distanced themselves from a "my country, right or wrong" nationalism in favor of what sociologist Alan Wolfe (1999) calls a "tempered internationalism." In their gut they know that we're "all connected now" (to use Walter Truett Anderson's [2001] memorable phrase) and that the irreversible mixing of the world's economies and cultures presents us with more opportunities to realize relatively higher degrees of creativity, contentment, justice, and sustainability than have been known in any human society before now. Rather than revert to a supposed golden era, they consider how to act responsibly in an integrated world of far greater complexity, where the apparently simple acts of traveling, serving, buying, and selling have repercussions that are far beyond the limits of their immediate experience and that they are morally obliged to take into account.

When Ethics Travel

Global learning is never completely innocent. It is saturated with difficult power relations, endemic to cultural difference, that can't be wished away or canceled out by a more "ethical" brand of travel. Even travel scenarios that allow us to serve others can make us feel good about ourselves without bringing to light their less-than-desirable side effects for both the destination community and ourselves.

What might be some of these unpleasant consequences? Consider the following fairly typical scenario: A faculty member at a private liberal arts college in the Midwest decides to offer a four-week course on tribal arts and social problems in Chiang Mai, northern Thailand. In the weeks that follow, 15 young adults, none of them Thai, are recruited to study traditional textiles and work with AIDS-infected girls. It matters little that no one on the team has any proficiency in Thai or can point to a close friendship with any Southeast Asian immigrant back home. Neither has there been a prefield, case-study analysis of the way commercial tourism often aggravates exploitative employment of women (i.e., prostitution), undermines women's human and social capital, and traps them in long-term poverty.

After a couple of meetings to review the travel itinerary and behavior expectations, the group takes off. On arriving in Chiang Mai, they are immediately besieged by hawkers and hustlers. They check into a local YMCA (arranged by their local host as part of a package deal) and are straight away identified with the resident tourist population. It so happens that their host is a well-known "culture broker" who has learned through much practice how to mediate between locals and foreigners. Each day he makes sure the group members have what they need, including flush toilets, village treks, meaningful service tasks, clear directions to the nearest Pizza Hut, and souvenirs for family and friends.

The host–guest relationship is mainly instrumental and impersonal, rarely colored by affective ties. Likewise, the behavior of foreign students and locals is almost always "on stage," each having prepared for his or her performances behind the scenes. The students have read their orientation materials, consulted with trip alums, and perhaps ransacked a *Lonely Planet* guide or phrasebook. The middleman and other locals have consulted with fellow performers; assessed the commercial or political benefits of associating with these "outsiders"; and, of course, rehearsed a friendly smile. Caught in a staged tourist space, the encounters between these parties are almost invariably marked by disparities of power and levels of stereotyping that would not exist among neighbors or peers. Each party knows that the transactions probably will be brief and temporary. This frees everybody from the constraints of mutual, long-term relationships and to act in terms of his or her own interests.

During the month of travel study, the foreign land fulfills its promise. Although the 15 foreign students may have only skimmed the surface of the regional culture, they succeed in meeting fellow travelers from around the world and forming deep bonds of friendship with trip mates. The fact that the *study* side of the study-abroad experience has been reduced to make room for assorted field visits virtually assures all participants of getting a passing grade. Service experiences also meet student expectations. They come away confirmed in their sense of being the ones who are healthy and strong, and the infected girls as being helpless and deficient.

Returning home, they're likely to speak and write of what they learned *about* or did *for* the locals rather than *with* them.

This simple—and perhaps simplistic—sketch serves to challenge the commonplace assumption that sojourns abroad automatically yield transformational results, either for "goers" or for "receivers." Much depends on specific program features and the choices that we as individual travelers make along the way.

Most of us are creatures of habit. Our tendency is to do things—including travel-related things—on automatic pilot, largely oblivious to the movements themselves and how they impact the world around us. While autopilot helps us stay "on course" in the rush and pressure of daily life with a minimum of expended energy, there is a major downside. It tends to undermine our capacity to be "mindful"—to consider *why*, *how*, and *with what effect* we do what we do. Instead, we simply go with the flow, even if that flow is shallow and trifling.

This chapter contends that we have the ability to choose whether our journeys will be mindful attempts to maximize benefits to ourselves and to host communities or yet another luxury commodity consumed more or less mindlessly. In Buddhist traditions, mindfulness (*sati* in the Pali language) is a moment-by-moment attentiveness to the world both within us and around us. To be a "mindful traveler" is to approach our field settings with a level of sensitivity and curiosity that raises our conscious awareness of how we affect the social and natural environments we enter and act upon. This intentional awareness finds its ground and inspiration in a "story" that clarifies our motivations and allows higher purposes to guide our attempt to grow in worldly wisdom while enriching the lives of others. Ultimately this is what distinguishes the mindful traveler from the carefree drifter or mass tourist.

Travel Worlds

A thirst for change and a more satisfying life underlies much of the travel that has occurred throughout history. During the medieval period, pilgrims endured hardship for months and even years on journeys they hoped would end in spiritual enlightenment. Religious scholars crossed national and cultural borders in search of new knowledge or to spread their faith. They were followed by the young elites who undertook "Grand Tours" through Europe starting in the 17th century. Following established trade routes, they would dedicate two or three years to expanding their intellectual and cultural horizons through travel study. Then there were the real explorers and adventurers—like Marco Polo, David Livingstone, Freya Stark, and Sir Wilfred Thesiger—who pioneered routes in uncharted lands. All that was left was for an eclectic and far more civilized swarm of colonists, merchants, and missioners to fill in the details and beat down tracks that would eventually appear in today's savvy travel guidebooks.

St. Augustine of Hippo once wrote, "The world is a book, and those who do not travel read only one page." Travel is a school for life, one that generates fresh insights and unforgettable memories. Nevertheless, it primarily enrolls a class of wandering elites. The explorer of the Amazon, the collegian studying abroad in Spain, and the religiously inspired volunteer to Haiti may each bring different personal backgrounds and goals to their travel. What they all share in common, however, is the expectation that travel will confer a certain social status and, perhaps, a much-needed break from the compulsiveness and tedium of bourgeois life.

We might like to think that educational travel is a special case, immune to this self-actualizing orientation. However, it probably has more in common with other "enlightened" forms of travel—like adventure travel, mission travel, and pro-poor travel—than we would like to think. This is evident both in the type of participants and in their travel expectations and consumption practices.

As noted previously, the numbers of those studying abroad is on the rise, especially in so-called nontraditional locations. In most cases, this involves transporting rich, White collegians into societies where the majority is poor and dark skinned. In common with others from their ethnoclass, they learn to distinguish themselves from others, not just by their education, income, and place of residence, but by the objects and experiences (what Pierre Bourdieu [Bourdieu & Passeron, 1990] called "cultural capital") they accumulate. This is particularly true for the more adventurous types of student travelers who often emerge from their ventures as figures of admiration, earning a certain cachet from having toughed it out in places marked not only by extreme climate conditions but also by brutal levels of poverty and inequality.

This admiration is often well deserved. Many of us venture out to distant lands in order to test the limits of our emotional maturity and world understanding. Through international service-learning programs, in particular, we also hope to contribute something of value to others. As an expression of sincere desire or obligation, there's nothing wrong and everything right with caring for AIDS orphans, dispensing medical supplies, and building shelters for the homeless. "The problem," contends John Hutnyk in *The Rumour of Calcutta*, "is that the technical apparatus and the conventional possibilities that are currently established for such expression tend easily towards servicing a grossly unequal exploitative system which affects us at every turn" (1996, p. 219). In other words, the collection of service experiences can be just one more form of consumerism, a "commodity" the volunteer actively "takes." This should come as no surprise in a world market where virtually everything is for sale. But it's still important to stand back and consider the links between the global economic system and our study or service abroad.

North-to-South educational travel certainly tends to highlight harsh social and economic imbalances. Contrary to quasi-Marxist analyses, these disparities are rooted not only in oppression by propertied classes but in poor soil, land shortage, primitive technologies, population growth, and despotic leadership (Diamond, 1999). Nevertheless, affluent westerners planning sojourns to third world destinations can discover that the price of their round-trip airfare alone represents a significant percentage of their host's annual income. Australian priest Ron O'Grady (1982), who has lived much of his life among Asia's poor, asks us to ponder their reality:

> They are people who will never be tourists. When they speak of travel they mean going on foot, or in a crowded bus, to the next village or town. . . . Family incomes are barely sufficient for survival and there is no extra money available for luxury travel. Indeed, when they think of luxury, their minds cannot stretch far beyond a bottle of soft drink or a better meal. The concept of a paid holiday or expenditure on leisure travel or visiting a foreign culture is totally outside their conceptual framework. (p. 1)

Ironically, the gross disparity in the life conditions of the poor and the nonpoor underlies much of the allure of third world destinations. The

© 2005 Paul Fitzgerald, Polyp Cartoons

inexpensive and unspoiled places that sojourners increasingly search out and appropriate into their personal worlds reflect, to a great extent, political and economic imbalances that originated under colonial rule. "Imperialism has left its edifices and markers of itself the world over," notes Caren Kaplan, "and tourism seeks these markers out, whether they consist of actual monuments to field marshals or the altered economies of former colonies. Tourism arises out of the economic disasters of other countries that make them 'affordable'" (1996, p. 63).

Living "on the cheap" isn't the only third world draw for affluent travelers. As hinted at earlier, the experience itself is seen as a form of liberation from the shallow and sometimes smothering "overdevelopment" of modern life. Authentic experience is assumed to lie elsewhere, in simple and spontaneous relationship with natural environments and supposedly purer cultures. The thought of braving it for six weeks in a "primitive" village among "traditional" peoples reflects this nostalgic search for a freedom and authenticity that the West lost centuries ago. Of course, the very act of Westerners visiting any remaining "remote and unusual" cultures ensures that those cultures, too, will eventually lose *their* simplicity.

All About Me?

It's often said that what we're attracted to in other people and places are those qualities we miss in ourselves or our homeland. If this is true, travel allows us to escape the banality of our own lives in order to seek satisfying experiences among those who can't escape the reality of their lives.

This is undoubtedly what led me to that remote Vietnamese village mentioned in the introduction to this text. Alighting from my motorbike, I was stunned to see the local community despoiled by U.S. media entertainment. But what was I expecting to find? Traditional forms of entertainment handed down from the elders to the young? An oral recounting of local history in story and verse? What a tale I could have told—of a simplified world where farmers experience antiquity, tranquility, communion with the earth, and all the other things missing in the West. Instead I discovered villagers in Levi's and Nikes intoxicated with images of paradise associated with my own natal land, Los Angeles.

Pico Iyer (1989) reminds us that "a kind of imperial arrogance underlies the very assumption that the people of the developing world should be happier without the TVs and motorbikes that we find so indispensable ourselves. If money does not buy happiness, neither does poverty" (p. 14). It was much easier for me to assume that these premodern villagers had freely chosen their way of life than to consider that maybe, just maybe, it was reflective of their place in the international economic order. My obliviousness was awkward enough, but it can take more pitiful forms. It's rather charmless to see Indian men gawking for hours at topless Swedes on the beaches of Goa, or obese Americans being hoisted onto the backs of camels in the middle of the Egyptian desert.

Images such as these underscore the speed at which traditional economies are converting from meeting their own basic needs to gratifying the leisure whims of foreigners. They also illustrate an astute observation first made by Karl Marx: that it is in the very nature of commodities to veil the social relations embodied in their production. When we eat a piece of fruit, buy an article of clothing, or participate in a study-abroad program, the economic conditions and social relationships of the many people responsible for producing that particular commodity or service are typically hidden from our view. We simply consume the product without giving the larger context a second thought.

Professor Ben Feinberg (2002) of Warren Wilson College was curious to know what, if any, "second thoughts" study-abroad participants actually had after spending months in another culture.

Doubting that a professor could elicit sincere responses from students, I invited one of my favorite undergraduates to work as my research assistant, interviewing 30 or so of her peers who had recently returned from courses in Central America, Europe, and Africa. The responses from Peter, who had spent 10 weeks studying and working on service projects with a group in South Africa, Zimbabwe, and Lesotho, were representative. When asked what he had learned from his African experience, Peter used the first-person pronoun seven times, eliminating Africans: "I learned that I'm a risk taker, um, that I don't put up with people's bull, uh, what else? That I can do anything that I put my mind to. I can do anything I want. You know, it's just—life is what you make of it." (B20)

Global learning became all about them. Feinberg goes on to suggest that a generation raised on reality shows like *Survivor* and *The Amazing Race* come to see exotic locations as personal playgrounds sealed off from real people in real places producing real goods under real conditions with real effects. In fact, the inequalities and injustices that we might experience in some parts of the world are subconsciously perceived to be there for voyeuristic "consumption" as part of the overall experience. Program "sites" become "sights" filled with colorful street scenes of modern skyscrapers towering over teeming shantytowns and scruffy street peddlers. The tourist gaze transforms all into aesthetic images of "nativeness" to be discovered, sighted, and "shot." The question of *how* outrageous wealth and horrendous poverty could share the same physical space is rarely considered. Our reflex is to observe the hardship of others' lives and then come away feeling "blessed" or "lucky" that divine providence or fate has permitted us to be born in privileged circumstances, and not as one of those "made to suffer."

This sense of gratitude, as mentioned earlier, may be heartfelt. But interpreting complex situations through a kind of "lotto logic" evades any serious analysis of the geographic conditions, historical relations, and real abuses (social, economic, political, and environmental) that explain the disparities we observe. And all too often an ignited sense of social responsibility is extinguished by a naive faith in the justice of fate. In either case, the structural relationships between communities of the North and South are sidestepped in favor of an exclusive focus on the individual.

This may partially explain why consistent growth in study-abroad participation has not necessarily met with a corresponding increase in longer-term cross-cultural engagement, whether at home or abroad. It's hard to call people to radical responses to a world that has served only as a backdrop for ephemeral episodes consumed purely for personal enrichment. As noted in the preceding chapter, one frequently hears program directors lament the embarrassingly high percentage of students who exchange the rare delight of engendering cross-cultural understanding for spending hours on end updating blogs and partying with other foreigners. Some commentators, in their call for greater accountability and "quality control," have gone so far as to question the moral propriety of sending culturally innocent first world youth to third world destinations at all. They challenge us to ponder uneasy questions: In what ways do ethnocentrism, racism, nationalism, and exoticism subtly operate within cross-cultural sojourns? Is it even possible for nonpoor students to "encounter" resource-poor residents in anything other than a paternal and intrusive mode?

The Journey Toward Mindfulness

Contentious questions like those above will probably be debated for many years to come. Far less controversial, however, is the expectation for international study and service programs to do everything in their power to protect fragile habitats and cultures and to provide direct financial and social benefits to host communities.

Such an "ethic" is especially evident among the expanding class of independent, educationally oriented travelers. They may be children of privilege, but their travel style is decidedly in the direction of being purposeful and "pro-poor." Some elect to backpack their way through regional circuits, *Lonely Planet* or *Moon* travel guide in hand, in a latter-day equivalent of the Grand Tour. Others prearrange volunteer-service placements through organizations like Action Without Borders (www

.idealist.org) and Wiser Earth (www.wiserearth.org). Still others enroll in programs that feature locally sponsored homestays and service projects organized around issues of conservation, human rights, and community education. What they all share in common is both an awareness of the downside of conventional tourism and a desire to make responsible choices about where and how to travel. If the "old" mass tourist was all about sun, sand, sea, and sex, the "new" mindful traveler aims to be sensible, sensitive, sophisticated, and sustainable.

Even so, the question of how educational travel might enrich an impoverished creation while also enhancing the learning of the nonpoor eludes easy answers. On one level it's becoming increasingly clear that tourism potentially carries both positive and negative effects for host communities. The more obvious of these are summarized in Figure 3.1.

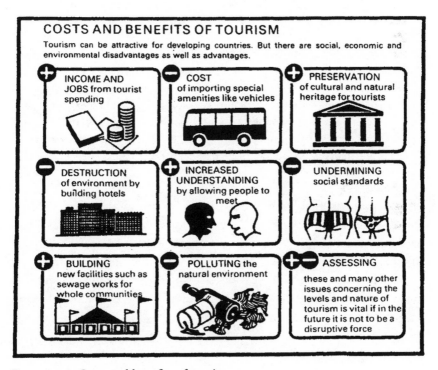

FIGURE 3.1   Costs and benefits of tourism

From the United Nations Environment Programme

On another level, though, a precise accounting of the complex pattern of gains and losses is difficult to achieve, for both technical and ideological reasons. One person might deem a given activity to be "just" and "beneficial" to a given community if it involves only X amount of disturbance to traditional lands and life ways. Another person may define it as involving Y number of new jobs and infrastructural improvements. A third may define it as involving all of these variables, as well as the cultivation of certain types of relationships between guests and hosts.

Instead of technical cost-benefit calculations, our focus is on practical strategies that might enable us, as educational travelers, to maximize benefit and minimize harm to host communities. Some of us may be quite sympathetic with those who argue that an immediate moratorium be placed on first world travel to the third world, at least until the most deleterious environmental and social effects are reversed. But is it realistic to expect that cross-cultural travel can *ever* totally be free of any undesirable effects? Deborah McLaren (2003) maintains that

> For a tourist to have truly minimal impact, she would have to walk to the destination, use no natural resources, and bring her own food that she grew and harvested. She would also have to carry along her own low-impact accommodations (a tent) or stay in a place that is locally-owned and uses alternative technologies and waste treatment. Of course, she would also leave the destination in no worse and perhaps in even better condition than she found it and contribute funds to local environmental protection and community development. (p. 93)

Like the traders and soldiers before us, we are all agents of cultural change. This is particularly so in those regions where sociocultural differences are greatest. Because culture is never static, the question is not whether we will introduce change but *in what direction?* How might we journey in ways that strengthen rather than undermine the goals of economic growth, cultural preservation, social harmony, environmental protection, and spiritual flourishing?

Economic Mindfulness

One in every five international tourists now travels from a "developed" country to a "developing" one. Many of these countries promote tourist activity as a means of generating new jobs and services, earning foreign exchange, and alleviating poverty. Nations like Thailand, Guatemala, and Nepal hope that their stunning landscape, distinctive culture, and low labor costs will attract a new generation of traveler, turning tourism into their "passport for development."

The logic is not hard to appreciate: Tourist demand creates much-needed jobs in various sectors, including construction, light manufacturing, transportation, telecommunications, and financial services. Residents then use their wages to buy the food, medicines, or school uniforms needed to improve their lives, or even to open a small business. New economic enterprises, especially when established in isolated locations, can also stimulate much-needed infrastructural improvements.

But these potential benefits are not automatically fulfilled. "Developing" economies drawn to tourism as a way of earning foreign exchange soon discover that only a relatively small amount of the nonwage revenues generated actually enters their national economy. Much of it ends up being repatriated ("leaked") to first world firms that own and operate the airlines, hotels, car-rental agencies, and food services that foreign travelers depend on. In fact, it's possible for that hypothetical group of 15 college students referred to earlier to book round-trip flights to Thailand on Chinese-owned Cathay Pacific (with commissions paid to a U.S.-based booking agency); enjoy a variety of onboard meals provided through a U.S. catering company; and then, following touchdown, rent a Mercedes or Toyota van that transports them to a hotel owned by a French transnational, before making their way to a local McDonald's or Pizza Hut for dinner.

This example may be generalized, but it highlights the money power held by foreign interests compared with local communities and national governments. In fact, the United Nations Environmental Programme (UNEP) estimates that an average of 55 percent of gross tourism revenues to the developing world actually leak back to developed countries. What does stay in the country is typically captured by domestic elites, with very little actually benefiting poor populations.

That's not all. To attract foreign exchange, governments of poor countries market their beaches and wildernesses, and the customs and festivals of their people, to the rich world. In the process, existing communities are often evicted from prized properties earmarked for tourist development. As real-estate prices soar, the local families that remain must spend a larger share of their income to meet housing needs. Displaced farmers and fisherfolk often have little choice but to reinvent themselves as seasonal tour guides or low-paying security guards for vacation homes that are locked up much of the year. Women are particularly vulnerable, having to find alternative ways of generating income as domestics, bar maids, or worse.

Mindfulness compels us to stay cognizant of who actually gains and loses financially from our presence abroad. Beyond that, it urges us to take practical measures to maximize economic benefits to those typically left out of tourism development. Some of us might decide to stay in locally owned and operated guesthouses and eco-lodges or—better yet—in the homes of the rural or urban poor. (I'm actually writing this from the home of a squatter family in Manila, Philippines, my accommodations having been prearranged by a local pastor I contacted over the Web. The money that would otherwise be paid to a financially secure hotel owner helps to meet the basic needs of a family of seven.) We can also elect to use forms of local transportation that employ poorer members of the community and provide rare opportunities for informal interaction. When essential goods and services are needed, we can opt to patronize resident-owned eateries, barbershops, and sidewalk vendors operating in the massive yet largely unregulated "informal sector." The habit of having one's daily needs supplied by paying a fair price to informal-sector workers provides a direct economic benefit to poor families. And the "circuit" of buying and selling can also evolve into a network of casual friendships that support one's learning of the local language and culture.

Cultural Mindfulness

Besides bringing money into the local community to purchase goods and services, we also introduce a new cultural reality. The languages we speak, the clothes we wear, the new ideas we share, the consumer habits we display—all of these send a message and carry an impact. That impact can be especially overwhelming in more traditional societies unaccustomed to foreign forms.

This doesn't mean that societies can—or should—exist completely independent of outside influences. Every community is enveloped in a complex process of continuity and change, with tourist flows being just one of many transformative effects. Some of those influences can be potentially quite positive. Educational travel, for instance, often facilitates the free exchange of ideas, allowing each party to become an access point to a more cosmopolitan identity and a more astute cultural perspective. At other times, cultural changes are the result, as anthropologist Davydd Greenwood (1989) notes, "of a lack of any other viable option; and some the result of choices that could be made differently" (p. 182). To the extent that we acquire an insider's point of view, we learn to appreciate those elements of the local cultural system that should be "approved" as promoting the well-being of human communities and ecosystems, and also those that might be "improved" or even "reproved" as harmful or unjust. Although evaluating the effects of tourism, much less homegrown cultural features, is riddled with complexity, are we to regard any cultural appraisal as "off limits" to foreigners? Many of the world's most vulnerable populations are protected today as a result of transnational movements that persist in addressing cultural practices that deserve to go, such as child slavery and domestic violence. Greenwood reminds us: "Some of what we see as destruction is construction."

On the positive side of the ledger, tourism can enable third world entrepreneurs to effectively market aspects of their way of life to foreign "culture vultures," thereby helping to revitalize traditional folk arts and instill a fresh sense of cultural pride. "With government or private grants," observes Miriam Adeney (2006), "traditional houses and community centers may be built. Local music and dance and storytelling may be valued and practiced. People may weave and throw pots and dive and trek and climb who otherwise would have become plantation or urban laborers. 'Lost' stories may be recovered and brought back into public discourse" (p. 467). Local traditions and material heritage are important for anyone wanting to gain a deeper appreciation for another culture, and educationally oriented travel can help preserve both.

There is a fine line, as you might expect, between the revitalization of culture and its "Disneyfication." To a greater or lesser extent, we all find ourselves inescapably complicit in the process of commercializing third world "otherness" within a global market economy. Witness the spectacle of indigenous residents-turned-actors in embalmed cultural rituals or artificially staged festivals. In the borderlands of Burma and Thailand, tour operators have set up human zoos featuring women from the Kayan tribal group—called "long necks" because they wear coiled brass rings that elongate their necks. Tourists pay 250 baht (about US$7) to take photos or just stare.

As we search out ever more remote and "authentic" destinations beyond the Eurocentric norm, the pressure for these areas to modernize only intensifies. Since 1975, Swedish linguist Helena Norberg-Hodge (2009) has carefully tracked changes that occurred in the western Himalayan land of Ladakh ("Little Tibet") as it opened to foreign tourists and modern goods. Within two decades, the traditional culture was being held up to scorn and ridicule by youth who began to see themselves as ugly, poor, and backward compared to the beautiful, rich, and culturally sophisticated foreigners.

The movement of affluents into resource-poor areas inevitably entails unequal cultural encounters. Mindful of this fact, we must do all we can to communicate respect for the distinguishing elements of the regional culture. Leading up to the trip, we can take it upon ourselves to learn about the area's political history, current events, religions, and customs (this will be the focus of chapter 5). We can also make sincere efforts to sort out the "unclaimed baggage" of cherished values and expectations— like time efficiency, technology dependence, and hyper-cleanliness—that are likely to perplex, if not annoy and upset, our hosts. Once settled in our destination communities, we will do well to follow the sage advice of vagabonder Rolf Potts (2008):

> Go slow. Respect people. Practice humility, and don't condescend with your good intentions. Make friends. Ask questions. Listen. Know that you are a visitor. Keep promises, even if that just means mailing a photograph a few weeks later. Be a personal ambassador of your home culture, and take your new perspectives home so that you can share them with your neighbors.

Given enough time, intentionality and program support, we may eventually become "accepted outsiders," even in places where regular tourists are rarely seen. Neighbors come to admire, not only our eagerness to adopt native ways without demanding modern amenities, but also our willingness to speak, however haltingly, in the local language. This type of empathetic movement toward the host culture places a needed restraint on potentially offensive cultural practices, whether it is stealth photography or condescending treatment of service workers. In the process, we discover the possibility of transcending the social and cultural patterns that have defined most of our lives in order to explore multiple definitions of what is common and what is good.

Social Mindfulness

Mindful global learning aspires to narrow the gap between "us" and "them," strengthening the bond of understanding and legitimate respect between strangers. Every intercultural program participant is potentially a bridge between peoples, enabling an empathetic, two-way learning process that can be deeply rewarding for host and guest alike. Each brings a different set of "eyes" to the local reality. Pico Iyer accurately observes that, especially in economically poor countries, "a foreigner tends to see paradise where a native sees purgatory, insofar as a foreigner is in a privileged position and has more appreciative eyes, undimmed by familiarity" (Powells.com, 2000). By exercising cultural appreciation, we open the door to forging rare cross-cultural bonds and alliances based on a common commitment to community betterment.

Most of the harmful social side effects of tourism result from the large numbers of visitors introducing a foreign sociocultural reality into a more vulnerable, receiving culture. It often happens that as soon as an unspoiled destination is discovered governments and multinationals rush in to build roads, hotels, restaurants, souvenir shops, and golf courses— "gilded ghettos" that enable temporarily leisured outsiders to enjoy a privileged separation from the mainstream culture.

All too often, the tourist's very presence serves only to exacerbate already existing tensions felt between the young and the old, the traditional and the modern, the beneficiaries of tourism and those marginalized by it. In response to tourists in their midst, locals may start thinking: "I like that these tourists spend money here. But I'm uncomfortable with the way our children want to imitate their tastes in clothes and music. Our children no longer value our local traditions or feel much sense of duty toward their elders. Also, I knew all the groups in our community weren't equal in wealth and power, but now I see how much greater it is in the outside world. The tourist I'm looking at may make in one year 500 or 600 times what I make. I didn't use to think of myself as poor, but now I do. Why do they have so much and most of us have so little? Where did they get all that money? It can't be by just working hard, because we also work hard and look how little we have. Maybe these people are rich because we're poor. Whether that's true or not, I resent them for having so much and then wanting to come see people who have so little" (Abernathy, 2006, pp. 22).

Affluent outsiders must work to understand and empathize with these feelings of resentment over unexplained social and economic disparities. We might experience it as a protective distancing and defensiveness from certain resident populations. At those moments, we come to realize that mere physical proximity in no way guarantees personal proximity; "natural" divisions of nationality, race, social class, language, gender, and social custom can act to keep "hosts" and "guests" worlds apart. Unless we learn to be consciously mindful of ways power and prestige are distributed in our host society, these dividing lines will tend to reinforce each other until a gap of difference becomes a gulf of separation.

Our first step toward social mindfulness is to understand and acknowledge the visible and invisible privileges and prerogatives that we as elite travelers take for granted but that often are denied to our third world hosts.[1] They won't expect us to stop being who we are or to individually "take responsibility" for the historical oppression they may have suffered. What they *do* expect is for us to be aware of our own culturally installed identities and behaviors, and how our perceptions and actions impact the people around us. What's obvious to them, but typically not registered by us, is that being rich and White in the contemporary world is to be "associated with" and "benefited by" a global social hierarchy that places people like us securely at the top and people like them firmly at the bottom.

Aware of the vast social chasm needing to be bridged, we might actually decide to begin our global education in our own backyard. In virtually every North American and European community, our near-neighbors highlight the complex interplay of race, class, language, religion, and immigrant status. In choosing to enter their social worlds, we learn to confront our stereotypes and false assumptions. We recognize our tendency to romanticize, rather than actually befriend and "neighbor" the stranger. And we begin to ask ourselves why we find it easier to struggle for cultural understanding and social justice everywhere else but in our own neighborhoods. Is it because we are drawn to the exotic and glamorous over the familiar and mundane? Or is it because we expect that third world peoples abroad will be less likely to question our motives and more likely to solicit our "help" than those at home? Whatever the reason might be, at some point we must learn to measure our commitment to justice abroad against the walls of our own house. This will inevitably involve close encounters with peripheral groups in our own communities, from whom we will gain a deeper appreciation for how power and privilege is distributed in the modern world.

Lacking this awareness, we can easily feel that some essential "cognitive hooks" are simply not available to "hang" critical incidences abroad. Talya Zemach-Bersin (2008), a study-abroad student in Tibet and Nepal, reports how her "program's curriculum focused on cultural and language studies while avoiding the very issues that were in many ways most compelling and relevant to our experiences." Disgruntled over not having the necessary conceptual tools to critically process what it meant to be a White American abroad, she asks, "Why had we not analyzed race, identity, and privilege when those factors were informing every one of our interactions?" Zemach-Bersin's chagrin (some might say naïveté) over being viewed, time and again, as a privileged Westerner only supports our main contention: that the quality of our relations abroad largely depends on the consciousness we carry with us. Which is why the shortest route to global understanding may actually run through the lives of strangers at home.

Ecological Mindfulness

Until recently, one of the most neglected areas of ethical reflection in global study and service programs has been the relation of the traveler to the ecosphere. The natural world was generally perceived as trivial, merely the stage for the interplay of cultural actors, with no particular moral questions or obligations. This general disposition has begun to change. After nearly three decades of environmental advocacy, and especially with the release of Al Gore's absorbing documentary *An Inconvenient Truth*, more and more of us are considering the ecological consequences of our actions.

Indeed, one of those "inconvenient truths" is that global travel is closely linked with climate change. Few of us stop to consider the enormous amount of jet fuel required to fly us from home to that colorful or "unspoiled" location abroad. Airplanes travel in the sensitive upper troposphere and lower stratosphere, where they release a cocktail of greenhouse-gas emissions that currently accounts for about 13 percent of total transportation-sector emissions of carbon dioxide (CO_2). A single trip from Toronto to Tokyo, for instance, produces over one ton of CO_2 *per passenger*. And this does not include the emissions from energy used in the airport buildings, facilities, baggage systems, airport service vehicles, concession facilities, aircraft fueling, airport construction, air navigation, and safety operations. "Fortunately for the climate," writes Ian Jack (2006), "a lot of the world's population is too poor to do much traveling at all."

As the situation with atmospheric CO_2 worsens, it's likely that national governments will be forced to impose some form of carbon tax or greenhouse-gas "allowance" in order to meet legally binding carbon-emissions-reduction targets. Until they do, respect for the aggregate rights of the biosphere calls us to embody personal lifestyles of restraint and frugality. "Love entails giving up at least some of our own interests and benefits for the sake of the well-being of others in communal relationships," notes ethicist James Nash (1991). To some, the idea of yielding up even *some* of our travel privileges in order to safeguard the well-being of others sounds like wishful thinking. After all, don't we have an indisputable "right" to travel, given sufficient time and money?

Ecological mindfulness calls us, first of all, to break through our obliviousness and indifference in relation to planet earth. It is, after all, our one and only home. Once this basic estrangement is healed we are in a position to weigh the educational benefits of our travel against the real harm done by it. This might lead us to ponder without denial or rationalization, whether the potential benefits justify the real costs. If we truly believe that global learning isn't just about us, how do we balance the moral good of broadening our cultural horizons and enjoying the planet's resources against the intrinsic rights of ecosystems and their associated life-forms?

I'm under no illusion that we can simply turn off our fossil-fuel-powered civilization and conserve our way to zero carbon emissions. At the same time, I've often wondered whether a greater "good" is achieved by transporting a team of 15 Americans to Ghana for three weeks of service-learning at a local orphanage at a combined cost of $35,000 and 40 tons of CO_2, when that same amount of money could support six full-time Ghanaians for an entire year without damaging the environment. I want to suppose that the intercultural encounters, together with exposure to a low-energy way of life, will significantly "globalize" the Americans' thinking and "green" their lifestyles back home. But I know this is far from automatic. The far more common tendency is to eschew any personal responsibility or to adopt a childlike faith that, in the end, better fuels and technologies will save us.

Perhaps a more promising strategy would be to manipulate those program features, like length of term and size of group, that bias participants toward maximizing benefits and minimizing potentially harmful effects to all stakeholders. We can also address the enormous challenge of global climate change by flying carbon-neutral. Essentially this involves calculating our "carbon footprint" (the approximate amount of carbon dioxide created by our flights), and then buying "offsets" calculated to equal the amount of CO_2 created by the trip per passenger.[2] While some argue that such "offsets" merely allow us to buy indulgences for our sins of emission, others see them as an indispensable, though not sufficient, means of pumping money into renewable-energy projects and reducing fossil-fuel dependence.

At the point when we actually take up residence abroad, mindfulness requires that we retain our eco-sense. Tourism development is notorious for thoughtlessly "paving over paradise" and overusing scarce resources to meet the heavy water and energy demands of its patrons. In Phuket, Thailand, the fresh water needed for showers, toilets, baths, swimming pools, and golf courses at 10 of the largest hotels equals the water used by the entire local population of 250,000 (McLaren, 2003, pp. 86–87). We can help reverse this trend by opting to live with local families and learning to consciously adjust our level of water and power consumption toward the local standard. Here in Manila, my host family expects me to turn off any fans or lights that are not in use, to take "bucket" showers that use just a few scoops of water, and to hand wash and line dry my clothes. Adopting these new habits of restrained consumption serves as a constant reminder that my study or service site is someone else's home, and that we all share a finite planet with exhaustible resources.

Spiritual Mindfulness

Every international sojourn brings us to a forking of paths. It can be yet one more "been there, done that" experience that pampers a spirit of pleasure and conquest. Or it can be something of a love story that romances our host community through empathetic acts of inquiry and caring. Spiritual mindfulness follows the latter path, inviting us to join local residents in pursuing insight and wholeness as a natural response to the spirit of life.

In most cities of the South, ethnic and religious heritages intermingle. Local residents manifest an enormous range of pieties and practices, both within particular religious traditions and at the interface between them. Each tradition has its own set of integrative norms that fundamentally influence their adherents' attitudes toward personal virtue, family, community, ecology, and political authority. This pervasive religiosity may take some getting used to, especially if the idea of divine transcendence has been eclipsed by human autonomy. But if we are willing to maintain a principled openness to evidences of the sacred, the deep continuity of religious belief among native populations can present us with rare opportunities to discover practical wisdom and vital spiritual resources for cultivating a deeper, richer sense of self.

Unfortunately, most modern travelers carry a reputation for being outgoing but insular, largely unreceptive to sources of value and virtue outside themselves and their own cultural traditions. By now it should be obvious that an ethnocentric, our-way-is-the-best-way orientation ultimately contributes little to us as travelers, much less to our host communities. Not only does it leave us at arm's length from some of the community's most important sources of meaning; it also unwittingly reproduces the imperial error of a previous generation. The traders and missionaries of the colonial era were, according to David Bosch (1993),

> predisposed not to appreciate the cultures of the people to whom they went—the unity of living and learning; the interdependence between individual, community, culture, and industry; the profundity of folk wisdom; the proprieties of traditional societies—all these were swept aside by a mentality shaped by the Enlightenment which tended to turn people into objects, reshaping the entire world into the image of the West, separating

humans from nature and from one another, and "developing" them according to Western standards and suppositions. (p. 294)

In a post-9/11 world, the margin of tolerance for repeating such errors has narrowed significantly. First world sojourners are especially at risk of being perceived as cultural imperialists interested only in extracting personal satisfactions from third world miseries. All the more reason why educational travel must dispose us, first of all, to seek out and welcome all reflections of truth, goodness, and beauty in the lives of those we meet. Reversing the natural tendency to denounce poorly understood ways of living, we stay poised to catch glimpses of the "holy" in even the most distressed places and peoples.

Imagine entering any one of the *favelas* of Rio de Janeiro (Brazil) or *umjondolos* of Durban (South Africa) as part of a global-learning term. Immediately we would be immersed in physical and social realities as far removed from the landscape of automobile suburbs, sterile office complexes, and megamalls as can be. Our natural impulse, as curious outsiders, might be to treat the slum community as something of a tragic spectacle, something merely to feed our appetite for the bizarre.

But what if we were to find meaningful ways to connect with residents—playing billiards or soccer with the young men, participating in a storefront religious service, or volunteering in one of the area's preschools? A self-aggrandizing and impersonal "poverty tour" might suddenly take on deeply human dimensions as we enter into the resilience, communal bonds, and spiritual vitality of those struggling against the insecurity of their environment. "In the slums of Dhaka," reports Jeremy Seabrook (1995), "there is an attempt to teach literacy to 60,000 adults. In the late evening, by the smoky flare of kerosene lamps, rag-pickers, brick workers, domestic servants, child laborers, and rickshaw-pullers meet to learn and to share their lives. They are delighted when others try to understand what motivates them" (p. 23).

By generously serving alongside people of different faiths but like passion, we share in the difficult but deeply rewarding task of making the world a better place to live. This shared commitment also provides the context for thinking much more clearly about ourselves in relation to other people and the root issues affecting their lives. Jackie's experience of having her cultural complacencies unsettled through serving alongside residents of a rural community in El Salvador suggests the transformative potential:

> Now I look at things through different eyes. Things I do and even things I buy, things I say, even just talking with people. And on the big level of what I am going to do with my life . . . I have been saying over and over that the people are not just numbers anymore. The poor are no longer just statistics. They have names and faces. They are friends. (Yonkers-Talz, n.d.)

Like Jackie, we might find that the initial confidence we exercise in commencing a journey abroad may unexpectedly evolve into a deeper unknowing. Everything may appear much more complex and less cut-and-dried than before. This is, after all, the genius of educational travel. As it arouses our passion and fascination with the unknown world, it also engages us in a constructive questioning of assumptions regarding our place in it. We find that there are no easy answers, especially as we face off with economic and political forces beyond our direct control. Grand, heroic acts are not necessary to participate in the process of change. Small acts, conducted in hope and with a certain mindfulness of our effect on a structurally unequal world, can quietly help to usher in a brighter future.

For Reflection and Discussion

1. What are some of the largely unintended impacts—both positive and negative—of international travel?
2. Explain *why* certain negative impacts occur and what you can do to minimize the negative and maximize the positive impacts. What, specifically, will you do to journey mindfully?

Notes

1. Resources for deciphering the mechanisms of power and privilege include "White Privilege and Male Privilege: A Personal Account of Coming to See Correspondences Through Work in Women's Studies," by P. McIntosh, 1992, in

M. L. Anderson & P. H. Collins (Eds.), *Race, Class, and Gender: An Anthology* (pp. 70–82), Belmont, CA: Wadsworth; *Privilege, Power, and Difference* (2nd ed.), by A. Johnson, 2005, New York: McGraw-Hill; and *White Like Me: Reflections on Race From a Privileged Son*, by T. Wise, 2004, New York: Soft Skull Press.

2. One of the best websites for calculating flight emissions, and then "neutralizing" them through community projects, is http://www.carbonneutral.com/cncalculators/flightcalculator.asp.

References

Abernathy, D. (2006). Ethical dilemmas and practical risks in tourist philanthropy. In *Responsible travel handbook 2006* (pp. 20–27). Retrieved June 25, 2009, from www.transitionsabroad.com/listings/travel/responsible/responsible_travel_handbook.pdf

Adeney, M. (2006). Shalom tourist: Loving your neighbor while using her. *Missiology: An International Review, 34*(4), pp. 463–476.

Anderson, W. T. (2001). *All connected now: Life in the first global civilization*. Boulder, CO: Westview Press.

Bosch, D. (1993). *Transforming mission*. Maryknoll, NY: Orbis Books.

Bourdieu, P., & Passeron, J. C. (1990). *Reproduction in education, society, and culture*. Thousand Oaks, CA: Sage.

Diamond, J. (1999). *Guns, germs and steel: The fate of human societies*. New York: W.W. Norton.

Feinberg, B. (2002, May 3). Point of view: What students don't learn abroad. *The Chronicle of Higher Education*, p. B20.

Greenwood, D. (1989). Culture by the pound: An anthropological perspective on tourism as cultural commoditization. In V. Smith (Ed.), *Hosts and guests: The anthropology of tourism* (2nd ed., pp. 171–186). Philadelphia: University of Pennsylvania Press.

Hutnyk, J. (1996). *The rumour of Calcutta: Tourism, charity and the poverty of representation*. London: Zed Books.

Iyer, P. (1989). *Video night in Kathmandu*. New York: Vintage.

Jack, I. (2006, Summer). Introduction. *Granta*, 94 ("On the Road Again").

Kaplan, C. (1996). *Questions of travel: Postmodern discourses of displacement*. Durham, NC: Duke University Press.

McLaren, D. (2003). *Rethinking tourism and ecotravel (2nd ed.)* Sterling, VA: Kumarian Press.

Nash, J. (1991). *Loving nature: Ecological integrity and Christian responsibility*. Nashville: Abingdon Press.

Norberg-Hodge, H. (2009). *Ancient futures: Lessons from Ladakh for a globalizing world.* San Francisco: Sierra Club/Counterpoint.

O'Grady, R. (1982). *Tourism in the third world.* Maryknoll, NY: Orbis Books.

Potts, R. (2008, January 14). *A slight rant about the rhetoric of "ethical travel."* Retrieved February 3, 2009, from http://www.vagablogging.net/a-slight-rant-about-the-rhetoric-of-ethical-travel.html#more-1272

Powells.com. (2000, March 27). *Pico Iyer's mongrel soul.* Retrieved October 3, 2008, from http://www.powells.com/authors/iyer.html

Seabrook, J. (1995). Far horizons. *New Statesman & Society, 8*(365), pp. 22–23.

Tagore, R. (1996). *English writings of Rabindranath Tagore, v.3: A miscellany.* New Delhi: Sahitya Akademi, India.

Wolfe, A. (1999). *One nation, after all.* New York: Penguin.

Yonkers-Talz, K. (n.d.). *The student's struggle for solidarity: How does immersion impact our students?* Retrieved February 25, 2008, from http://www.scu.edu/ignatiancenter/bannan/publications/explore/spring06/section02.cfm

Zemach-Bersin, T. (2008). American students abroad can't be "global citizens." *The Chronicle of Higher Education, 54*(26), p. A34.

MAKING PREPARATIONS

Congratulations!
Today is your day.
You're off to Great Places!
You're off and away!
You have brains in your head.
You have feet in your shoes.
You can steer yourself any direction you choose.
You're on your own. And you know what you know.
And YOU are the guy who'll decide where to go . . .
And will you succeed?
Yes! You will, indeed! (98 and ³/₄ percent guaranteed.)
Kid, You'll Move Mountains!
—DR. SEUSS, *Oh! The Places You'll Go*

I REMEMBER MY CHILDHOOD as a time when I was encouraged to achieve all that I could. Life challenges were to be met head-on with an intensely pragmatic, can-do spirit. By marshaling enough energy and making the necessary sacrifices, I could "move mountains," achieve any goal.

Especially in the United States, young people are trained to stand alone, think independently, and become their own person. In fact, adulthood dictates that we rediscover and re-create ourselves *apart from* family and inherited traditions. In the process we learn to be our own source of necessary information and to believe that we should make decisions and solve problems without consulting with or depending on others. Our wildest dreams can be fulfilled by simply venturing out into the world and overcoming all obstacles. The future is bright. The sky's the limit. The time is now. Take the necessary risks and . . . just do it!

No wonder many of us chafe at making certain preparations for our sojourn abroad. Expending effort in detailing every facet of the trip may seem like an awful waste of time. Like modern-day nomad Rita Golden Gelman (2002), we may wish to "move through the world without a plan, guided by instinct, connecting through trust, and constantly watching for serendipitous opportunities" (p. vii). Our fear is that deliberate preparation will only detract from the chance encounters that catch us by surprise and yield the most wonderful memories.

But planning and providence need not be mutually exclusive. As Phil Cousineau maintains in *The Art of Pilgrimage* (2000), "Preparation no more spoils the chance for spontaneity and serendipity than discipline ruins the opportunity for genuine self-expression in sports, acting, or the tea ceremony" (p. 71). Thousands of other experienced travelers make a similar claim: that attention given to patient preparation actually allows one to leave with peace of mind and to learn with focused attention. Rather than encumbering us, putting things in order serves to lighten our load and ready us for the many "teachable moments" that we don't anticipate. We prepare for spontaneity and serendipity.

Of course, no predeparture process can ready us for *every* experience we will encounter abroad. Travelers experience and react to situations in vastly different ways. But whoever we are and wherever we go, we are more likely to minimize frustration and maximize learning if we treat "getting ready" as an integral part of the total travel experience—a type of journey in its own right. Learn to approach travel preparations not as obstacles to the "real" goals of cross-cultural living and learning, but as opportunities to interact with folk who might have something to teach us about the art of travel. The discipline of making preparations also serves to organize the transition between "home" and "field" into a sort of ritual by which we allow ourselves time to gradually adjust to another frame of mind. From the moment we commit to the act of leaving, we begin to prime ourselves emotionally, physically, and spiritually for new regions, new relationships, and new responsibilities. The sooner we begin planning, the richer the potential metamorphosis.

Preparations are highly personalized and can take various forms. Throughout the world, purifying rites of fasting and spiritual contemplation prepare group members for challenging life passages. Cousineau notes the Muslim practices of head shaving, nail trimming, and donning of all-white robes before undertaking a sacred pilgrimage. Many Native American tribes conduct special prayer meetings for members leaving for college or military service. In like manner, Jesus enjoins his pilgrim followers to pray long and travel light as they begin their hazardous journey (Luke 10:1–3).

What follows is simply one means for managing the practical aspects of your global-learning term. It supplements other preparation rituals by leading us through a number of "conversations" addressing matters that range from selecting an appropriate program and obtaining a passport to making travel arrangements and packing gear. Most topical discussions include a set of select websites as vital resources for completing preparation in a self-paced manner. Expect to be inspired and perhaps overwhelmed by the volume of available information. Patiently sift through the contents of each site for what is most useful. Then record relevant information in a journal or field book of some kind so that you'll have ready access to it.

What Type of Program Is Best for Me?

Any cross-cultural study and service plan begins by reflecting on some basic questions: *What* type of experiences will help meet my learning goals? *Where* do I want to study or serve, and *for how long*—a summer, a semester, or an entire year? Finally, *how* do I best learn: solo or with a group, through classroom lectures, or through community immersion?

Literally thousands of study and service programs exist for global learners to choose from. They differ widely in terms of program length, extent of prefield preparation, level of sociocultural difference, degree of cultural immersion, and use of host language. One way of bringing some organization to the immense variety of program types is to think of global learning at three levels: exposure, encounter, and integration.

Exposure programs can range from the short (one to three weeks) study tour or mission trip to the four- to six-week summer course. These experiences provide a first contact with another way of life in a cross-cultural setting. No language or culture training is normally required (apart from a brief orientation), and in most cases, faculty or staff accompany the student group and arrange academic credit. A classic example is the art-history tour, with group hotel accommodations, morning lectures, guided museum visits, and perhaps some directed reading and writing assignments. Competency goals are usually limited to acquiring specialized knowledge. An institutionalized "tourist culture" typically caters to the group's travel needs, narrowing the sociocultural distance between hosts and guests and minimizing the degree of contact with the mainstream society. Given the predetermined itinerary, participant self-direction is low, but costs—which include group transportation, hotel accommodation, and site visits—can be quite high. The value of exposure programs is that they offer a level of intellectual, aesthetic, and intercultural enrichment beyond that of simple tourism, with the potential to act as a springboard for longer, more culturally challenging experiences.

The next level, the cross-cultural *encounter*, is perhaps best represented by semesterlong programs operating in either national or international settings. Sponsored by either a student's "home" institution or an in-country "host" institution or agency, encounter-type programs are often organized around the investigation of a particular issue of global consequence (e.g., "Ecology and Conservation," "Culture and Development," "Peace and Conflict"). An on-field director is responsible for providing academic and personal counseling, as well as arranging housing, lectures, service placements, and language- and field-study opportunities for groups of 15 to 50 participants. In-country coursework is typically organized through the host institution and conducted in English. Few, if any, prerequisites (like language-study or area-studies courses) are generally required, and participant self-direction and cultural immersion can range from low to medium. Participants draw their most positive memories from experiences shared with others in the student group.

The most challenging program type features a significant amount of cross-cultural *integration*. The term abroad can extend to 6 to 12 months, enabling learners to fully participate either in the daily life of national students via direct enrollment in a host university, or in direct immersion in the daily life of a local resident (i.e., nonstudent) community. Some programs combine elements of both models. In the "direct enrollment" model, students enroll directly in a foreign university, completing course-work in the local language with local students and local professors. Integration is achieved by immersion—at least into an elite academic sub-culture. Although the potential for intercultural learning is great, much depends on whether they receive the coaching and support necessary to make sense of and function effectively in their new environment. Students participating in the "community immersion" model often complete extensive training in the host language and in field-study methods (i.e., learning how to learn). They integrate directly into the host society through family homestays, voluntary service placements within community organizations, and independent research on development-related topics. Drawing on a repertoire of linguistic and cultural skills, their challenge is to adapt themselves to local routines and relationships as the prerequisite to a deepening understanding of another way of life.

More and more students are electing to include two, three, and sometimes more global-learning ventures in their postsecondary education. One of my own students, Robert, completed an exposure-type travel/study seminar along the Nile River valley in Egypt during a "gap" year between high school and college. He followed with an encounter-type urban field-study program in central Los Angeles during his sophomore year. By junior year he was ready to immerse himself in Freetown, Sierra Leone for six months in an integration-type process. He lived with a local family and joined UNICEF in their efforts to demobilize and reintegrate child soldiers back into society.

WEB RESOURCES

◊ GoAbroad.com: www.goabroad.com
◊ StudyAbroad.com: www.studyabroad.com
◊ Council on International Educational Exchange: www.ciee.org
◊ Institute for International Education: www.iiepassport.org
◊ *Transitions Abroad* magazine: www.transitionsabroad.com

Should I Travel Alone or With Companions?

The decision to travel solo or with one or more companions is one of a handful of factors that can profoundly affect one's intercultural learning.

The mere presence of 15 to 20 other copatriots at a program site, all sharing the same language and cultural habits, often discourages one from making real connections with local residents. As strangers in a strange land, it's only natural to "cocoon" with cultural similars in order to meet our social and emotional needs. But there is a downside. "Grouping shields the individual from the discomfort of host culture and language contact," explain John and Lilli Engle (2003), "while travel serves up a comfortably neutral, generally English-speaking world" (p. 29). For travel to be deeply educative it must render certain familiar things—like physical settings, cultural habits, and social relationships—unfamiliar. Without authentic encounters with alternative frames of reference, much of the learning potential of our sojourns drops out. English cleric and writer Charles Caleb Colton reached a similar conclusion nearly 100 years ago. In *Lacon* he wrote: "Those who visit foreign nations, but associate only with their own countrymen, change their climate, but not their customs. They see new meridians, but with the same men; and with heads as empty as their pockets, return home with traveled bodies, but untraveled minds."

If banding together with our own tends to produce "untraveled minds," is traveling solo the answer, especially for a woman? Maybe not. Maybe so. It's certainly true that in much of the world, "single women traveling alone" is a cultural anomaly. In places like India and Vietnam it rarely takes place, and the very idea can, quite frankly, mystify locals. Rarely would an unmarried woman think of traveling unaccompanied, even if her family would tolerate it. At the same time, as Susan Griffith (n.d.) rejoins,

> There is a pernicious mythology surrounding the lone female traveler, whether it be as a hitchhiker around Britain or a traveler in Southeast Asia. Many people instantly exaggerate the perils and dwell on a single woman's vulnerability. Often this doom-ridden response is just an excuse for their own timidity of spirit. In fact, traveling around most of Asia is far safer, and more pleasant, than traveling on the Lexington Avenue line in New York City. (para. 3)

The on-the-ground experience of an increasing number of intrepid female travelers suggests that concerns about potential perils are more than offset by the unexpected delights opened up by an independent mode of travel. Marybeth Bond (n.d.), who has traveled solo through six continents and more than 70 countries, narrates the type of serendipitous encounters that can become almost daily occurrences:

> On a beach in Bali I asked an American woman to watch my bag while I went swimming. After a short conversation, we became friends and explored the island together—renting a motorcycle to discover remote villages set among green terraced rice fields, even changing flights to continue traveling together. Later, I met a Swiss woman on a plane to Delhi and ended up renting a houseboat with her in Kashmir. This voyage taught me that women connect easily when traveling and rely on each other for advice and companionship. (para. 2)

Many cross-cultural programs answer the independent versus group-travel question for participants by their very design. Nevertheless, there may still be some "wiggle room" for personal choice, and we do well to process the pros and cons in advance. Pertinent questions include these: Is my personality introverted or outgoing? Has my past experience as a group or solo traveler been pleasurable or torturous? Is my proposed destination isolated or more cosmopolitan? Are women's roles there rigid or flexible? Is the English language dominant or are there few speakers? Is my program structured in ways that encourage cultural immersion or separation?

As you sort out these issues, keep in mind that our natural desire is always for what we don't have. Gertrude Stein's observation applies to even the most seasoned travelers: "When they are alone they want to be with others, and when they are with others they want to be alone. After all, human beings are like that" (2003, p. 107). That said, returning sojourners have, over the years, highlighted a number of potential benefits *and* drawbacks of traveling in a more self-directed and culturally immersed style. Their own words capture some of the singular advantages:

◊ *Reliance on locals.* "Of course, 'going alone' is all relative; you're never really alone. You're surrounded by family members, greeted by neighbors, and shoulder to shoulder with coworkers in your service organization."

- ◊ *Freedom to form friendships with nationals.* "Not being attached to another foreign student forced me to make friends with locals, which was the main reason for me to travel abroad in the first place."
- ◊ *Openness to new experiences.* "The day I was about to leave India, there was a huge transportation strike. No mode of transit moved. So I spent three days in the Calcutta airport with hundreds of people from all over. We shared food from the airport eateries, and talked and talked. I connected with a family from Malaysia and ended up going to Malaysia and living with them for a couple of weeks. I'm not sure any of this would have happened had someone else been traveling with me."
- ◊ *Self-understanding.* "It's hard to put into words how difficult it was to be stuck with myself in such an unrelenting way. But I feel that through it I finally became an adult."
- ◊ *Confronting and conquering fears.* "To say I'm being stretched out of my comfort zone doesn't quite capture it. Almost every day I'm doing and feeling things that I've never done or felt before. I'm finding myself changing, becoming a more confident and independent kind of person."

There are, however, potential downsides. They cluster around the natural apprehensions that prevent some sojourners from completely embracing an independent travel style:

- ◊ *"I don't like being alone."* For some, being alone is torturous. We crave the company of others, whether eating, studying, or just hanging out.
- ◊ *"I'll feel too vulnerable and afraid."* The world has become a more dangerous place, especially for White Westerners. In many cultures, women walking alone are frequently gawked at and harassed by men.
- ◊ *"I'll be in trouble if I get sick."* Illness is a drag wherever you are, but protracted bouts of malaria or dysentery can be grueling, especially in a place where you lack facility in the language and the comfort of familiar friends.

◊ *"I won't have anyone to share the experience with."* In order to make sense out of our experience, we need the opportunity to dialogue with others going through similar experiences.

◊ *"I'll have to make all the decisions, and I don't trust my judgment."* Some of us dread taking the kind of responsibility and initiative necessary to truly take charge of our own education. We prefer the predictability, ego safety, and ready companionship provided by traveling and learning with others.

Taken together, feedback from fellow travelers points to the need to achieve an optimal balance between *challenge* and *support* during our term abroad (Sanford, 1966; Vande Berg, 2009). One of the creative ways that some learners accomplish this is by combining the security and companionship of group travel with the freedom and cultural-integration potential of solo travel into what might be called the "independent duo." Writing from Cochabamba, Bolivia, Stephanie commends this arrangement and leaves us to consider how it might be adapted within our own field programs.

> In the past, I assumed that traveling with another person and having them live in the same city would surely inhibit the learning experience and make it much harder to develop relationships with locals. Interestingly enough I'm discovering that, in reality, the opposite is true. By having a companion in the same city, you have a support system that enables you to remain emotionally healthy so that you are then able to develop relationships with locals.

How Do I Obtain a Passport and Any Necessary Visas?

All international travel requires proper documentation and identification. Each country has its own special requirements for entry, typically based on one's citizenship, purpose of visit, and length of stay. It's our responsibility to find out which requirements pertain to our situation and to obtain the appropriate documents in advance.

Passports

A valid passport is your official identification as a citizen of a particular nation. As such, it is also your single most important travel document. Even land or sea travel by Americans to Canada and Mexico may require at least a high-security, wallet-size tourist card. A passport or tourist card must be on your person to show border and customs authorities whenever you enter or leave other nations, or on various other occasions that require official verification of your citizenship. Pay special attention to the expiration date. A current U.S. passport, for example, needs to be valid at least six months *beyond* the time of your travel. If it is due to expire prior to the end of travel, be sure to apply for a new passport before leaving home.

Applications typically take at least two months, so apply far ahead of your departure (and longer if you're going to need visas). In the United States, passports are issued by the Department of State through any office of the U.S. Passport Services or through one of the several thousand federal or state courts, U.S. post offices, or public libraries authorized to accept passport applications. The State Department website provides the latest policy information and allows you to search, by zip code, the nearest location for submitting your application.

If it is your first passport application, you'll need to apply in person. Be sure to bring some proof of U.S. citizenship (e.g., a certified copy of a birth certificate or naturalization certificate); two identical photographs taken within six months of applying (measuring two inches square, with a white background); and proof of identity, such as a valid driver's license (not a Social Security or credit card). Finally, you must complete Form DS-11, "Application for a U.S. Passport." The application and execution fees for a 10-year passport total around $100; renewals run $75. If you're in a real hurry, for an extra fee you can request "expedited service" from the U.S. State Department or the over 100 private organizations.

Once you obtain your passport, put it away in a safe but accessible place. Losing a passport while overseas can be nerve-wracking; procedures for obtaining a replacement are complicated and time-consuming. Be sure to carry with you—separate from your passport—two extra passport pictures, along with your passport number and the date and place it was issued. If your passport is lost or stolen while abroad, immediately notify your country's consulate or embassy, local police authorities, and your program supervisor.

Visas

A visa is a document provided by officials of a foreign government that permits you to enter that country for a specified purpose and for a limited time. Whether you need a visa or not depends on what country you visit and the length and purpose of your stay. The visa generally takes the form of an endorsement or stamp placed inside the passport, so you need to have a passport already before applying for a visa. Some visas are free and easy to acquire, but others may cost over $100 and require extensive documentation and wait time.

Prior to departure, chart out what travel you'll do beyond your host country and whether a visa is needed for those countries. Visas are not always available at the border or on arrival at a main airport, in which case you'll need to obtain them from the embassy in a neighboring country's major city. Doing so will typically involve less hassle and expense than applying from your home nation. But be prepared: Besides a valid passport, you may need one or more photos, proof of sufficient travel funds, and an invitation letter (provided by a university, a family, or an in-country organization).

WEB RESOURCES

◊ U.S. State Department Passport Services: http://travel.state.gov/pass port/passport_1738.html
◊ Visa information: http://travel.state.gov/travel/cis_pa_tw/cis/cis_ 1765.html
◊ National Association of Passport and Visa Services: http://napvs .info/

How Should I Prepare for Potential Health Risks?

Every year more than a third of the estimated 45 million U.S. citizens who travel abroad experience a travel-related illness. The risk is greatest throughout the developing world, where simple exposure to contaminated food or water can suddenly leave you with unwanted souvenirs: parasites, diarrhea, intestinal problems, or an upper-respiratory infection. Of course, these and many other illnesses—such as malaria, yellow fever, and tick-borne encephalitis—are endemic to whole regions of the world and a part of the daily life of local residents. If this is the reality for those with a lifetime of built-up immunities, how much more vigilant should nonnatives like us be in learning all necessary precautions as part of our trip preparation?

As a first line of defense, consider your general health and other personal circumstances when deciding where, how, and for how long to travel. As a general rule, you should not suffer from any special mental or physical condition that would prevent you from fulfilling personal or program expectations. Plan to have a travel-medicine specialist assess your overall health status in relation to the destination location, travel season, and type of travel. This checkup should be completed at least four weeks prior to departure in order to allow any necessary vaccinations and immunizations to take effect. Vaccines are designed to protect against the most prevalent diseases, including hepatitis A, typhoid, yellow fever, dengue, and malaria. They expose your body to a little bit of a disease germ that is weak or dead, allowing the body's defense system to build up its own protection (i.e., antibodies) to fight the disease.

Have your university's campus health-service office or travel doctor stamp each vaccination on an International Certificate of Vaccinations, or "yellow card." This is an official proof of vaccinations and may occasionally be required as a condition of entry into some countries. Most of the important "jabs" you actually receive will be boosters of shots you had as a child, but even boosters will leave you feeling a bit groggy afterward. Because travelers can't acquire effective resistance to malaria, most doctors will advise one of two prophylactic regimes (mefloquine or doxycycline) that start prior to travel and end several weeks after leaving the malaria zone. For comprehensive health information and country-specific recommendations, peruse the websites of the Centers for Disease Control and Prevention (CDC) and the World Health Organization (WHO).

Finally, be certain to carry adequate health and accident insurance. An "adequate" level of coverage is determined either *by you*, independently, or *for you* by the chosen field program. Overseas programs typically include insurance coverage in their fee structure, but whether you are buying a policy on your own or paying for a program policy, find out exactly what is and what is not covered by the plan. Does the coverage extend overseas for the entire duration of your study or service term? Can you extend the policy online? Do you have to be a full-time student to qualify? Some policies cover high-risk activities like river rafting and mountain biking but others do not. Some cover dental and optical care but others limit coverage to medical illness or injury. Carefully examine and evaluate terms and rates related to preexisting conditions, emergency evacuation, overseas legal assistance, lost or stolen baggage, kidnapping or terrorism, and accidental death and dismemberment. Rates for each of these coverages may vary with geographic region.

Most important, review your policy for its claim process. Insurance companies require that you submit claims "by the book," including contacting the company immediately after an incident. It is especially important to know whether the carrier will make payments directly to the service provider (i.e., the hospital and/or physician overseas) or whether you, the traveler, are first required to obtain preauthorizations or second opinions, pay in advance for services, and then submit claims for later reimbursement. If the latter is true, *it is imperative that you retain any and all receipts* (including ATM slips).

WEB RESOURCES

- ◊ U.S. Centers for Disease Control and Prevention: http://wwwnc.cdc .gov/travel
- ◊ *International Travel and Health* (WHO publication): www.who.int/ ith/en
- ◊ Canadian Society for International Health: http://www.csih.org/
- ◊ "Health Insurance Options Abroad" article: www.transitionsabroad .com/publications/magazine/0801/health_insurance_options_abroad .shtml

What Should I Do to Stay Safe
and Secure in the Country?

In the spring of 1996, on a six-hour side trip on the fabled Grand Trunk Road in India, four U.S. college students tumbled to their death as their tour bus lost control, swerved, and careened off the dimly lit highway into a ditch. They, with a group of 60 other foreign students, were en route to the Taj Mahal. That same year numerous other incidents were reported to study-abroad offices in the United States. Among them: an alleged rape in a host home in Morocco; a debilitating case of dengue fever in Lima, Peru; and a mugging in Lagos, Nigeria that resulted in a stolen wallet and passport but, fortunately, no bodily harm.

Security concerns have taken on a new urgency with the increased popularity of travel to ever more remote and risk-prone areas of the world. Off the beaten path of global tourism, sickness and disease are more prevalent. Roads are often treacherous and buses old and over-crowded. Thieves are ever on the prowl for unsuspecting innocents. Women—especially *foreign* women—are easy targets for verbal sexual harassment, groping, and even physical assault. These are only some of the conditions that give rise to the tragic stories we often hear: of student-travelers being bedridden with dysentery or malaria, being robbed of all they have, or narrowly avoiding rape or a serious motor-vehicle accident.

I'd like to tell you that these things *don't* ever happen, but unfortunately they do. The good news is that, statistically, the overwhelming majority of the tens of thousands of adults who travel abroad for educational purposes each year have safe and enjoyable journeys. United Educators, which insures almost 900 U.S. colleges and universities, processed fewer than 100 claims over a 10-year period ending in 2004. Nevertheless, even one incident is one too many. To minimize potential harm and travel with peace of mind, we do well to arm ourselves with basic precautions, awareness, and a healthy dose of common sense.

First off, it's important not to confuse a place being *theft prone* with a place being *physically dangerous*. In many of the places alleged to be "dangerous" there is actually little risk of being physically assaulted. In fact, in most resource-poor countries you can expect to feel as safe or safer than you do at home—especially if "home" is somewhere urban in the United States. The random acts of violence that occur in the West are nearly nonexistent in Thailand, Peru, and Tanzania. Common criminals in places like these are usually after one thing: your money. Most are pickpockets or "sneak thieves" with no interest in harming you or even confronting you. In the unlikely event of being mugged, immediately give up your money or valuables.

Ironically, the best protection you have against physical harm or political unrest is the fact that you are a foreigner. Like gang fighting back home, most victims of violence are those from their own or opposing ethnic, religious, or political groups. If a political disturbance were to occur, and you found yourself caught in the cross fire, you would probably be hustled away and protected by the local people and the police.

The greatest risks to foreign travelers are actually those over which they have the most control. Each year, thousands of European and North American travelers are arrested abroad, either on narcotics charges (including possession of very small amounts of illegal substances) or for raucous behavior while "under the influence." Many are the sad tales of intoxicated and culturally naive students who, finding themselves in unfamiliar pubs or clubs, were unable to defend themselves against "date rape" or robbery.

The regrettable reality is that women must travel with special care, ever aware of how local men perceive them (often as naive, unattached, and "easy"), and what effect those perceptions will have on the men's actions. A western woman may innocently jog in a Jakarta park or wear shorts or a tank top in Mexico City and suddenly find herself the subject of incessant stares and catcalls. Another woman might find herself on a crowded subway in Rome or Tokyo with men pressing up against her, even fondling her. The helplessness and anger that wells up toward a few predators can easily become projected on the entire male population of the country as a practical defense against the false image that is objectifying and degrading her.

To brave a world wracked with inequality, gender oppression, and exploitation is to subject oneself to uncertain risks and dangers. But those of us wishing to insert ourselves into the world's woes should keep the larger context in proper perspective. Gary Haugen (2005) of International Justice Mission poses a searching question regarding danger:

> "Dangerous" for whom? While the dangers for us are a *risk*, for the victims we seek to serve, the dangers are a *certainty*. For the girls locked away in

brothels, they will certainly be raped. For the husband illegally detained in prison, he will certainly be beaten if he stands up for his innocence or dignity. For the 19 year old boy held in bonded slavery, he will certainly not go to school today, he will certainly not play today, and will certainly suffer if he doesn't make his quota of bricks today . . . *unless* someone steps into place between the oppressor and his vulnerable prey. (para. 3)

Given these realities, our choice is either to stay at home, to create expatriate bubbles abroad that attempt to avert inherent risks, or to enter into the world with suitable caution and common sense. Yes, there are risks, but they are *necessary* risks that *must* be taken *if* we are to find freedom from our own fears, much less support the freedom of others. And they are generally no worse than the physical risks any of us would encounter traveling with a backpack at home. It's impossible to control everything that happens to us, whether at home *or* abroad. But we can sway the odds by staying abreast of any travel advisories that might be in effect, and by conducting ourselves in a culturally sensitive and responsible manner. The following guidelines summarize hard-learned lessons from hundreds of fellow travelers:

- ◊ Complete a self-defense course prior to departure.
- ◊ Read a book or two about the unique risks *and* opportunities facing female travelers. Try *A Journey of One's Own* by Thalia Zepatos or Beth Whitman's *Wanderlust and Lipstick: The Essential Guide for Women Traveling Solo.*
- ◊ Avoid flights that arrive late at night or require that you wait for hours in airports or train stations.
- ◊ During daylight hours, thoroughly explore the area where you are staying. Learn to be aware of what and who is around you. Stay on well-traveled routes, avoiding seedy areas and political hot spots. Don't venture home late at night alone unless absolutely necessary, and then use only registered or government-run taxis.
- ◊ Immediately learn to communicate basic information (including "help!" and "no!") in the local language.
- ◊ Learn and adapt to local role expectations and dress customs. Find out what messages are conveyed by eye contact, body distance, catcalls, and the like.

- Travel light and try not to look conspicuously wealthy. The less you have, and the less you show off to others, the fewer problems you will have with theft. (Your digital camera may be someone's monthly salary.) Some solo female travelers even downgrade their looks (wearing caps and no makeup, even the Muslim *hijab*) and wear a cheap substitute wedding ring to reduce their "availability aura."
- Don't rent a room that is not secure; lock it every time you leave.
- Develop a network of friendships through your host family, campus community, or service organization that can provide a social and emotional "safety net." Become a regular and expected part of the immediate community by participating in local associations and events (like religious services, dance clubs, and university lectures).
- Whenever possible, stay in physical contact with your bags. Carry all your bags onto the bus or train *with you* instead of having them stored on top or below. (A good reason to travel light!) On a train, if you get up and walk around, make sure someone you trust is watching your bags. If you are alone, either stay put or use a large padlock to secure your bag to a rack.
- Carry your money, passport, and credit cards in a money pouch or belt at all times (unless it's at your place of residence). Keep them in front of you and next to your skin (not exposed). Take them to the shower with you. Sleep on top of them.
- Carry only the amount of money you expect to use during the day. Should you be one of the unlucky few who are threatened at knife- or gunpoint for your money, don't think twice—just give it up!
- Stay aware of what's happening around you at all times, and especially as you cross roadways. In the developing world, pedestrians are at the bottom of the food chain—below bicyclists, auto rickshaws, cars, buses, and trucks. Learn how to cross busy streets by watching locals.
- Be immediately suspicious of anyone who walks up to you and asks you to talk to them, go with them, use their service, buy their product, or give them money—*especially* if they speak good English. In general, those who approach you on the street are *not* the kind of people you want to get to know. Most are con artists, not genuinely friendly people. When approached by strangers, *keep moving* and

just ignore them. If they continue to harass you, be assertive with a firm "no" or "leave me alone."

◊ If you're a woman, never—*never!*—accept a ride from or give your local address to anyone you don't know. And don't tell them to meet you later in order to get rid of them. They're likely to turn up again and again. Firmly say "no" the first time, and just walk away. Observe how local women rarely respond to strangers and protect themselves by walking arm in arm or holding hands.

◊ Ladies, avoid smiling at guys or dressing "sexy." Ladies and gents, avoid entering into romantic relationships with local men or women. Most are fleeting, often initiated by seasoned opportunists who charm foreigners with insincere flattery. What they want is money, a green card, or easy sex; you'll be left with a broken heart and, quite possibly, some STDs.

WEB RESOURCES

◊ "A Safe Trip Abroad" article: http://travel.state.gov/travel/tips/safety/safety_1747.html
◊ Travel advisor: www.fco.gov.uk/travel
◊ Travel advisories: U.S.: http://travel.state.gov/travel/cis_pa_tw/tw/tw_1764.html; Canada: www.voyage.gc.ca/
◊ World Travel Watch: www.worldtravelwatch.com

How Do I Go About Making Travel Arrangements?

Depending on the program, you may have to arrange for some or all of your travel to and from the program site. This may involve purchasing airline tickets, arranging transportation from the airport to the program site and back, and finding a place to stay. Making these arrangements takes time and planning, so *start early*, at least three months in advance. Begin by reviewing the "Getting There" section of a good country-specific travel guide (like *Rough Guides, Lonely Planet*, and *Moon*) to get a general idea of international travel options to and from your destination. With that basic information, you can begin to compare online fares or consult with a reputable travel agent specializing in low-cost student travel (such as STA Travel).

Getting the best airfares normally requires booking several months prior to departure and being flexible with dates and times. The cheapest tickets are normally available only before or after "peak season" (i.e., June through September) and on flights that are inconvenient (red-eye), nondirect (e.g., Asia routed through Gulf states), and with less-known airlines. If you plan to do much regional travel at the tail end of your program, you might wish to weigh the pros and cons of purchasing a *one-way* or *open-jaw* ticket that allows you to fly in to one destination and out of another. While this can save you from backtracking, these tickets are usually more expensive than the return half of a round-trip ticket. Oftentimes the best bet is to identify your host country's national carrier and determine which destinations they serve within your region of interest.

With this basic information in hand, search online sites like Kayak, Cheap Flights, or Sidestep with as many combinations of destinations and dates as you can. Quick comparison shopping can sometimes uncover some great deals. Begin searching as early as possible because cheap flights fill up fast, especially during peak travel times. If you are enrolled in a frequent-flyer program, consider flying with an international partner of that domestic airline; the miles may apply.

Paper tickets have now gone the way of milkmen and cassette tapes, having been replaced by e-tickets. This allows your online vendor and the airline you're flying with to store your ticket on their respective computer systems. The e-ticket can even be delivered to your cell phone, relieving you of having to worry about carrying or possibly losing a ticket. Simply bring a copy of your e-ticket receipt and government-issued identification (driver's license or passport) to the airline check-in counter or self-service kiosk.

Web Resources

- Airlines of the Web: http://flyaow.com
- STA Travel: www.statravel.com
- Kayak: www.kayak.com
- Cheap Flights: www.cheapflights.com
- Sidestep: www.sidestep.com
- Last Minute: www.lastminute.com

What's the Best Way to Handle Mail and Money?

If you plan on being away for more than a couple weeks, you'll need to think through how you'll access mail and money. Consider asking a friend, relative, or neighbor to sort through your mail for pieces that need to be sent to you while abroad. If your program or host family doesn't have a mailing address (most do), you can arrange to have mail forwarded to you in care of "general delivery" at the central post office in the cities where you'll be staying. Upon arrival, inquire at the community's post office.

International travelers today may use at least four forms of money: credit cards, ATM cards, traveler's checks, and cash. Dollars, for example, can be exchanged for foreign currency at the international airport or any major bank in your destination country. While you'll want to have some local cash on hand to pay for transport, food, and other incidentals, cash has one major drawback: Once it's stolen or lost, it's usually gone for good. As previously mentioned, make a habit of never carrying large amounts of cash with you; keep the small amount you need at any time in a neck wallet or money belt.

Traveler's checks have been replaced almost completely by ATMs, which allow you to obtain national currency from foreign ATM units with a minimum surcharge (for the use of an out-of-network ATM) at a fair exchange rate. While there's a limit on how much can be withdrawn per day, most budget travelers find that the limit is enough to cover normal expenses for several days. Those in extended (year or longer) residence abroad may want to establish an in-country bank account.

Major purchases can be covered by credit cards, recognized the world over as the new international currency. Not only do credit cards make foreign currency transactions easy; they also offer the best exchange rate, reduce perishable cash, provide an exact accounting of money spent, and are invaluable in a financial emergency. If a card is lost or stolen, it can be canceled and replaced. American Express and Visa have even created a debit-style travel card that can be loaded in advance in U.S. dollars, euros, or pounds.

One caution: Take only the credit cards you will use on the trip, and learn to *use them wisely.* Overspending is easy to do, and foreign-transaction fees and interest charges can mount up quickly. Great care should also be taken to protect the card from loss or theft. One student volunteer in the highlands of Guatemala had his wallet and passport stolen, leaving him penniless until his passport could be replaced and money could be sent, via cable transfer, from his home bank to an internationally recognized bank in a town several hours away. Fortunately, he had kept a separate photocopy of his passport, along with a listing of cards, numbers, and emergency replacement procedures.

WEB RESOURCES

◊ Money Matters: http://www.cie.uci.edu/prepare/money.shtml
◊ Currency converter: www.oanda.com/convert/classic
◊ American Express: www.americanexpress.com
◊ Visa/Plus ATM finder: www.visa.com
◊ Mastercard/Cirrus ATM finder: www.mastercard.com

What Personal Details Do I Need to Settle Prior to Departure?

As your date of departure approaches, it is easy to get overwhelmed with all the last-minute details that must get settled before your mind can be truly free to focus on what lies ahead. The following checklist can help:

ADVICE FOR STUDENT TRAVELERS

◊ Obtain all required approvals for major and/or elective credit for courses completed abroad.
◊ Make sure your academic advisor has the names, phone numbers, and postal/e-mail addresses of those persons (i.e., parents or guardians) who should be contacted in the event of an emergency.
◊ If you will be graduating at the end of your term abroad, fill out an "Intent to Graduate" form (if applicable). If you are not graduating, determine whether you need to apply for a leave of absence.
◊ If you wish to have grades from your last term sent to you, leave a stamped, self-addressed envelope with the registrar's office.
◊ Make sure you pay off any school housing, bookstore, or library accounts.

◊ Terminate all current contracts with residence-life and dining services. Notify the housing and registrar's offices of your readmittance plans.

◊ Sign the Perkins Loan, Stafford Loan, or University Loan promissory note. If you receive financial aid, submit the Student Aid Report (SAR) to your campus financial aid office for certification.

◊ Record the names and postal/e-mail addresses of campus personnel whom you may need to contact while abroad.

◊ Arrange for your campus mail center to have your mail forwarded to your home address.

Advice for All Travelers

◊ Gather important papers for yourself and family members: medical records (including vaccination data, prescriptions, and histories of past illnesses), dental records, lens prescriptions for eyeglasses (take a spare pair, if possible), and insurance-policy information and identification cards.

◊ Leave copies of your passport, credit card information, airline and travel itinerary, and host-family contact information with a family member or trusted friend.

◊ Give notice to your landlord/landlady at least 30 days in advance of the date you will be leaving. Have your phone and utilities disconnected on moving day, and pay the final bill (or make arrangements to pay the final bill if it will arrive after you've left).

◊ Collect any items that are being cleaned or repaired or have been loaned to friends or neighbors. Return library books and other loaned or rented items. Decide what to do with your potted houseplants.

◊ Cancel newspaper and magazine subscriptions, or arrange to have some of these materials shipped overseas.

◊ If you plan to be away for an extended period, close your charge accounts with local stores and cancel any credit cards you don't plan to use abroad. Arrange to make online payments on any outstanding bills.

◊ If you want another person to have access to your assets and other personal information in your stead (e.g., to sign an official or legal document during your absence), arrange for an appropriate person to have "power of attorney." Power of attorney enables the person you designate to withdraw your money, deposit money for you, and write your checks; her or his signature counts as your signature.

How Do I Decide What and How to Pack?

One of the final and most absorbing steps in your preparation process is deciding what to bring and what to leave at home. Because of the variety of cross-cultural settings, that decision will depend on the particular environment you will be in and the resources that will be available to you. For example, it's senseless to pack toilet paper and dress clothes if they're either available in your host community or impractical in your context. On the other hand, it may be more difficult to come by some items (like a computer) that can make the difference between a fruitful or inefficient learning experience.

Rick Steves, in *Europe Through the Back Door*, claims, "You'll never meet a traveler who, after five trips, brags, 'Every year I pack heavier'" (2007, p. 36). Almost without exception they wish they had traveled lighter, having learned by hard experience that any extra gear ends up either being lugged around, given away, or thrown away. But during the preparation phase our inclination is just the opposite. Our almost uncontainable impulse is to overestimate what we can't do without and to underestimate what is available in-country (often for much less than we'd pay back home).

How we pack can literally define our journey, both physically and psychologically. It can encourage us either to shed our foreigner mindset and adapt to local ways of life or to stay culturally "at arm's length." How might we overcome the "better safe than sorry" mentality that leads us to overstuff our bags with all the trappings of "home"?

Let's assume our goal is to "travel light"—to be comfortable, unassuming, secure, and free of dead weight. Begin the packing process by visualizing yourself in your new surroundings. What items will help you feel relaxed and settled? Will you need to transport them to one location or carry them from place to place? (Imagine carting your belongings in and out of small taxicabs or rickshaws, on and off crowded buses and trains, and up and down long flights of stairs without any assistance.) How "heavy" or "light" are you willing to travel? What baggage limitations are specified by your domestic and overseas airlines? Do you want to bring things that would be difficult or expensive to replace if lost or stolen? Carefully evaluate the constraints of space, mobility, and expense.

Now you're ready to make a paper list of packable belongings. Begin by sorting them into "must takes" (items you absolutely cannot do without), "could takes" (items it would be nice to take but you could live without), and "must *not* takes" (items too large, heavy, valuable, or inappropriate to take). At this point, you're not trying to lighten your load to a minimum but simply establishing your preferences. With your belongings sorted in this way, take your "must takes" list and try to *reduce it by half.* That's right, half. Try to imagine being a typical resident in your host community. How would *they* feel about your "must take" clothes, electronic gadgets, and other personal items? Aim to pare down the list to about 25 "essentials" distributed among a neck pouch or money belt, one checked bag, and one carry-on bag.

Neck Pouch or Money Belt

This is where you pack vital documents and other valuables: passport with visas, vaccination certificate, credit/ATM cards, travel itinerary, large bills in local currency, and emergency foreign currency. Look for a neck pouch that is strong and durable, with moisture protection, zippered pockets, and slots for your boarding pass or passport. Alternatively, you can opt for a thin cloth money belt that fits easily inside the waist of your pants.

Checked Bag

The era of free checked baggage is officially over. In order to compensate for the soaring cost of jet fuel, most major airlines now charge extra fees for each piece of checked luggage (ranging from $15 to $50 per bag), and for bags that are overweight. Rachel discovered this the hard way:

> As I was moving to Poland for a full year, I decided to check two bags—a medium-sized suitcase and a second, quite small suitcase—which seemed

very manageable and presumably would be within most airlines' allowance of two free checked bags. To my dismay, as I hadn't read the fine print closely enough, I wound up paying $40 extra for *each* leg of my domestic travel. Then, once I got to Europe, I had to pay nearly twice the amount of my plane ticket going from London to Wroclaw for bags alone, due to the airline's strict policies and exorbitant fees! Books alone can put one over the [weight] limit very quickly. . . .

To avoid these surcharges, pack light enough to fit almost all of your gear in a single checked bag measuring less than 62 linear inches (length, width, and depth added together) and weighing less than 50 pounds. The best bet is a 25- to 29-inch soft-sided case made of lightweight materials with a graphite frame, often called a Pullman or trolley. (Hard-sided cases, though durable and water-resistant, weigh more.) As you pack, be sure to inform yourself about permitted and prohibited items. (American travelers should check the Transportation Security Administration [TSA] website.) Then attach identification tags, both outside and inside the bag, with your name, e-mail address, and phone number on them.

- ◊ *Lightweight clothing.* Clothing needs obviously depend on the destination's particular climatic and cultural contexts. In most tropical locations you'll want trousers, shirts, and skirts that are lightweight, quick drying, and wrinkle resistant. Two of each is better than one, reducing the frequency of washing and allowing you to wear a fresh pair of pants or shirt when the other is soiled. If wearing shorts is frowned on in the host society, look for lightweight (nylon or synthetic) pants that can keep you cool and offer sun protection for your legs. Many feature zip-off legs that for men eliminate the need for a bathing suit. Make sure they have at least one "security" zip pocket to thwart pickpockets. Other clothing items to pack in your bag include one nice outfit (for formal occasions), two sets of underwear, and perhaps a microfiber Windbreaker or light sweater for those rainy or chilly days.

- ◊ *Waterproof sandals.* Wherever you set up your study and service term, one thing is certain: You probably will do a great deal of walking. In tropical regions (most of the developing world) all you'll need is a pair of rugged, waterproof sandals. Of course, serious trekking or formal work roles might require additional footwear. But unless you're an avid runner, leave those running shoes at home; they're bulky, smelly, and in humid climates, they can breed nasty fungal infections. Waterproof sandals with back straps offer adequate foot protection, allow your feet to breathe, and can be worn anywhere. Some (like those by Keen, Teva, or Chaco) are pricey but virtually indestructible.

◊ *Toiletry bag.* Use basic but sturdy containers (even ziploc bags) to store toiletries and essentials: a thin bath towel, toothpaste, a toothbrush, floss, a razor, a hairbrush, sunscreen, a laundry soap bar, earplugs, a sleep mask, DEET insect repellent, contact-lens supplies, and any medicines. An antibacterial inner lining will prevent the growth of odor-, mildew-, and mold-causing bacteria and germs. All other toiletry items can be picked up in-country (including feminine hygiene products; however, options may be extremely limited in remote areas).

◊ *Sarong.* This is essentially a large, lightweight sheet of brightly colored or printed fabric, often wrapped around the waist and worn as a type of "skirt" by men and women alike throughout much of South and Southeast Asia and on many Pacific islands. It can be used as a lightweight skirt or shawl for women, a comfortable pajama for guys, or a quick-drying towel.

◊ *Sleep sheet.* Indispensable to many travelers is a travel or sleep sheet—a piece of fabric sewn together in a sleeping bag configuration that protects against bedbugs, mosquitoes, unclean bedding, lice, and scabies. Many hostels require guests to use one. Although silk "dreamsacks" are truly compact and quick-drying (and yes, luxurious), you can make your own by simply taking a queen-size sheet, folding it in half, and stitching up the bottom and two thirds of the side.

◊ *Leatherman.* Consider packing this multi-use tool to cut bread or fruit, spread jams, open bottles, cut cloth, complete minor repairs, and much more.

◊ *Locks.* A padlock (to keep your room secure), a lock and chain (to secure your bags at night), and a luggage lock (for the checked bag).

◊ *Reminders of home.* Take along a few items that create a shared "at home" feeling and can serve as conversation starters with hosts and friends: a DVD of family photos and videos, pictures or posters of your homeland, or a favorite book or food item.

◊ *Gift items.* Gift-giving etiquette varies across cultures, but expect to "repay" unexpected assistance and hospitality in some way. Lewis Hyde in *The Gift* counsels against monetary and material items and in favor of consumable gifts (such as a basket of fruit) which become a shared experience for family and community members.

◊ *Pepper spray.* This is a valuable men's and women's self-defense tool, but be sure to practice your aim *before* you have to spray a predator while panicked.

◊ *Photocopies of vital documents.* Include copies of your passport, credit cards, ATM card, airline itinerary, and insurance policy.

◊ *Program materials.* Depending on program requirements, you may need to pack a number of academic texts and other study materials.

Carry-on Bag

Besides your own person, the bag or backpack that accompanies you will be the first thing people will notice when they meet you. New, brightly colored bags with brand-name patches immediately tag you as a wealthy foreigner. Consider picking up a well-worn but functional shoulder bag that will be less of an invitation to thieves. As you pack it, keep in mind that most commercial airlines ban sharp items like scissors, razors, and nail files in carry-ons.

◊ *Wristwatch with alarm.* Ensure that you catch those early morning buses!

◊ *Address book.* Organize the names and addresses of new friends made along the way.

◊ *Sunglasses* (with UV protection) and extra *eyeglasses* or *contact lenses.* You'll need the backup pairs in the event of loss or breakage.

◊ *Journal.* Use a durable journal to jot down observations, spontaneous impressions, shapeless ideas, local information, and phrases. Writing helps travelers to organize raw experience into a coherent form that, ultimately, can be transformed into documented learning.

◊ *Current phrasebook and guidebook.* Both are indispensable on-the-road accessories. Pocket phrasebooks are available for almost any language, enabling even the linguistically challenged to use simple phrases on the bus, at home, or in the marketplace. Dating back to the medieval Arab world, travel guidebooks serve as the written equivalent of a local tour guide. Granted, they are bulky reminders to everyone around that you're a tourist, and they run the risk of overguiding travelers—drawing them away from things that, ideally, they would have discovered by accident. But their convenient maps, language glossaries, well-researched cultural information, and savvy recommendations can spare us from having to endlessly experiment and improvise on our own. In addition to or instead of print versions, many publishers offer downloadable documents that can be read on a portable computer or handheld device.

◊ *Electronic tools.* Most educational travelers depend on electronic tools like laptop computers, digital recorders, and compact cameras to systematically document their learning and update their blogs. Fortunately, most portable devices today come with power supplies that can be used in almost any part of the world, assuming you have the appropriate plug adaptor. Under certain circumstances, however, these devices could prove useless on one day (because of lack of power supply), a source of social discomfort on another day (being luxuries that few in the host community could ever afford), and an encumbrance (because of weight and fear of breakage or theft) over the length of your program.

In making final packing decisions, keep in mind that the residents of your destination community will have most of the same day-to-day needs as you. Virtually any essential items—from clothes and notepads to toiletries and towels—will be available on arrival. This includes cell phones and calling cards. Unless your own cell phone is "unlocked" to use the GSM standard of your destination country, it won't work. Even if it does, you'll want to avoid incurring high per-minute "roaming" charges. One alternative is to buy or rent a prepaid, low-cost cell phone locally that allows you to make and receive in-country calls (e.g., the Talk Abroad travel phone, www.cellularabroad.com). For out-of-country calling, an international calling card can be purchased in various denominations either online (e.g., at www.callingcards.com/ccads) or through in-country post offices or general stores.

◊ World Climate: www.worldclimate.com
◊ Transportation Security Administration (TSA): www.tsa.gov/travelers/
  airtravel/prohibited/permitted-prohibited-items.shtm
◊ Organization and packing: www.artoftravel.com/20organization.htm
◊ Travel guidebooks: www.artoftravel.com/11guides.htm

Conclusion

We can expect the months leading up to our term abroad to be filled with great anticipation and many practical preparations that require advanced planning and focused attention. Instead of regarding this groundwork as an onerous but necessary duty, try to embrace it as an adventure in its own right. The world is at once more accessible and more threatening than ever before. If executed well, these preparations can reward us with an informed, safe, and smooth "entry" into a new social world where, once established, we can use our creative gifts to confer benefit to the community in which we live, study, and serve.

FOR REFLECTION AND DISCUSSION

1. Do you agree or disagree with Phil Cousineau's idea that "preparation no more spoils the chance for spontaneity and serendipity than discipline ruins the opportunity for genuine self-expression"? What evidence drawn from your life experience supports your opinion?
2. What two or three travel-planning questions are, right now, "front burner" for you? How are you going about answering them?

References

Bond, M. (n.d.). Solo travel. *Women's travel tips*. Retrieved September 15, 2009, from http://www.womentraveltips.com/tips7.shtml
Cousineau, P. (2000). *The art of pilgrimage: The seeker's guide to making travel sacred*. San Francisco: Conari Press.

Engle, J., & Engle, L. (2003). Neither international nor educative: Study abroad in the time of globalization. In W. Grunzweig & N. Rinehart (Eds.), *Rockin' in Red Square: Critical approaches to international education in the age of cyberculture* (pp. 25–39). Hamburg: Lit Verlag.

Gelman, R. G. (2002). *Tales of a female nomad: Living at large in the world.* New York: Three Rivers Press.

Griffith, S. (n.d.). Traveling solo as a woman in Asia. *Transitions Abroad.* Retrieved June 17, 2009, from http://www.transitionsabroad.com/publica tions/solowomantraveler/travelingsoloinasia.shtml

Haugen, G. (2005). *But isn't that dangerous?* Retrieved June 23, 2009, from http://216.128.18.195/IJMarticles/ButIsntThatDangerous.pdf

Sanford, N. (1966). *Self and society: Social change and individual development.* New York: Atherton.

Stein, G. (2003). *Paris France: Personal recollections.* London: Peter Owen.

Steves, R. (2007). *Europe through the back door 2008.* Berkeley, CA: Avalon Travel.

Vande Berg, M. (2009). Intervening in student learning abroad: A research-based inquiry. *Intercultural Education, 20*(4), S15–S27.

CARRYING KNOWLEDGE

In traveling, man must carry knowledge with him if he would bring home knowledge.
—SAMUEL JOHNSON (Boswell, *Life of Johnson*, 1791)

THE JOURNEY OF WISE and resourceful travelers doesn't begin at the point of taking up residence in a foreign country. Besides making logistical arrangements, the prefield phase of our journey requires that we also complete certain preparations of the mind. "Doing our homework" prior to departure enables us to comprehend some of the most important historical events, as well as existing social, economic, and political systems, that shape the cultural realities within our destination country. Carrying along this knowledge can save us weeks, even months, of haphazard field activity. Not only will we be better prepared to interact intelligently with residents, we will more naturally act in ways that dispel the stereotype of the clueless and self-absorbed "Ugly American" (or equivalent) that persists in many parts of the world. Within only a week of arriving in Delhi, India, Kerrie discovered that deliberate prefield learning enabled her to break through common misperceptions held by her hosts:

> When I arrived in India, I was surprised at how much I didn't know about some things, but thankful that I had done my homework, particularly about religion. Showing knowledge of and interest in the Hindu religion gave me a way to relate to the family I stayed with. They expected me to be a demanding American, and to want to do things a certain way. Being open to learning their approach to life gave me a lot of cultural insight I could have missed.

Carrying knowledge conveys a curious and concerned self, one who *cares enough* about the peoples and places in one's destination country to invest the time learning about them. This, in itself, may not be enough to distinguish us from the camera-toting and culturally clueless tourists piling in and out of tour buses, but it's a good start. Because respect and trust are essential prerequisites to building rare cross-cultural friendships, our deliberate efforts to honor the beauty and specialness of our hosts' way of life acts to smooth the way toward gaining their acceptance and cooperation.

While seasoned travelers prepare in many different ways, this chapter will recommend five primary methods:

1. Cultivating relationships with cultural group members
2. Contacting experts of the host society
3. Reading model ethnographies
4. Viewing select films
5. Conducting electronic searches

After a brief look at the first four, this chapter will then explore strategic, responsible, and discerning ways of searching for information through online sources and electronic searches.

Cultivating Relationships

Among the many benefits arising from the global movement of people across national borders is the unprecedented opportunity for face-to-face encounters with different cultures in our own backyard. International students at a local college or university; immigrant shop or restaurant owners; and congregants of local temples, mosques, or churches—each are potential aids, even mentors, for the adventure ahead. Consider devoting an extended period of time finding and befriending members of your destination culture who might be residing close by. Most will be eager to oblige you with stories, encouragement, and practical advice. Some may even offer to put you in touch with relatives and friends in their homeland. On numerous occasions, global learners have successfully arranged international homestays with the friends or family members of those they met in their own hometown.

Contacting Experts

A second way to begin field study while yet at home is to contact, and consult with, those possessing expert knowledge of your destination culture. Sometimes group representatives—for example, the students, business owners, and religious practitioners just mentioned—can refer you to others with specialized knowledge of particular cultural issues or service opportunities. Especially in multiethnic and multireligious urban centers, leaders of the many *diaspora* communities represent an extraordinary, though often overlooked, resource for global learning. Most are keen to help cultural outsiders appreciate their unique history, language, musical forms, religious practices, and political concerns.

Other, more academic, experts can be contacted through a university that sponsors special regional study programs. Using your favorite search engine, type in the relevant region-specific terms (e.g., "Latin American studies," "Middle Eastern studies," "Slavic studies"). Search the program websites for faculty contact information and then contact them by e-mail or phone.

Alternatively, search the Worldwide Email Directory of Anthropologists (http://wings.buffalo.edu/WEDA/) by geographic location or research interest. Identify anthropologists with professional involvements in your destination country and attempt to make contact with them. Make your requests brief and specific, being careful not to ask for too much. Many will be delighted to offer advice in the form of book recommendations, service opportunities, or reputable language schools. If for some reason they can't help you, ask if they can suggest someone else who can.

Reading Ethnographies

Traditionally, anthropologists would step outside their own social worlds and brave unfamiliar climates and customs in order to describe the way other people live or have lived. The written accounts of these ways of life are known as ethnographies. A fine-grained ethnography, specific to a particular people or place, is usually based on extended involvement in a host community, as well as fluency in the local language. As such, it offers a valuable window into the mindset and methods associated with cross-cultural field study. In reading these accounts, we are led to discover, through vicarious experience, the everyday life of others in radically different contexts. Of course, no two fieldwork experiences are alike. Nevertheless, much can be learned from reflecting on others' experiences (including their *faux pas*) in advance of our own field study.

Headed for a destination in the Muslim world? Pick up Elizabeth Fernea's account of her field experience in *Guests of the Sheik* (Anchor, 1995). In the 1950s, this newly married American woman accompanied her husband to a rural Iraqi village where she learned to live in a mud hut with no indoor plumbing, speak the local language, and adopt behaviors (like wearing the veil) that would help her become an "accepted outsider" within a conservative Islamic community. In her story, Fernea narrates the day-to-day life of village women, including the process of slowly making friends and participating in local religious observances. Each chapter brims with insights for adapting to and learning from another culture.

While ethnographies like Fernea's may not provide all the technical guidance necessary for doing fieldwork, one is left with an appetite for the deep connections and intercultural insights that are possible through the global-learning experience. There are many excellent examples to choose from, including Lila Abu-Lughod's *Veiled Sentiments* (Bedouins of Egypt), Elenore Smith Bowen's *Return to Laughter* (Tiv of Nigeria), Jean Briggs's *Never in Anger* (Inuit Eskimo), Anne Fadiman's *The Spirit Catches You and You Fall Down* (Hmong in America), Alma Gottlieb and Philip Graham's *Parallel Worlds* (West Africa), and Paul Rabinow's *Reflections on Fieldwork in Morocco* (Morocco).

Viewing Select Films

Another rich source of world knowledge is available to us in ethnographic films, documentary projects, Hollywood movies, and even YouTube videos. Ethnographic and documentary films allow us to visually encounter living persons in their cultural context in ways not possible through written texts. In contrast to most fictional (Hollywood) films, they are neither scripted nor staged. With little control over the action or the event being filmed, the filmmaker attempts to *document* the "real life" of a culture and *interpret* some representative aspect of it.

Some well-crafted dramatic narrative films may also transport us mentally to the geographic and cultural worlds of distant peoples and allow us to imagine ourselves embedded within a radically different way of life. Many also present complex themes of colonial rule, political repression, courtship and marriage, Westernization, and social inequality in sensitive and enlightening ways.

Pay a visit to your local Blockbuster or a large public or academic library, and search its database for DVDs and other media related to a particular destination. Or just view a range of random films from different countries, allowing images of far-flung peoples and places to sensitize you to the ways cultural motifs are symbolized in visible behavior. Recommendations made by educational travelers include the Netsilik Eskimo Series, *Women and Men Apart* (Grecian village), *Out of Africa* (Kenya), *The Legend of Suriyothai* (Thailand), *Buena Vista Social Club* (Cuba), *The Year of Living Dangerously* (Indonesia), *Slumdog Millionaire* (Mumbai, India), *Lost in Translation* (Japan), *Not Without My Daughter* (Iran), *The Cup* (Tibet), *Kandahar* (Afghanistan), *Hotel Rwanda* (Rwanda), *When You Say Four Thousand Good-Byes* (African village), *Monsoon Wedding* (New Delhi, India), *Born Into Brothels* (Kolkata, India), *City of God* (Rio de Janeiro, Brazil), and *Paradise Now* (Palestine).

Conducting Electronic Searches

Much of the cultural knowledge available today can be accessed electronically. With the advent of the CD-ROM, online databases, and the Internet, it has never been easier to gather and process vast amounts of place- and people-specific information. High-speed Internet connections are now deeply integrated into our home, school, and work environments. New search technologies, social networks like Facebook and Twitter, blogs, virtual classes, and digital libraries are becoming ubiquitous features of modern life. Though the Internet is unlikely to ever contain everything written, filmed, photographed, or recorded, it certainly has become one of the most dynamic travel resources available. Coupled with the hundreds of independent journals available through library-owned

electronic indexes and databases, we have the electronic means for searching out information on virtually any subject.

The two "guides" that follow organize these searches, first with the
Internet and then with electronic databases. Both are designed to assist
us in gathering and carrying knowledge that can support the educational
goals of our global learning. But first a word of caution. For serious culture learners, there appear to be at least two dangers inherent in the
online universe. The first relates to the Web's knack, in the words of Max
Frisch, "of so arranging the world that we do not have to experience it."
With access to huge amounts of secondhand information *about* people,
we may be tempted to conclude that we no longer need to use all of
our primary senses—sight, hearing, touch, smell, and taste—to directly
explore the world for ourselves. Our immersion in the technology-
mediated universe of smartphones, iPads, laptops, and digital cameras
has shrunk our sensory world. The richness of life, including novel
human encounters within mystery-filled places, has gradually narrowed
to secondary, vicarious, and one-way experiences delivered via machines,
typically a touch-screen device or flat-panel TV (albeit in high-def, 3-D,
and surround sound). Who needs to undergo the rigors of India or Ant-
arctica when IMAX or the Discovery and National Geographic channels
offer a full-color, sight-and-sound experience? And what more does one
need to know about other places and peoples that isn't already available
on the Internet? The fact remains that much of the world can only be
known directly, face-to-face, and from touching and doing with our
hands. "Though many of us would like to believe otherwise," writes Richard Louv, "the world is not entirely available from a keyboard" (2008, p.
67). We should exercise great care not to sever cultural understanding
from authentic, primary experience.

A second danger is the tendency for the Web to reduce information to
a mere commodity—a "thing" to be collected and consumed apart from
any certain moral direction and social purpose. As noted in chapter 2,
human life is narratively rooted. We require "grounding" stories to tell
us where we've come from, where we're going, and why. Our stories also
advise us on what we need to know and what we do not need to know.
One of the things that becomes all too apparent through open-eyed travel
is that most of the world's fractures are human—not technical—in
nature. The best hope for alleviating sorrow in the world lies not with a

better supply of information or more wondrous technologies, but with individuals and institutions that have learned to recognize and respect a common human bond of dignity and justice. This is not to suggest that it's either possible or desirable to withdraw from a high-tech world, only that a virtual world is no substitute for the quest for authentic relationships and ultimate meanings.

Guide 1: Searching the Internet

That said, there are several features of the Internet that make it especially useful for educational travelers. Not only are many Web-based documents almost instantly available, they are also timely, being revised and updated on a regular basis. They also represent an astounding range of topics unrivaled by the world's finest library collections. That is the Internet's blessing but also its bane. While the Web contains a wealth of information on countless topics contributed by people from all over the world, content quality is uneven and often contradictory. This is because no one actually owns the Internet or the services (e.g., the Web) communicated through it. Instead of being a central organization to enforce quality or editorial standards, the Web is a self-publishing medium that enables *anyone* with Internet access and the right software to disseminate information. Some sites represent expert knowledge; others mix polished prose with informal conversation, art with advertising, and careful research with wild hearsay. Generally, websites are considered less authoritative sources of information than materials available through library-subscribed electronic databases (more on those later).

Basic searches of the Internet are typically conducted using a Web *search engine* like Google or Yahoo! Each search-index company owns thousands of computers that use software (called spiders or bots) that scans the Web at certain intervals and grabs new sites for the index. When you use a search engine, you are asking it to look in its index to find matches with the words you have typed in. Many search engines are also reference sites that supplement their search capability with news, weather, picture indexes, and other features. GoodSearch (www.goodsearch.com), powered by Yahoo!, contributes pennies from each search to the nonprofit or school of your choice.

In addition to search engines there are *search directories*. Instead of using spiders or bots to download and index pages, they use human editors to evaluate sites submitted by site owners. The editors evaluate, edit, and list these sites by categories and subcategories. For example, the Google Directory and World Wide Web Virtual Library (informally referred to as "the VL") are both run by a loose confederation of experts in particular areas. This results in directory databases being much smaller than those of search engines. But the fact that the sites are hand-picked often means that searches will yield higher-quality results.

Gathering information through a search engine or search directory is done by using *keywords*. A keyword is a word or phrase that describes the main concepts of a topic. For example, if our topic is pollution, other keywords might include *toxic waste, smog,* and *global warming*. Most search engines offer a keyword search by default: It simply finds all pages that contain any of the words specified, in any order, and at any location. Most search engines also allow us to perform an exact *phrase search* that locates pages with only the exact words we type in, in that exact order. Typing in a general-topic word like *environment* probably will return thousands of hits, most of them irrelevant. But typing in an exact phrase like *"environmental pollution"* (with the quotation marks) will significantly narrow a broad or general topic. One can even combine various phrases (e.g., *"air water pollution cities Thailand"*) to narrow the search even further.

In order to expand or to limit search results, some search engines allow you to use the *Boolean operators* AND, OR, and NOT. The operator OR expands the search; the others contract it. For example, if you type into the search engine *domestic violence,* you will get a hit on every page that has either the word *domestic* or the word *violence* on it. On the other hand, if you type in *"domestic violence" AND "Dominican Republic,"* only pages with both terms will be returned. As you might imagine, this approach will result in a much smaller and more refined set of hits. If you type in *"domestic" NOT "violence,"* then only pages with the word *domestic* and not with the word *violence* will be found.

Read the search tips or "help" information provided by each search engine to determine how to perform more advanced searches, how to restrict or expand searches, and how to use the site more efficiently. For example, Google has an automatic "and" search, is not case sensitive, and uses quotation marks for phrases. Knowing this, you might create the following search:

"child soldiers" Uganda trauma

Every resulting webpage will contain the exact phrase *child soldiers* (rather than just the two words anywhere in the document), as well as the terms *Uganda* and *trauma*. Other online search tools may have automatic phrase searches.

Once you've performed a search, practice saving relevant sites for future reference by creating *bookmarks* in a series of folders. The "Bookmarks" or "Favorites" feature in major browsers allows users to compile lists of frequently visited pages without having to write each one down or memorize the URL (i.e., Uniform Resource Locator, or webpage address). When you wish to return to these pages, you can simply find it on the list and click on the bookmark. If you are not able to add bookmarks for some reason, note some of the best websites for future reference.

Furnished with this basic technical know-how, you're now ready to walk through several tasks designed to give you a broad framework for more focused online research.

Task 1: Explore prospective regions and countries. Search the directories below for sites related to one or more prospective regions and/or countries of interest. Browse numerous subcategories nested under the main general categories of "Regional" or "Regions of the World." Do this for at least *three countries* within *two different regions* selected from Table 5.1. Choose "Bookmarks" or "Favorites" on your menu bar to bookmark some of your favorite sites. Add submenus (folders) to organize these sites under your three countries. Your bookmarks are "live," so you can return to them anytime with a simple double-click.

Google Directory: http://directory.google.com
Yahoo! Search Directory: http://dir.yahoo.com
Librarians' Internet Index: www.lii.org

Task 2: Compile general information on your host country. If you were an astronaut and just approved to participate in a mission to Mars, what would you want to know about your destination? Near the top of your "need to know" list would undoubtedly be space conditions and potential

Table 5.1   Regions and Representative Countries

Region	Representative Countries
Africa	Eastern Africa (e.g. (e.g., Ethiopia, Kenya, Rwanda, Tanzania)
	Middle and Southern Africa (e.g. Angola, Chad, South Africa)
	Western Africa (e.g. Ghana, Côte d'Ivoire, Nigeria, Sierra Leone)
Americas	Northern America (e.g. Canada, Greenland, the United States
	Latin America and the Caribbean (e.g. Mexico, Costa Rica, Ecuador, Brazil, Haiti)
Asia	Eastern Asia (e.g. China, Japan, Korea)
	South Central Asia (e.g. India, Sri Lanka, Bangladesh, Afghanistan, Kazakhstan)
	South-Eastern Asia (e.g. Philippines, Indonesia, Thailand, Cambodia)
	Western Asia and Northern Africa (e.g. Turkey, Iraq, Israel, Palestine, Egypt, Morocco)
Europe	Eastern Europe (e.g. Romania, Russia, Czech Republic, Hungary)
	Northern Europe (e.g. Lithuania, Sweden, the United Kingdom)
	Southern and Western Europe (e.g. Spain, Greece, Yugoslavia)
Oceania	Melanesia, Micronesia and Polynesia (e.g. Fiji, Papua New Guinea, Samoa)
	Australia and New Zealand

hazards, followed by the planet's geography and climate, and your exploration strategy.

While our own sojourns will probably be restricted to earth, there will be times when we'll feel as if we've landed on another planet! To live knowledgeably and respectfully within our destination culture, good intentions are not enough; we also need to absorb enough background knowledge to project an informed, culturally sensitive self.

A remarkable breadth of information, both country and culture specific, can be assessed through interlinked websites. Net travelers soon discover that one site connects to the next, which leads to yet other useful resources. Consider your region(s) of interest. Find relevant information on at least five national features (e.g., geography, groups, religion, current events, and language) by browsing the Web resources listed after the following descriptions of these and more national features. Jot notes in a physical or electronic notebook and bookmark the most useful sites.

◊ *Geography:* In what region of the world does your host country lie? What are its neighboring countries? What is the climate in each of your host country's main regions? What are its major natural resources (e.g., forestry, fishing, minerals)? What are the names and locations of the country's major states/provinces? What are the names of the major urban centers in each? What is the national capital?

◊ *Political history:* What are the major periods and watershed events in your host country's history? Was there a classical era or "golden age"? Describe the experience of colonialism or foreign domination: How was colonial rule imposed? How was independence won? What historical events are annually commemorated? Who are the nation's heroes and heroines? For what are they best known?

◊ *Economy:* What percentage of the labor force is involved, respectively, in agriculture, industry, services, and the military? What is the country's annual per-capita income and gross national product? What are its primary agricultural and industrial products? Where are they produced? What are the leading exports and imports?

◊ *Groups:* What are the various groups in the country called, and where are they concentrated? What groups occupy the service sector and which make up the elite? Is there an indigenous population? Are there any intergroup tensions based on race, religion, territory, or language? Among what group(s) will you be living and serving?

◊ *Current politics:* What is the form of the national government? What are the majority and minority parties, and what issues and perspectives do they represent? Who are their leaders? Does any one group or family dominate local politics? What is the political relationship between your host country and your homeland? What countries are important to them and why?

◊ *Religion:* What religions are practiced? What proportion of the people are followers of each faith tradition? Is there one national religion? What are the most important religious ceremonies? Have you read any of their sacred writings?

◊ *Arts and sports:* What are some of the most popular music and dance styles? What traditional or popular sports are regularly played? What cultural festivals will be held during the time of your residence in the country?

◊ *Environment:* What factors affect the productivity of the land and the quality of life of those who farm it? (Consider climate, overpopulation, pests, land ownership, farming methods, indebtedness, seed varieties, deforestation, and desertification.) What environmental factors—like climate, rainfall, calamity, and land productivity—negatively affect the country?

◊ *Education:* What indigenous, premodern institutions and practices have historically served educational functions? Currently, what are the major divisions of the public and private education system? How many grades are there in each division? Is the school system modeled after that of another country? What are the most pressing issues (e.g., relevant curriculum, competent teachers, better books and equipment) facing modern education?

◊ *Current events:* Judging from current newspaper articles, what are some of the most important issues and problems engaging the minds of the people?

◊ *Languages:* What languages are spoken in your host country? Are these official or unofficial? Do these languages represent any ethnic, geographical, or socioeconomic divisions? List and learn five essential phrases in the local language.

WEB RESOURCES

◊ Background Notes: www.state.gov/r/pa/ei/bgn
Full-text reports from the U.S. State Department containing detailed country information.

◊ Country Studies: http://lcweb2.loc.gov/frd/cs/cshome.html
A series of over 100 online handbooks published by the Library of Congress under the auspices of the Department of the Army.

◊ Virtual Library: www.vlib.org

One of the highest quality guides to particular sections of the Web. See especially the "Regional Studies," "International Affairs," and "Social and Behavioral Studies" pages.

◊ Economist.com Country Briefings: www.economist.com/countries
   Covering approximately 60 countries, this site offers authoritative news stories, country fact sheets, and forecasts.

◊ Portals to the World: www.loc.gov/rr/international/portals.html
   Selected links to Internet resources on over 120 countries and regions compiled by area specialists of the Library of Congress.

◊ World Factbook: https://www.cia.gov/library/publications/the-world-factbook/index.html
   Basic information on over 250 countries published annually by the Central Intelligence Agency (CIA).

◊ National Geographic: Travel and Cultures: http://www3.national geographic.com/places/
   Includes blogs, Traveler *magazine, country and city guides, and stunning photography.*

◊ Anthropological Index Online: http://aio.anthropology.org.uk/aio search
   Includes more than 4,000 periodical titles from over 780 journals in more than 40 languages, held at the Anthropology Library at the British Museum.

◊ RootsWorld: www.rootsworld.com/rw
   One of the most extensive collections of world music available on the Web.

◊ World-Newspapers.com: www.world-newspapers.com
   Browse world newspapers, magazines, and news sites in English, sorted by country and region.

◊ U.N. News Centre: www.un.org/News/dh/infocus
   Essential resources on United Nations issues in world news.

◊ Online phrasebooks: http://wikitravel.org/en/Wikitravel:List_of_ phrasebooks/
   Learn basic words, numbers, colors, phrases, and more from phrasebooks organized for tens of languages.

Task 3: Identify a researchable issue. Education-abroad programs increasingly encourage participants to design and carry out individualized field research projects. These projects enable students to investigate specific topics of global concern and personal interest while deepening the learning of coursework or service-learning experiences. This task invites you to survey a full range of quality-of-life issues, and to identify one or two topics that might be explored in more detail within your field setting (see Table 5.2). Many of these issues, as you might expect, cross national borders and affect the everyday lives of millions of people.

International nongovernmental organizations, magazines, and academic journals sponsor the following websites. Each one indexes and analyzes a variety of global issues through news reports and perceptive articles. Peruse three or four of the sites. Ask yourself: Which issues appear to be of greatest concern within my destination country or community? Which might I investigate further through a community-service project or small-scale research project?

WEB RESOURCES

◊ ELDIS gateway to development information: www.eldis.org
  Sponsored by the Institute for Development Studies in Sussex, this site provides access to over 26,000 full-text documents from over 7,500 development organizations.
◊ Human Rights Watch: www.hrw.org
  In-depth reporting aimed at exerting diplomatic and economic pressure around specific human rights issues.
◊ New Internationalist: www.newint.com.au
  An Oxford-based independent monthly magazine that publishes reports relating to social justice and human rights in the Majority world.
◊ The Economist: www.economist.com
  One of the leading sources of analysis on world affairs, published weekly and searchable by country and topic.

Table 5.2   Researchable Global Issues

Biotechnology	Domestic violenceHuman rights	Informal economy
Child labor	Education	Informal settlements
Civil society (NGOs)	Environmental harm	Malnutrition
Conflict & war	Globalization	Organized crime
Digital divide	Human rights	Relief & development
Disaster prevention	Ideologies & religions	Sex tourism
Discrimination	Infectious disease	Street children

◆ Foreign Policy: www.foreignpolicy.com
A monthly magazine of global politics, economics, and ideas published by the Carnegie Endowment for International Peace, searchable by country and topic.

◆ Sociosite: www.sociosite.net
A comprehensive listing of all social science resources based at the University of Amsterdam, searchable by subject areas.

Task 4: Search for issue-specific information. Once two or three issues are identified, you are ready to deepen your search for relevant information about them. First, using the Google search engine (www.google .com), practice typing in keywords and phrases, and see what kinds of documents come up. Remember: Google uses AND as the automatic Boolean operator, so select your search terms with care before clicking the Search button. When a list of "hits" comes up, scroll through them to see what looks useful. Then click on several for closer examination. Bookmark "keepers" for future reference.

If you intend to live with national families, you may also wish to search for Web-based resources that illuminate various aspects of family life. Information can be collected on everything from house construction and courtship practices to daily routines and role relations. First, decide on relevant keywords or phrases you will use to search country-specific family materials. Refer to Table 5.3 for keywords and synonyms to use in the search. (Remember: There are *billions* of websites out there, so try to be as specific as possible in naming the information you desire.) Practice dropping keywords and phrases like *Thailand house, Thailand family,* and *Thailand children* into Google. Then scroll through one or two screens of matches for the most useful results.

Guide 2: Searching Databases

There was once a time when research articles published in thousands of academic journals—be they in sociology, anthropology, psychology, or political science—could be found only by searching through cards in wooden drawers and on shelves of hard-copy periodicals. Not anymore. Public and academic libraries throughout the world now subscribe to electronic databases that already have done the arduous task of sifting

Table 5.3   Key words and Synonyms

Keywords/Phrases	Synonyms/Related Terms
House	home, dwelling, residence
Family	family life, household
Gender roles	sex roles, gender relations
Women	female, child bearing, motherhood
Children	youth, teenagers, socialization
Adolescents	adolescence, teens, youth
Kinship	kin, kinfolk, relatives
Courtship	dating, engagement, marriage
Patriarchy	authority, domestic violence, divorce

through, indexing, and abstracting information from magazines and journals for you. These subscription databases are licensed to libraries for a hefty fee and are not accessible through conventional search engines. The good news is that your regional public library will likely subscribe to the most popular databases, allowing library-card holders to have immediate remote access to all of its electronic resources, including magazine databases and downloadable audio, video, and music.

Electronic databases have yet to completely replace print sources, but the trend seems to be in that direction. (A notable example is *Encyclopaedia Britannica Online*, the electronic version of the monumental *Encyclopaedia Britannica*.) Until that day arrives, our information-collecting strategy should combine hard-copy reference reading with Internet and library-database research. Whereas Google and Wikipedia may enable you to access a vast wealth of information, they generally give you little control over the quality and type of search results. Research databases, on the other hand, organize materials that generally involve more careful scholarship and analytic depth than those available on the Web. They also offer a wider date range of items available.

Research databases share some basic vocabulary. A *database* is a collection of digitized facts or information stored in a computer. Databases are made up of *records* that display important elements of information related to a particular item. Those elements of information are called *fields* and may include the title, author, abstract, source, and subject of the record. The information itself can be presented in several *formats*, such as text, pictures, or sound.

Task 5: Organize and perform a library database search. This next task requires you to obtain access to online databases within a public or academic library. Some libraries are restricted to state residents or enrolled students, but others are either freely available to anyone or allow for special "guest" use. Students enrolled in a college or university can access restricted library resources including databases and online journals from off-campus computers through their school's proxy server. An identification code authenticates you as a valid member of the university community.

This task will take you through the following seven steps:

1. Do background reading on tentative topics.
2. Define your research topics and identify the main concepts.
3. Familiarize yourself with databases must appropriate to your topic.
4. Refine the search terms.
5. Document searches on a search log.
6. Save and file results.
7. Properly document electronic sources.

If you are brand new to searching electronic databases, expect to be a bit confused and even lost in the beginning. Don't hesitate to consult with librarians or other experts who specialize in electronic-reference (i.e., e-reference) or research assistance. They can assist you in selecting the databases and keywords most relevant to your research topic. Appointments can also be made with the librarians for in-depth consultation and assistance.

Step 1: *Do background reading on tentative topics.* Research on the Internet will have undoubtedly raised your awareness of the varied and interrelated dimensions of social life within your host country. Now supplement that knowledge by searching through the pages of an electronic encyclopedia. As a full-text database, an online encyclopedia like *Britannica Online* or *Funk & Wagnall's* provides summary articles with valuable hyperlinked outlines on a wide range of subjects. Within the encyclopedia interface, you can search by keyword, browse topics, or filter by media types (e.g., animations, photos, audio, or maps). Returned articles are full text, indexed, and cross-referenced.

By way of illustration, assume your interest is to research something related to the country of India. Begin by calling up the *Encyclopaedia Britannica Online* homepage. Type *India* into the search bar and click "Go." By clicking on *India*, you will be taken to the main article for India, a useful bibliography, and a hyperlinked outline of various historical, political, social, and cultural topics. Under "The Arts," for instance, you'll find links to "Architecture" and "Theater, film, and literature" that could support your study of the Indian family.

Repeat this process for your prospective host country. Work your way to the main article and scan it for three to four general subjects that interest you. Click on the subjects to do background reading on topics that you'd like to explore firsthand while abroad.

Step 2: *Define your research topics and identify the main concepts.* After identifying topics of special interest, the next step in a database search is to more clearly define what you want to know about those topics. Think about where you'll be and what you'll be doing. Learners intending to live with a host family in a rural area of Kenya might want to search for information that could be stated as "Family life in rural Kenya." Those wanting to collect information on an issue or problem associated with a community internship or research project might state their research topic as "Hindu women's organizations in Bangalore, India," "Daily life among street children of Rio de Janeiro, Brazil," or "The impact of Western popular culture among teenage Muslim girls in Izmir, Turkey."

Each of these research topics contains one or more related ideas or concepts that combine to form a *query*. Consider a potential research project that you might undertake during your term abroad. With the topic stated in appropriate natural language, jot down several related concepts (and their synonyms) that could be used to search one or more databases for pertinent articles or books (see Table 5.4 for examples).

Table 5.4 Sample Research Topics and Concepts

Research Topic	Concept 1	Concept 2	Concept 3
1. *Family life in rural Kenya*			
Family organization	Family	Rural	Kenya
2. *Muslim women's organizations in Bangalore, India*			
Women's rights	Muslim	Women's associations	Bangalore
3. *Daily life among street children in Rio de Janeiro*			
Vulnerable children	Activities	Street children	Brazil

As mentioned earlier, key terms are literally *key* (significant) words that are used singly or combined to find information about a given subject. Be aware, however, that in a keyword search you may retrieve a number of irrelevant records because the search engine is looking for the *exact* word you typed, not for the meaning or context of the word. For example, a search on AIDS may retrieve items on "Aids for the hearing impaired," "School aids," and "AIDS" (the disease). For this reason, it's best to begin thinking and searching broadly and then to gradually narrow your focus. The more common the word you search for, the more irrelevant hits you will produce. That's why searching for *acquired immune deficiency syndrome* is likely to produce relatively fewer but more relevant hits than searching for *sexually transmitted diseases*. Similarly, searching for *dance* probably will give you a more tightly focused set of results than searching for *arts*.

Step 3: *Familiarize yourself with databases most appropriate to your topic.* The number of databases available through community or academic libraries is continually expanding, and many of them provide instant information on issues of both global and local importance. By seeking professional assistance *before* actually conducting a search, you will know what databases they own, what each offers, and whether they can be accessed from home. With this information in mind, consider various angles on your topic. For example, research on Muslim women's organizations in Bangalore could be done in various databases: cross-discipline (ProQuest), specialized (Contemporary Women's Issues), and social science (SocINDEX). Be careful not to content yourself with one or two familiar databases, overlooking other, more specialized resources. Conduct a number of experimental searches in both general *and* specialized databases (see Table 5.5) to determine which are most germane to your information needs.

Step 4: *Refine the search terms.* Once you've selected the databases most appropriate to your search, it's time to figure out how they can be best used to find the information you need.

Table 5.5   Library Databases

Field	Database	Description
Cross-discipline	WorldCat	Over 52 million records of books and other materials in over 400 languages
Cross-discipline	EBSCOhost databases	Full text of over 2,000 magazine and journal articles
Cross-discipline	ProQuest databases	Full text of 2,800 magazine and journal articles
Women's studies	Contemporary Women's Issues	An international, full-text database of articles from women-focused sources
Sociology	SocINDEX	Full text of articles from more than 300 sociology journals on social topics worldwide
Interdisciplinary	CQ Global Researcher	In-depth, single-topic reports on a wide range of world issues from a number of international viewpoints
Social sciences	Social Sciences Full Text (Wilson Web)	Full-text articles and citations from thousands of sources with coverage from 1982
Humanities	Humanities Full Text (Wilson Web)	Indexes and abstracts of over 1,700 international journals, books, and other important reference sources
Humanities	Project Muse	Scholarly full-text database in the humanities and social sciences
Dissertations and theses	ProQuest Digital Dissertations & Theses	Abstracts of doctoral dissertations and master's theses from 1,000 institutions
Current events	LexisNexis Academic	Full text of authoritative world news, public records, and business information
Education	ERIC	Full text and abstracts of journal articles and reports on all aspects of education for all age groups
Religion	ATLA Religion	Abstracts of international titles in the fields of religion and theology
Art	Art Index	Index of publications in all art subjects in international perspective
Economics	EconLit	Indexes of the world's economic literature for more than 450 journals
Psychology	PsycINFO	Over 1 million citations of international literature in psychology and related disciplines
Language	Linguistics and Language Behavior Abstracts	Abstracts of articles and books on language and language learning

♦ *Familiarize yourself with the database.* For each database, find out if and how you can use the "advanced search" option to help you limit your search results by keyword, subject heading, language of publication, publication type, and specific published date or date ranges. Familiarize yourself with limits and other basic techniques *before* entering a keyword or phrase and launching your search. There is a great deal to learn about each database. Fortunately, almost all have a "Help" or "Tips" menu that provides valuable information about how to perform searches effectively and efficiently.

♦ *Identify alternate search terms.* Launch your search using the key terms drafted during step 2. Once in the database, you can modify your strategy and improve results by looking for alternate search terms within the records themselves. Database indexers use a specific, predetermined set of terms to define concepts for each item that is indexed. These terms, usually called *subjects, subject headings,* or *descriptors,* are found in the subject or descriptor field of the record. By using the subject headings assigned to books and articles by the indexers (in what is known as a "database thesaurus"), you can be assured that all items about the same topic have consistent subject headings. Subject-headings searches are best used when you have a specific subject in mind and are looking for specific articles focused on that topic. For instance, a search on *family life in Kenya* (search terms: family life + Kenya) in SocINDEX might generate a number of librarian-assigned subject categories from which to choose articles:

> Family relations
> Social networks
> Bride price
> Marital relations
> Manners and customs

Select the subject headings from the list that are most applicable to your research topic. In addition to a list of articles, the database will often direct you to *additional* subject headings. Select one or more of these additional headings (e.g., "Family relations") and you will see how one search can build on another with a "snowball effect," eventually exhausting relevant records.

Step 5: *Document searches on a search log.* To keep track of all the key terms and subject headings used to generate records, you'll need to maintain a careful record of your literature searches. Subject headings tend to vary from database to database, and keywords that generate numerous hits on one database may give you few or none on others. Try out several keyword combinations for each database, then document these searches in a written search log. Patiently recording each database, along with the keywords used in it, encourages you to customize your search strategy for different databases and to retrace your steps if necessary (Table 5.6).

Step 6: *Save and file results.* Determine the value of particular records by reading the abstracts or full-length text. After identifying useful items, you have four options for preserving them for future reference:

1. *Print your results.* If your workstation is connected to a printer, you can use your browser's "print" button to print. Only what you see on the screen will print. Consult with a librarian for pricing and procedure.
2. *Save to flash drive.* If no printer is available, you have the option of saving your results onto a personal USB flash drive. To save records to your drive, choose "Save as" from the file menu on your browser. Be careful to save all files in text (.txt), not HTML (.html), format and to assign a new file name each time you download; otherwise you will overwrite any information in the file.
3. *Forward to a personal e-mail address.* Many databases provide the option of sending any full citation or "tagged" records to your personal e-mail address. To ensure that the entire article is delivered to your mailbox, choose the "e-mail" button on the screen that shows the full article. Store articles for each topic in a separate folder on your webmail service (e.g., Gmail or Outlook).

Table 5.6 Search Log

Database	Keywords	# Results	Keywords	# Results	Keywords	# Results

4. *Order materials through interlibrary loan.* What if only the citation or abstract of a desired item is available through the database, and the library doesn't own the book, journal, or magazine? In such cases, most libraries will assist you in ordering the full-text article through their interlibrary loan (ILL) service. The ILL office will determine, via an online database, which library has the item you need and proceed to borrow it from the most convenient location. It is important to give the ILL office *at least* two weeks to locate and receive your requested item. Again, inquire about pricing and procedure.

Step 7: *Properly document electronic sources.* As information increasingly has become a commodity that can be sought and sold, copyright laws have come into effect to protect personal property. These laws require researchers to document (i.e., give credit to) the sources of their information. If your discipline follows an official style manual, consult that first. In general, you will document electronic sources as you do printed sources, beginning with the author's name (if available), date of publication (or date of retrieval) in parentheses, title or description of document, other relevant information (volume number, page numbers, etc.), retrieval-date statement, and URL. A research report, accessed online and conforming to the style conventions of the American Psychological Association (APA), would be documented as follows:

> Humphrey, K., & Koester, H. (2005, Fall). On the street: International research takes education beyond the classroom. *Abroad View*. Retrieved February 21, 2010, from http://www.abroadview.org/latinamerica/humphry_koester.htm

Citation styles vary considerably, but whatever format you decide to follow, *be consistent.* Also be sure to type every letter, number, symbol, and space accurately; even a discreet error makes retrieving your source impossible.

Conclusion

The Beach, Alex Garland's 1996 cult novel, depicts a group of Western wanderers adrift on a remote, untrammeled island in the Gulf of Thailand attempting to create their own paradise. In their idyllic beach community untouched by tourism, there is little effort made to understand Thailand's history or explore its cultural traditions, much less establish friendships with the Thai farmers on the other side of the island. Removed from the complex reality of Bangkok, both psychologically and physically, the drifters simply have nothing new to discover. All that's left is to indulge a shallow, beach-bum existence, with days spent fishing, gardening, playing with a Game Boy, and smoking lots of cannibas on the white sand beaches.

There was once a time when wanderlust was driven more by a thirst for authentic local knowledge than by hedonistic possibilities. Travel was virtually synonymous with education. Paul Fussell reminds us in *Abroad* (1982), "Before the development of tourism travel was conceived to be like study, and its fruits were considered to be the adornment of the mind and formation of the judgment. The traveler was a student of what she or he sought" (p. 39). Sometime in the 1970s things changed. The planet was transformed from a powerful classroom to instruct us into a huge playground to entertain us. Today we can all be grateful for the opportunity to travel more *widely* than ever before. But our real frontier lies elsewhere, in traveling more *wisely*—transforming fragments of information into real knowledge that can then be applied to forming cross-cultural friendships, cultivating understanding, and addressing the most pressing problems that confront humankind.

For Reflection and Discussion

1. Do you agree that *carrying knowledge* about particular peoples or places is central to both *maximizing field learning* and *bringing home knowledge* that can be used to positively impact the world? Explain.
2. Through a combination of simple searches, prepare a "culture/country briefing" on at least five culture/country features (e.g., geography, political history, religion, current events, and language).

References

Fussell, P. (1982). *Abroad: British literary traveling between the wars.* New York: Oxford University Press.
Louv, R. (2008). *Last child in the woods.* Chapel Hill, NC: Algonquin Books.

LIVING WITH PARADOX

*The test of a first-rate intelligence is the ability to hold two
opposing ideas in mind at the same time and still retain
the ability to function.*
—F. SCOTT FITZGERALD, *The Crack-Up*

THE DREAM OF COMPLETING an international study and service term
in Morocco had occupied Hanna for years. To prepare, she had taken
various foundational courses—such as world geography, intercultural
communication, and comparative religions—and compiled hundreds of
pages of culture-specific academic materials. She had even carved out
time to complete an audio course in elementary Arabic. Everything was
now set: plane tickets purchased, bags packed, and field arrangements
confirmed. Planning could not have been more systematic or thorough.

After final good-byes to family and close friends, Hanna finally boards
the plane that will take her to Paris en route to Fez. Her dream of learning
in a new culture is about to come true. But for all her preparedness,
Hanna isn't ready for what she's about to experience.

> I'm at the airport in Paris waiting in line to check in. I'm the only person
> at the terminal with a fair complexion. Mothers with children, men with
> business partners, I seem to be the only person traveling alone. Not for
> long. A man taps me on the shoulder. Surprised by this foreign touch, I
> turn around. "Bonjour Madame"—that is all I can understand. I'm not
> flattered. In truth, I'm afraid. I don't know what's going on. He obviously
> wants to help me to the gate and sit next to me. I turn away, looking in
> vain for someone who can understand my plight.

Before I proceed any farther, I find a bathroom and don my head covering. Although women in the bathroom stare at me, I feel a sense of security
and seclusion with the scarf. Tightly drawn around my face, I seek ano-
nymity amidst the crowd. I want to blend in and escape the stares and
"Bonjour Madams." If I feel this insecure in a Paris airport, how will I ever
make it off the plane in Morocco?

An elderly couple sitting next to me at the boarding gate shyly smile at
me. In my best French (which is pathetically limited) I ask them if they
speak English. No response, only shy smiles. I try again in very poor Arabic. Again, there's no response. Desperate to make some kind of vocal
contact, I ask them in Spanish. This time they look away. What am I doing
wrong? I thought everyone in Europe at least spoke French, Spanish, or
Arabic.

Cigarette smoke fills the airport despite the "No Smoking" signs. Everyone seems to be smoking except for this elderly couple and me. A wave of
nausea comes over me. I suddenly don't want to go to this country that I
have longed for and dreamed of for so many years. My tense body doesn't
want to board the plane. I hesitate as they call all passengers to board. I sit
there frozen with fear of the unknown. What's wrong with me? Slowly, I
make my way towards the boarding ramp. I'm the last person to board the
plane.

I'm also the last person off the plane. My light backpack suddenly
becomes unbearably heavy. For the first time I notice the intense heat and
the perspiration dripping off my brow. I can't go any further. I sit down
in silence, hands shaking, knees trembling, tears silently streaming down
my face. No friend to talk to. No guide to direct me. I am a stranger in a
strange land.

Losing Cultural Footing

Smooth transitions and trial-free sojourns are rarities. No matter how
well prepared, broad minded, or full of good intentions we may be, entering a new culture knocks our cultural props out from under us. We spend
decades learning the "ropes" for effective functioning within our own
society. Then, without warning, our mental programming is upset. What
we've come to know as "normal" and "natural" isn't normal or natural
anymore. Immediately upon arrival, the foreign setting confronts us with
a steady stream of new sights, sounds, and smells. *Everything* seems so

different: the slow pace of life, the intimidating stares, the strange language, and so much more. And without sufficient knowledge of the cultural code, and fearing offense, we must attend to *everything*. Days of doing so can leave us feeling exhausted.

Amazingly, native residents hardly seem bothered by what produces, for us, such consternation. A lifetime of experience has taught them how to unconsciously "blend," how to filter out some stimuli and focus on others. Their stares, their whispers, and their pointed figures continuously signal to us that they're not foreign, *we* are. Our own experience comes to painfully validate Clifton Fadiman's perceptive observation: "A foreign country is not designed to make [us] comfortable; it is designed to make its own people comfortable" (in Travel, n.d.).

This condition, commonly referred to as "culture shock," implies a state of relatively short-term emotional, mental, and physical *dis-ease* that we suffer when transitioning from an environment in which we have learned how to function effortlessly and successfully to one where we have not.[1] In this movement from the familiar to the unfamiliar, expected signs and symbols for relating to others are disrupted. We lose our sense of when to do what and how, leaving us in a state of ambiguity and, at times, acute disorientation. How does one greet someone he or she doesn't know? While talking to that person, does one look him or her in the eye or avoid direct eye contact? In someone's home, are shoes taken off or left on? Do male guests help clean up after a meal or leave that for the womenfolk? Back "home" the answers to these and a thousand other cultural questions were second nature to us, part of our internalized cultural code. Then we enter a strange culture, and most of the familiar signs and symbols simply don't work. We're like a fish out of water.

If you were to trade places with Hanna, what would *you* do to bring the cultural turbulence under control? Who would you be in this new situation? How would you determine what is socially appropriate or inappropriate to do or say? How much of your personal identity would you give up in order to be accepted by locals? Almost predictably you would find yourself caught in the paradox of wanting to adapt to the new setting in order to be accepted and successful without relinquishing cherished values and perspectives from home. Explains intercultural expert Janet Bennett (1998): "At one and the same time, we value our old belief system as well as adaptation to the new; we seek a way to survive within our former worldview, and yet recognize the necessity for a new perspective. . . . It is not merely 'not knowing what to do,' but it is more a case of not being *able* to do what one has come to value doing" (p. 218).

The Belly of the Whale

In *Hero With a Thousand Faces*, Joseph Campbell (1949) charts the journey of the archetypal hero endlessly retold in world mythologies. According to Campbell, "A hero ventures forth from the world of common day into a region of supernatural wonder: fabulous forces are there encountered and a decisive victory is won: the hero comes back from this mysterious adventure with the power to bestow boons on his fellow man" (p. 30).

Like the hero in ancient legends, our path begins in the ordinary world, only to lead us into an unusual world of unknown forces that present us tasks and trials that must be faced head-on. We find ourselves having to mediate two worlds and selves, what Campbell represents as "the belly of the whale." At this point in our hero path, we often feel ourselves being swallowed up by opposition forces much larger and stronger than ourselves. We can hardly imagine the belly of separation and self-death being turned into a womb of rebirth and transformation.

How *are* we to harness the transformative potential of the "whale's belly"? Do we listen for echoes of familiar voices? Count the ribs? Dream of the mainland? Curse the whale? The second half of this chapter will suggest strategies for converting challenging circumstances into vital learning opportunities. But the key thing to bear in mind is this: The "belly" of the local culture will remain strange to us—and us to it—until we acquire a culturally appropriate frame of reference and repertoire of behaviors that enable us, despite our circumstances, to be an accepted and respected outsider.

A first step in this direction is to mentally brace ourselves for passage into the realm of the unknown. This transition will not look the same for everyone. Every hero-traveler is affected by cultural contrasts in different ways and to different degrees. For some, the symptoms may be severe and protracted, and for others, quite mild and short-lived, even nonexistent. How each of us reacts depends on a complex set of psychological and social influences that include our travel motivations and purposes, our prior travel experience, our local language ability, the compatibility of home and host cultures, and the presence or absence of support structures (like a host family or local mentors). Furthermore, individual personality traits interact with these factors to either restrain or ease cross-cultural adjustment. Someone who is outgoing and ever ready to try something new is likely to fare better in stressful situations than an introverted and culturally cautious perfectionist.

The Path of Transformation

It is through struggle and change that life shapes us. "Change means movement and movement means friction," said Saul Alinsky, the great grassroots organizer. Few of us invite or welcome that movement and friction—the breakup we didn't see coming, the sudden death of a loved one, or some other deep disappointment or humiliation. But it's such shocks and losses that especially form us, despite our resistance.

This is especially true as we cross into another culture. To be transformative, our path must necessarily take turns and present obstacles that are, at times, greater than our ability to navigate them. It's only when givens change and old rules no longer apply that we become aware of the special lens through which we look at life. As anthropologist Clyde Kluckhohn (1949) famously stated, "It would hardly be fish who discovered the existence of water. Students who had not yet gone beyond the horizon of their own society could not be expected to perceive custom which was the stuff of their own thinking" (p. 11). It seems that in order to see life—and ourselves—differently than when we did before, we need to contend with contrasts, and with the disorientation and confusion that typically follows.

In most cases, we won't have to seek out disorienting experiences. Anyone entering a distinctly different culture for an extended period of time, and without all the protective supports of home, can expect to be confronted by stress-inducing situations. While it's true that the initial decision to uproot is ours, soon afterward, much of our life abroad happens under our feet and without our permission. Cultural quakes happen. Our foundations suddenly shift, and nothing—not family, not friends, not language, not customs—seems fixed anymore.

Deep intercultural learning depends on this kind of dissonance, but it need not debilitate us, leaving us feeling defeated and depressed. Although the path of transformation rarely follows a predictable and linear course, it requires that we keep walking. The goal of being able to "step into" and "imaginatively participate in the other's worldview," as Jane Bennett (1998, p. 221) puts it, is not achieved all at once. It unfolds over time, typically as a result of a journey that cycles through several distinct phases.

Phase 1: Anticipation

Our journey commences as we leave behind the everyday world we've been nurtured by and spent decades learning to function in. We eagerly embrace the prospect of challenging our interpersonal, intellectual, and physical abilities with an "I just can't wait to . . ." kind of anticipation. A sense of adventure and freedom runs high. Although there is some natural trepidation over waking up to the unknown, for the most part the differences or difficulties only heighten our sense of expectancy.

Phase 2: Contact

Touching down at our destination, we enter a new physical and social space—one with its own unique history, social identity, and natural habitats. The fact that we bring foreign qualities into our hosts' cultural and natural world renders us "strangers"—displaced persons—who must now learn to live in a state of cultural and ecological limbo, between two worlds. To our hosts we are largely an unknown quantity needing to be put in some familiar category of persons: tourist, trader, teacher, development worker, even spy. For our part, we are "fish out of water," needing to figure out how to accomplish simple, ordinary tasks like going to the bathroom, bathing, and getting a good night's sleep. This can prove far more challenging than we might expect, as the following report back to Jesse's friends and family from Bangalore (India) illustrates:

> As most of you know, Indians don't use toilet paper. That is why you always use the right hand for eating; the left is for splashing water on yourself after using the toilet. I'm still trying to get the hang of that one! I'm also learning to bathe with a bucket of water . . . which brings me to the cockroaches. Two huge ones were watching me from the doorframe the other night when I was trying to bathe out of the bucket. I wasn't going to worry too much as long as they stayed put. But when I was brushing my teeth, a huge one ran across my foot! That started a nightlong war between me and the cockroaches. At first there were two, then three. By the end of the night, three turned into seven. Needless to say, I got no sleep whatsoever that night.

Like Jesse, some of us may find the initial euphoria associated with a supposed "honeymoon" period to be short-lived. Immediately immersed in homestay and work settings that require myriad physical and cultural issues to be sorted out, we may be pressed, straightaway, to crack the cultural code and confront our fear of the unfamiliar.

Others of us can expect to more gradually ease into our field settings, especially if our field program or backpacker enclave provides us something of a "halfway house" between complete strangeness and homespun familiarity. Though not necessarily optimal for culture learning, it does guard us against having to cope with too many cultural tests too soon. A degree of cultural insulation can allow us to absorb the "new" with a tourist's enthusiasm. Local sights and sounds exude charming novelty. The indigenous population, enjoyed at arm's length, presents no challenge to our status, identity, and well-being. Sure, we may have to deal with minor intestinal disturbances and insomnia, but negative stereotyping is largely absent. E-mails home might read: "This place is *so* amazing, and the people *so* friendly."

Phase 3: Disintegration

Assuming that we don't remain safely sealed off from the local people, the cultural novelty that marked our arrival to the country will begin to wear off. With each passing day we become more and more aware of how *different* this place is from home. Unfamiliar foods, unwanted critters, struggles with the language, transportation hassles, water and power shortages, continuous gawking, and chronic homesickness—all of this and more conspire to produce feelings of inadequacy and acute frustration. What some researchers describe as "field work blues" becomes a daily experience. This was the case for Michael, who, during a six-month stint in the highlands of Guatemala, had to negotiate a relentless stream of cultural differences, not the least of which was the radically different value attached to time.

> The phrase *mas o menos* (more or less) has become all too familiar to me. Among my new friends in Santa Anita, the concept of time doesn't seem to be based on clocks, numbers, or agendas at all, but on relationships, daily routines, and weather patterns. If it's raining outside, time doesn't seem to matter; work will wait until it stops raining. If you run into someone on the street and a conversation ensues, time stops until the conversation is finished. This is something that drives me to points of major confusion and frustration.

As aggravating as it can sometimes be, learning to think and act within a new frame of reference is central to turning parochials into cosmopolitans. The emotionally intense nature of learning to cope with distinct cultural differences tends to quickly bring grandiose aspirations to "global citizenship" back down to earth. The salient questions become: Can we—both hosts and guests—learn to sympathetically adapt to each other? Can our substantial differences be a source of mutual enrichment rather than separation? And can we both make enough space for each other to appreciate each other's perspectives and approach common dilemmas with a wider horizon?

In every society, culturally approved rules standardize everything from nose blowing and bodily distance to "punctuality" and friend making. We must patiently, sometimes painstakingly, learn these rules; simply "being there" isn't enough. Developing an amphibious ability to inhabit two different worlds simultaneously requires a determined spirit, a good sense of humor, and the effective use of particular language and culture learning skills (Paige, Cohen, Kappler, Chi, & Lassegard, 2002). When we lack these abilities, relatively minor irritations tend to pile up until the weight of it all becomes overwhelming. At the point that we hit bottom, only sources of identity and value located deep within ourselves can keep us from feeling totally helpless and undone.

Given a certain set of circumstances, both within and without, a gutting sense of cultural and physical disintegration can overtake us. Writing from Lagos, Nigeria, soon after arrival, Lena manages to put her angst into words:

> I know I have been here for just under two weeks, but I feel like I'm trapped, like I could never have belonged in Africa. I am too ill to have the patience to cope with everything and am trying desperately to not count the days until I'm scheduled to leave. I don't like Lagos at all. There's no way for me to "fit in" and I'm taken advantage of constantly. The people will not sell to me at regular prices because they know I can pay more. My hosts tell me not to trust anyone, but all I want to do is build trust relationships. I do not know how to deal with this. I fear I'm on the brink of disengaging myself entirely from the community in order to maintain emotional stability.

The experience of "hitting the wall," especially in intense cross-cultural settings, tends to defy simple remedies. Nevertheless, we may still be tempted to dispense armchair advice. Michael in Guatemala should simply move in the direction of his hosts' concept of time. Lena, for her part, should first see a doctor and then try to empathize with the local culture at a deeper level. But when you are in the center of the cultural storm, there appears to be no ready "fix" for conflicts that reach down and threaten our core values and self-identity. Sometimes the best we can do is to remind ourselves that we're not going crazy—that we are reacting in normal and even predictable ways to circumstances over which we have little control.

When we discover that things in our destination culture are profoundly different from things at home, our natural tendency is not to move toward them but to flee away from them. Flight typically occurs in one of two directions. The first is to defend ourselves against a threatening environment by idealizing our home culture and ridiculing the native way of life. "Can you believe these backward people?" we complain to other foreigners. "Why can't they just . . . ?" Instead of seeking to *under-stand why* certain practices so irritate us, our immediate impulse is to simply spurn them as primitive and uncivilized, even immoral. Doing so justifies our escape from the culturally disagreeable environment into behaviors where we can feel protected and affirmed: calling home frequently, sleeping either too much or too little, reading romance novels (or seeking romantic relationships), blogging or listening to music for hours on end, watching movies, eating chocolate, seeking refuge in the company of other foreigners . . . the list goes on. We may not "return home" in a physical sense, but psychologically we're a world away.

This is not to discount other foreigners as a source of much-needed companionship and consolation. During our lowest times, national hosts may be largely oblivious to our plight, wondering why we just can't "get over it." Empathetic compatriots give us a chance to recount struggles, release frustrations, and recover a sense of hope and strength. Speaking developmentally, they provide the external support needed for us to negotiate the challenges of our environment, to resolve unfamiliar and clashing ways, and to ultimately integrate new cultural understandings into a higher or more appropriate way of functioning (Evans, Forney, & Guido-DiBrito, 1998; Sanford, 1967).

But emotional dependence on cultural similars is double-edged. Although it may provide vital social support, it can easily lead to stagnation in terms of cultural adjustment and learning. The dynamic is self-reinforcing: "The more we retreat from the culture and the people," notes Craig Storti (1990), "the less we learn about them; the less we learn about them, the more uncomfortable we feel among them; the more uncomfortable we feel among them, the more inclined we are to with-draw" (p. 32). Continual retreat into a foreigner bubble runs the risk of reinforcing a sense of "being in control" *apart from* having to adjust ourselves to native expectations. Until we're able to actually risk *new* ways of thinking and behaving, our general well-being and field learning are likely to be hindered.

There is a second, though far less common, way that stressed-out sojourners signal retreat from the frustrations inherent in living between two cultures: It is to "go native." Going native is driven by an exaggerated longing for cultural acceptance and approval. But instead of finding that social security in the company of other foreigners, nativists renounce their home culture in favor of an indiscriminate submersion into the host culture. They will typically shun the company of other foreigners and embrace, wholesale, the very way of life that has caused so much anxiety. Those who react to culture stress in this manner are, in most cases, looking to weld themselves to those cultural elements—like simplicity, mystery, spiritual vitality, and "color"—that they perceive to be missing in their own society. Indian author Geta Mehta (1994) recalls such a "going native" obsession among Westerners on pilgrimages to India during the 1960s:

> What an entrance. Thousands and thousands of them, clashing cymbals, ringing bells, playing flutes, wearing bright colors and weird clothes, singing, dancing and speaking in tongues . . . [a] caravanserai of libertine celebrants who were wiping away the proprieties of caste, race, and sex by sheer stoned incomprehension. The seduction lay in the chaos. They thought we were simple. We thought they were neon. They thought we were profound. We knew we were provincial. Everyone thought everybody else was ridiculously exotic and everybody got it wrong. (p. 19)

The blame for "getting it wrong" cannot be placed entirely on the naïveté of would-be global souls. The western tourist industry, embedded within a global consumer culture, has made a fine art out of commodifying exotica for innocents abroad—while supplies lasts. Masked by these fantasized and often fetishized images, however, are the brutal subjugation and unequal power relations that, in many cases, have confirmed "exotic" peoples in their native splendor (Huggan, 2001; Hutnyk, 2000). Suffice it to say that "going native," as a response option to the experience of disintegration (see Figure 6.1), is not likely to help us achieve the equilibrium we seek.

Phase 4: Recovery

What are we to do, when we find ourselves tempted to either withdraw into a homelike subculture or reject our home culture altogether and "go native"? The short answer is that we need to *step back* and *think about* the actual conditions triggering our mental and emotional disorientation, and our physical response to it.

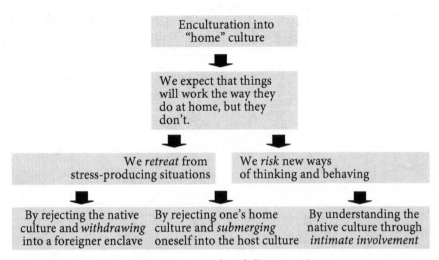

FIGURE 6.1   Alternative responses to cultural disintegration

Some find this reflective process best facilitated through face-to-face conversations where they make their experiences intelligible to sympathetic listeners. The hope is that narration plus reflection will yield deeper comprehension. Others find self-conscious writing to be the most productive means of sorting out complex emotions and getting at the true sources of their alienation (Wagner & Magistrale, 2000). Writing in an analytic mode helps us to calm down, gain some objectivity, and ask the critical questions: What provoked this reaction from me? How do locals interpret this act or event? And what does my reaction tell me about myself? Especially as we learn to put personal experiences and reactions into a larger social and theoretical context (typically through instructive readings and lectures), our writing takes on a distinctive character—one that joins personal expression with cultural analysis—and encourages a more rigorous cognitive process than is common in conversation.

Through the process of analytic reflection we come to realize a simple truth: The only way *over* culture stress is *through* it. This insight emerges for Katie in El Salvador as she pauses long enough to take stock of her situation:

I have been gone for a month now. During this period I've moved from denying that I'm an extremely prideful being who could never really feel helpless and vulnerable, to forcing myself to reflect on all that I'm feeling in hopes of understanding it better. It's odd how there can be a crowd of people surrounding me, and yet I feel so incongruous with the setting. This week has partially been spent wishing I could either hibernate until my departure date or catch some terrible illness that would force me to return early. But life has begun to turn around. I'm realizing there are times in our lives when we should simply ignore ourselves. Being out of control has put me in touch with my need for others and some deep-seated feelings of inadequacy that have remained hidden behind self-protective walls. I'm seeing that this trip is a test for me. Will I persist here just to fulfill a school requirement by "studying" these people from a distance? Or will I learn to "be" in this community in such a way as to allow the Salvadorean people to teach me with their lives?

It's often the case that those experiences that are the most difficult incidentally lead us to our deepest lessons, if only we can hold our emotional reactions in check long enough to uncover their cultural meanings. Peter Adler (1987) contends that it is only through situations that evoke disintegration and introspection that "the individual experiences himself and other people in a new way distinct from previous situations, and is consequently forced into new levels of consciousness and understanding" (p. 31). New self-awareness allows us to recognize not only our own feelings but also how those feelings affect other people. Our thought processes also become more sophisticated as we construct new and more complex cognitive maps, allowing us to factor in multiple points of view and cultural norms to our everyday living.

The transformative potential of global learning requires that we not waste our sorrows. Instead of treating them with disdain, as unexpected and unwanted foes, we can learn to welcome them as inevitable and indispensable friends. No longer do we stay on guard and keep the local culture at arm's length. We make the fateful decision to enter the cultural fray and to risk alternative ways of thinking and acting—things not expected of the casual tourist or even the typical study-abroad student. This doesn't mean, though, that we go it alone. Expect to encounter gurus, companions, and mentors along the way—trustworthy "insiders" who accept us within their sphere of activity and offer wisdom and guidance for the journey through our new world.

Phase 5: Integration

If we learn to actively participate in our host culture without rejecting or romanticizing it, our global learning can enter a phase of emotional, mental, and physical adaptation and integration. In time our circumstances begin to "normalize," and we experience an unexpected sense of ease with our surroundings. No longer do we require therapeutic havens to blunt the edge of living and learning outside our comfort zone. Instead of immediately withdrawing from unpleasant situations, our habit now is to mentally step back and become critically aware of our context and ourselves. Not only do we learn to manage our own fluctuating emotional states; we also come to recognize and respond to the subtle social signals of others in our host culture. The environment hasn't changed, but our self-awareness, cultural knowledge, and empathic ability have. Most of the differences between "our" ways and "their" ways are understood and appreciated as different but morally neutral means of doing life.

Unlike going native, cultural integration is not driven by a desperate need for acceptance and belonging for their own sake. Neither is it motivated by the prospect of being able to rehearse, upon our return home, harrowing tales of deprivations endured. Rather, we allow ourselves to be affected by the host culture in ways that yield new insights, fresh perspectives, and richer cultural comparisons—the "bricks and mortar" for constructing a better life, whether on an individual, national, or global level. In order to make fair and illuminating comparisons between cultures, we must temporarily suspend our largely inherited values and beliefs without flaunting *or* renouncing them. We maintain a conscious awareness and acceptance of our self as a "center," a cultural being ultimately responsible for its own thoughts and behaviors. This is critical. Without a properly centered self, we have no stable root for our identity apart from our fluctuating mental, emotional, and physical states. We must be able to think new *and* old thoughts, to experience new *and* old emotions. This doesn't mean that certain aspects of the host culture will magically cease to unsettle and confuse us. Or that we won't end up confirmed in our own ways and disapproving of the other. It simply means, at a minimum, that we will have learned to adjust our own behavior so it doesn't unsettle, confuse, or offend *others*.

From Travail to Transformation

There is a certain reward for enduring extended periods of intense disorientation in settings where we're continually confronted by our inadequacy and vulnerability. It is to make progress in learning how to walk in two distinctly different worlds. In time we acquire a knack for passing, in Campbell's (1949) words, "back and forth across the world division . . . permitting the mind to know the one by virtue of the other" (p. 229). This aspiration may not be realized in 1, 2, or even 10 cross-cultural ventures. Our present sojourn is just one in a lifelong journey toward becoming a certain type of person for a certain type of world. Whether or not we ultimately achieve what specialists call "global competence" or "cultural intelligence," our journey has served to enrich our minds, to rectify at least some of our prejudices, and to sharpen our ability to see through the cultural myths that can so easily command us.

The paradox of educational travel is that we rarely unearth its hidden treasures apart from deeply personal and often painful costs. "Few of us ever forget the connection between 'travel' and 'travail,'" writes Pico Iyer (2000), "and I know that I travel in large part in search of hardship—both my own, which I want to feel, and others', which I need to see." Our sojourns can potentially reveal whole new worlds, both within and outside ourselves. But those worlds tend to be revealed only through the involuntary displacements and discomforts that accompany our movement from familiar to unfamiliar environments. The question is whether those travails will make us bitter or better. Will they produce sour resentment, keeping us locked into psychological defenses or fresh revelation that frees us from overattachment to previous ways of thinking? Much depends on our success in following six pieces of seasoned advice.

1. Mentally prepare with cultural information.

The preceding chapter advocated for a basic toolbox of cultural information as the necessary foundation for attempting to crack the "code" of our host culture. Intellectual preparations help sensitize us to the cultural complexity that awaits us in distant lands, helping us form realistic expectations. What they can't do, of course, is guarantee that we will be open-minded and responsive in the face of the unfamiliar. In fact, an exclusive reliance on "book learning" runs the risk of fixing expectations, making it difficult to cope with the unpredictable and unexpected.

Aim to strike a balance between staying open-minded without leaving home empty-headed. Take the time to cull *specific information* from websites, guidebooks, and academic databases. That information then becomes the basis for constructing *strategic knowledge*: the ability to consciously select which behaviors to use in which situations and to understand *why* those behaviors might be appropriate in one setting and not in another. It's one thing to understand, on a cognitive level, that Thai or Japanese persons hold elders in high regard. It's quite another to learn how and when to initiate an interaction with the appropriate *wai*, or bow.

2. Evaluate the conditions that influence cultural adaptation.

One of the most important steps in our personal preparation is to take stock of the numerous variables that determine whether our global experience will carry transformative impact or return us home relatively unchanged. Certain conditions may either drive or restrain deep learning. Entering our field settings with "both eyes open" enables us not only to set reasonable learning goals but also to take appropriate measures to build on the strengths and compensate for the weaknesses inherent in each set of influences.

The model presented in Figure 6.2 synthesizes a wide range of factors that appear to influence the outcome of global-learning experiences. Although the process of cross-cultural adjustment and learning is far too complex to systematize in any rigid way, there are distinct sets of factors that influence our ability to cope effectively with a broad spectrum of demanding and disorienting situations. Some of these influences reside within us; others, in the local context; still others, in the foreign-study or service program. Each factor set interacts with the others to color how we might react to—and potentially learn from—unfamiliar and, often, stressful situations.

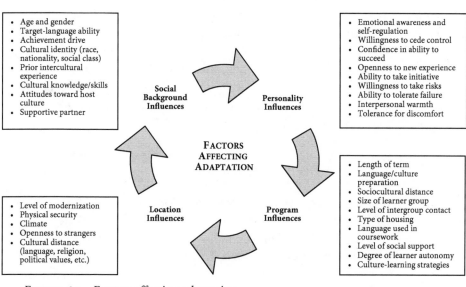

FIGURE 6.2   Factors affecting adaptation

On an individual level, there are a variety of social-background and personality characteristics that shape the way we will interact with cultural differences. These include our age and gender, life experience, knowledge of host culture, motivational mix, language ability, emotional maturity, cognitive flexibility, and general sociability.

Each of us must also navigate influences that reside within our new location abroad. The foreign context shapes our expectations and how we choose to act in relation to others. It may or may not be welcoming to foreigners. It may or may not have language, laws, foods, religious values, and climate in common with our home culture. Similarities to our own culture simplify acclimation, while cultural contrasts act to "raise the bar" that we have to clear in order to eventually find cultural footing. Characteristics in the host culture help to explain why the outcomes of a four-month term in Ethiopia or Angola, other factors being equal, are likely to be quite different from those resulting from a four-month term in England or Australia. It also suggests that certain types of sojourners will succeed in some environments better than in others.

Finally, there are certain aspects of the program itself that impact the level of cultural integration we are likely to achieve. A one-month study tour in Western Europe that requires little or no advanced preparation, that is conducted in English, and that supplies group housing for 25 co-nationals in an international dorm presents a much different integration challenge for participants than a six-month term rooted in a Central American community where participants, traveling either solo or in pairs, must learn to communicate and collaborate with local families and service organizations.

3. Cultivate personal traits that maximize involvement.

Some factors bearing on cultural adjustment—like choosing where we'll travel, how, and with what type of program—are clearly within our control. Other factors, especially those intrinsic to us, may not be so easily manipulated. But there are certain personal variables that we *do* have power over. We can decide, for example, to enhance our knowledge base, develop additional skill sets, or adjust our motivations and relational behavior. In particular, the attitudes we carry with us can also make a profound difference in how we interact with, and what we learn from, our new environment. For instance, a humble and nonjudgmental attitude toward the sight of veiled women or begging street children can guard us against rushing to premature conclusions and closing off further learning. It's good to remind ourselves that locals must also exercise tolerance toward the ambiguities surrounding *our* presence—like why we're so conscious of time or so protective of private space.

Cultivating personal traits that positively influence cross-cultural integration can begin prior to departure. In fact, many of these traits may *already* have been tested through stress-provoking transitional experiences within our home culture. Our reactions to a family move or our first full-time job can make us suddenly aware of our unique strengths and weaknesses. Our abilities and deficiencies may either aggravate or relieve stress as we adapt ourselves to new peoples and places.

The exercise in Table 6.1 lists 15 personality-related abilities related to notions of social, emotional, cultural, and spiritual "intelligence" (Earley & Mosakowski, 2004; Gardner, 1993; Goleman, 1995; Zohar & Marshall, 2000). These personal traits appear to positively influence cultural integration and are typically formed through "transitional" life experiences like sojourns abroad. As you read each behavioral description, ask yourself:

Table 6.1 Self-Screening Exercise

Capabilities	Rating
• My ability to identify and assess personal strengths and weaknesses [Integrity]	
• My interest in learning about new cultures [Inquisitiveness]	
• My ability to think positively about the cross-cultural situation [Optimism]	
• My confidence in being able (mentally and physically) to accomplish goals [Self-confidence]	
• My ability to self-start and approach unfamiliar situations in a proactive manner [Initiative]	
• My ability to remain composed in stressful situations [Emotional stability]	
• My ability to "laugh things off," including my own cultural blunders [Sense of humor]	
• My ability to withhold judgments until I can absolutely "see" behind the scenes [Open-mindedness]	
• My ability to "read" local situations based on knowledge of the country's social, cultural, and political systems [Context awareness]	
• My ability to form effective working relationships with people from different cultures [Collaboration]	
• My ability to "feel into" the experiences of others and to "see" from their perspective [Empathy]	
• My ability to "try on" different ways of speaking, valuing, believing, and behaving [Experimentation]	
• My ability to appreciate what's good and true in other cultural traditions [Respect]	
• My ability to follow through on self-directed tasks [Conscientiousness]	
• My ability to persevere in the face of unfavorable conditions and failures [Hardiness]	

How well developed is this ability in my life? What life experiences have helped form this ability? Then, on a scale of 1 (low) to 5 (high), assign a rating beside each attribute.

Once you finish the exercise, go back and "self-screen" your highest and lowest ratings. How might you build on your strong areas and improve in the areas where you are weakest? What additional "supports" at the situational (i.e., program and location) level might be necessary to compensate for the "challenges" you face at the individual (i.e., social background and personality) level? For example, if you find that you are risk averse and overly concerned about diet and "proper" hygiene, you might want to think twice about participating in programs located in resource-poor countries. Conversely, you may consider yourself a fearless "supertraveler" who sets high goals and embraces hardship with a singular focus. A high level of self-confidence may help you organize your mental and emotional faculties in order to tackle new challenges. But there is a flip side: Those who are goal oriented and task driven within more relationship-based societies tend to do worse, not better, than those who take delays and other annoyances in stride. What personality traits need to be cultivated in order to maximize learning at your program site?

4. Sustain involvement in the host community.

During the ups and downs of our initial adjustment period, we may naturally look to fellow foreigners to help stabilize our emotional state and affirm some of the values of "home." This was the case with Sarah after spending weeks without in-person communication with other Westerners.

> I've now been in Bangalore [India] for a little over a month. . . . After returning to campus, I met up with two girls from the UK, Laura and Julia. We went to Rayasandra and had lunch, a rest, and a tour. It was so good to be able to bounce things off the girls that can only be understood by those from the West. I think this would be a similar situation if someone from the East came to the West alone, and suddenly, after a few weeks, had an Easterner to talk to.

In-country connections with cultural similars can be a much-needed source of emotional refreshment. Nevertheless, a productive level of cultural integration ultimately depends on us establishing a network of supportive relationships with host nationals: extended family members, internship staff, shopkeepers, national students, language helpers, and cultural mentors who agree to welcome you into their lives.

Only as we become a functioning part of the local community does its strangeness begin to wear off. But it takes work. It requires that we step outside of our relational comfort zone and begin to take some risks. Successful culture learners find imaginative ways to invite the unknown and cultivate a network of close-knit and supportive friends. Their most common recommendations include the following:

◊ Decide not to resort to a cell phone (at least in the beginning) to tell time. Instead, ask the time from people on the street or bus.

◊ Actively explore the host community in order to figure out how to get around and meet everyday needs through local markets, shops, banks, post offices, and the like (see chapter 7). Along the way, solicit local knowledge from random residents who agree to serve as temporary guides and cultural informants.

◊ Frequent many of the same bus lines, grocery stores, restaurants, Internet cafes, and money changers to establish a regular and expected "presence." Acquainting yourself with local residents opens up unexpected opportunities and invitations.

◊ Join a local club or association as a way to get exercise or renew your spirit, and to meet residents who share common interests. Soccer, cycling, baseball, birding, dancing, martial arts, yoga, worship, swimming, cooking, and classical music are just a few of the group activities available in most communities.

◊ Take advantage of scheduled community events or seasonal festivals that are off the path beaten by tourists. Examples include sponsored lectures, town-council meetings, school dances, yodeling contests, parades, and public wedding ceremonies.

5. Get below the surface of local scenes.

Making sense of an unfamiliar world is the central cognitive process in intercultural learning and a critical part of successful adaptation. We've already mentioned the role that analytic writing plays in helping us take stock of complex emotional responses to field experiences. But writing is also an indispensable tool for thinking our way out of our negative reactions. The discipline of putting our experiences into written words pushes us to pay attention to things we otherwise would tend to ignore. Noelle's journal entry, written while serving with the Grameen Bank in Dhaka, Bangladesh, reveals this heightened level of attentiveness to both the local culture and to herself:

> After going to the market today, if anyone had asked me how I like it in this country, I probably would have burst into tears. Maybe you would have too, if live chickens, tied together by the feet and hanging like a poultry bouquet were thrust in front of your face by a scrawny old man who shouted to you in a strange language that you were trying to learn but cannot seem to get a handle on. Here—choose a chicken! Two? Okay . . . we'll stick them in a bucket and weigh them, slowly cut off their heads in front of you, then throw them into a huge pot to kick around while the blood from their necks splatters the wall, the other chickens, maybe even you. Here, have a seat. This will only take a minute. Sit and watch and listen as they prepare your chicken, put it in a plastic bag, and hand it to you.
>
> As I write this I wonder why I am so disturbed by this scene. In the U.S. we're so distanced from such realities. Everything is packaged so neatly so that we don't have to witness the death or suffering that food has to go through. When I think about it, isn't it more disgusting to eat chicken from a mega-market that sits in my freezer for months and months after sitting at the store for who knows how long? But to do otherwise would be too inconvenient, too messy. It would force us to face the sacrifice involved in sustaining our lives. It seems we've turned everything about the pain of life into a sterile practice. We rarely ever watch people die, and never prepare the dead for burial ourselves. We fight old age with everything in us, dedicating science and personal finance to the cause of looking young. Bangladeshis see the processes involved; I only see the final (often fabricated) product. Which should I cry over now, I wonder?

Noelle's introspections take on an analytic quality by including not just incident descriptions but also comparisons and musings as attempts to probe below the surface of disturbing cultural scenes. For her it was open-air meat processing. For us it might be loud and incessant "calls to prayer" or enthusiastic belches by family members following an evening meal. Some native practices will always be a source of frustration, if not offense. Writing allows us to think systematically about the meanings that locals attach to these practices, and to project those meanings onto life within our home environment. Self-conscious cultural *description* ("What is happening here and how do I feel about it?") is linked to contextual *interpretation* ("Why is it this way?") in a spiraling movement aimed at "seeing" behind local scenes with greater and greater clarity.

6. Try on new ways of thinking and behaving.

Attempts at cultural "sense making" set the stage for cultural experimentation. Riches are to be found in every culture—in its customs and rituals, language and stories, intellectual and ethical achievements—and offer us, as global learners, vast resources for nourishing a more transcultural consciousness. The act of "trying on" new ways of thinking and living enables us to understand, via direct experience, the deep meanings these cultural treasures hold for community members. At a deeper level, it expresses a fundamental belief: that "all human cultures that have animated whole societies over some considerable stretch of time have something important to say to all human beings" (Taylor & Gutman, 1992, p. 66). Cultural experimentation leads us to reach down into the soil of our host culture through empathetic involvement with local residents, and to pick out those virtues and values that have universal resonance.

Recall Jesse's struggle to cope with her physical and cultural environment in Bangalore. Even though learning to bucket-bathe and use squat toilets challenged 20 years of mental and physical conditioning, in time the new behaviors normalized and may even have become preferable. Making these necessary lifestyle adjustments was awkward enough. Nevertheless, like learning to wear a sari or eat with her hands, bucket-bathing and squatting posed no threat to her sense of right and wrong. In time she came to understand and accept these behaviors as morally neutral expressions of a distinctive way of life.

Other behaviors, however, are not that innocent. At a much deeper level they may challenge fundamental assumptions and values. Residing in virtually any Middle Eastern society, we're likely to observe local women living in *purdah*; wearing a *hijab*; serving their husband's coffee or tea; and doing most, if not all, of the household cooking and cleaning. Given our cultural training, such behaviors probably would present us with irrefutable evidence of "male domination" and "female oppression." Or imagine yourself a sole female traveler in a Latin American city. As you walk to language school, a group of young men decide to make pincers of their hands, tuck them into the corners of their mouths, and relentlessly "wolf whistle" at you. What should you do? Assuming you don't take it as some kind of compliment and smile back, you'd probably want to flip them off and walk on.

When confronted by behaviors that violate fundamental notions of right and wrong, thinking our way out of our negative reactions is a tall order, requiring considerable emotional self-regulation and cognitive flexibility. In the case of the wolf whistling, it would take us searching out the local meanings associated with the act. Are behaviors that would be defined in the West as forms of sexual harassment and gender discrimination *necessarily* be perceived or defined that way here? How do local women explain it? What is their subjective experience of it?

Cultural explanations might help, at least on a cognitive level. But emotionally we may still be stuck in disgust, or at least disapproval. In every culture (including our own) there will be behaviors we simply cannot accept even after we have uncovered the reasons behind them. In other words, even though we *expect* them, and even understand them, we are still not able to *like*—much less adopt—them. That's because they violate deep-seated beliefs and values that are so fundamental to our identity that our continued sense of self-respect demands we reject them (Storti, 1990).

As a general rule, the process of cultural adaptation follows the wise maxim, "When in Rome do as the Romans do," albeit without actually "going Roman." It involves living *with* the people, *as* the people, and *for* the people, without indulging the illusion of ever *becoming* the people. How far do we actually move toward resident expectations? That will depend on prudence, good judgment, and the expectations of the local people. But unlike "going native," our movement toward local norms won't ultimately be about gaining personal approval or acceptance. It aims to construct a platform of respect and credibility from which the totality of our living, studying, and serving can be oriented toward the common good.

Conclusion

The journey toward a more global sensibility proceeds along a fairly predictable road—one marked by singular joys and open-eyed wonder, but also by cultural incompatibilities and struggles. Some experience of painful *un*-learning always accompanies new cultural learning. The question is not *whether* we will face it but *how* we will maximize its transformative potential. Rather than signal retreat from the sources of sorrow, we can choose to take the road less traveled by learning to press through the obstacles to the deeper self-awareness and worldly wisdom needed to work for positive change.

FOR REFLECTION AND DISCUSSION

1. Consider the various factors listed in Figure 6.1 and Table 6.1 that influence adjustment to a new cultural milieu. How might certain personality and social-background factors have either a positive or a negative effect on your own adaptation? Which program factors are likely to heighten or to reduce your level of cultural stress?
2. We're encouraged to regard cultural stress not as an adversary to somehow "manage" but as a rare opportunity for deep personal growth, both emotional and intellectual. Discuss how the strategies outlined in the "From Travail to Transformation" section might be applied to your field setting in order to foster fundamental changes in self-understanding, cultural beliefs, and personal lifestyle.

Note

1. Anthropologist Cora DuBois first coined the term *culture shock* in 1951 to describe the cultural confusion experienced by professional investigators suddenly immersed in a strange milieu. Since that time, a variety of specialists have

sought to refine the concept. Kalvero Oberg (1960) popularized the notion of culture shock as an "occupational disease" that all international sojourners, not just anthropologists, must contend with. He was followed by John T. Gullahorn and Jeanne E. Gullahorn (1963), A. Cesar Garza-Guerrero (1974), Peter S. Adler (1975), Ingemar Torbiorn (1982), Stephen H. Rhinesmith (1986), Michael Kim Zapf (1991), Paul Pederson (1995), Janet Bennett (1998), Young Yun Kim (2001), and Colleen Ward, Stephen Bochner, and Adrian Furnham (2001). More recently, Linda Chisholm (2002) has drawn parallels between Campbell's "hero's journey" and the stages of intercultural adjustment described in the professional literature.

References

Adler, P. (1975). The transitional experience: An alternative view of culture shock. *Journal of Humanistic Psychology, 4*, 13–23.

Adler, P. (1987). Culture shock and the cross-cultural learning experience. In L. Luce & E. C. Smith (Eds.), *Toward internationalism* (pp. 24–35). Cambridge, MA: Newbury House.

Bennett, J. (1998). Transition shock: Putting culture shock in perspective. In M. Bennett (Ed.), *Basic concepts in intercultural communication: Selected readings* (pp. 215–224). Yarmouth, ME: Intercultural Press.

Campbell, J. (1949). *The hero with a thousand faces.* New York: Bollingen.

Chisholm, L. (2002). *Charting the hero's journey.* New York: International Partnership for Service-Learning.

Earley, C., & Mosakowski, E. (2004). Cultural intelligence. *Harvard Business Review, 82*, 139–153.

Evans, N. J., Forney, D. S., & Guido-DiBrito, F. (1998). *Student development in college: Theory, research, and practice.* San Francisco: Jossey-Bass.

Gardner, H. (1993). *Frames of mind: The theory of multiple intelligences.* New York: Basic Books.

Garza-Guerrero, A. (1974). Culture shock: Its mourning and the vicissitudes of identity. *Journal of American Psychoanalytic Association, 22*, 408–429.

Goleman, D. (1995). *Emotional intelligence.* New York: Bantam Books.

Gullahorn, J. T., & Gullahorn, J. E. (1963). An extension of the U-curve hypothesis. *Journal of Social Issues, 19*(3), 33–47.

Huggan, G. (2001). *The postcolonial exotic: Marketing the margins.* New York: Routledge.

Hutnyk, J. (2000). *Critique of exotica: Music, politics and the culture industry.* London: Pluto Press.

Iyer, P. (2000). *Why we travel.* Retrieved July 15, 2008, from http://archive.salon .com/travel/feature/2000/03/18/why/index.html

Kim, Y. Y. (2001). *Becoming intercultural: An integrated theory of communication and cross-cultural adaptation.* Newbury Park, CA: Sage.

Kluckhohn, C. (1949). *Mirror for man.* New York: McGraw-Hill.

Mehta, G. (1994). *Karma cola: Marketing the mystic east.* New York: Vintage.

Oberg, K. (1960). Cultural shock: Adjustment to new cultural environments. *Practical Anthropology, 7*(4), 177–182.

Paige, R. M., Cohen, A. D., Kappler, B., Chi, J. C., & Lassegard, J. (2002). *Maximizing study abroad: A student's guide to strategies for language and culture learning and use.* University of Minnesota: Center for Advanced Research on Language Acquisition.

Pedersen, P. (1995). *The five stages of culture shock: Critical incidents around the world.* Westport, CT: Greenwood.

Rhinesmith, S. (1986). *Bring home the world.* New York: Walker.

Sanford, N. (1967). *Self and society: Social change and individual development.* New York: Atherton Press.

Storti, C. (1990). *The art of crossing cultures.* Yarmouth, ME: Intercultural Press.

Taylor, C., & Gutman, A. (1992). *Multiculturalism and the politics of recognition: An essay.* Princeton, NJ: Princeton University Press.

Torbiorn, I. (1982). *Leaving abroad: Personal adjustment and personnel policy in the overseas setting.* Chichester, England: Wiley & Sons.

Travel. (n.d.). In *Wikiquote.* Retrieved April 12, 2010, from http://en.wikiquote .org/wiki/Travel

Wagner, K., & Magistrale, T. (2000). *Writing across culture: An introduction to study abroad and the writing process.* New York: Peter Lang.

Ward, C., Bochner, S., & Furnham, A. (2001). *The psychology of culture shock.* London: Routledge.

Zapf, M. K. (1991). Cross-cultural transitions and wellness: Dealing with culture shock. *International Journal for the Advancement of Counseling, 14*, 105–119.

Zohar, D., & Marshall, I. (2000). *SQ: Connecting with our spiritual intelligence.* New York: Bloomsbury USA.

GETTING ORIENTED

Toto, I've [got] a feeling we're not in Kansas anymore.
—DOROTHY, from *The Wizard of Oz*

IN THE BELOVED FANTASY MUSICAL *The Wizard of Oz*, a tornado transports Dorothy and her little dog, Toto, from their house in Kansas to the magical Land of Oz. She immediately recognizes that she is "out of her element," a stranger in a strange land. But her sober declaration to Toto carries significance beyond the enchanting fable. Like Dorothy, we are embarking on a step-by-step journey. We are on the verge of change. Dorothy's words speak to that process of change, especially the disorienting angst so many of us feel as we move from "home" to "abroad."

Kansas represents home—everything that is safe, stable, familiar, and predictable. It may be flat and gray and ordinary, but for Dorothy (and I suspect the rest of us) it's a "comfort zone," a place of least resistance. The Land of Oz, on the other hand, represents the strange, unstable, and unknown world afield. In Oz, anything can happen—scarecrows talk, horses change color, monkeys fly—and few of the familiar rules of Kansas apply. It's a land of "not knowing."

It's precisely this plunge into the unknown that awakens the sleeper in us, exciting a sense of childlike wonder. "Of the gladdest moments in human life," Sir Richard Burton writes in *The Devil Drives*, "is the departure upon a distant journey into unknown lands. Shaking off with one mighty effort the fetters of Habit, the leaden weight of Routine, the cloak of many Cares, and the slavery of Home, man feels once more happy. The blood flows with the fast circulation of childhood. Afresh dawns the morn of life." In this transitional space between home and program site, Kansas and Oz, our field orientation begins.

The flight to our chosen field is often filled with built-up anticipation. At the same time, it can be marked by discomforts and uncertainties (as discussed in chapter 6). Long-distance air travel is often exhausting, as jumbo jets offer precious little legroom, much less sleep, during the time warp of traversing the globe at 550 miles per hour. Even exiting an aircraft can sometimes be an ordeal. Aika, a Japanese study-abroad student, along with several hundred other passengers, was prevented from disembarking at Melbourne Airport. "Two passengers complained of a high fever and the captain was afraid that we all might be infected with bird flu. It was hours before we were finally released from the airplane."

Once we're off the plane, we face the challenge of negotiating formal entry into another country, all the while stranded in that netherworld known as jet lag. No longer in the air but not quite on the ground, it's hard to imagine being in a state of mind *less* prepared to gather our bags, pass customs, and defend against the horde of besieging porters and cabbies lying in wait just outside the airport doors. No wonder a cyclone had to pick up Dorothy and Toto and drop them in Oz. Who would willingly subject themselves to the disorienting confusion involved in getting there?

The First 48 Hours

If you're not traveling with a chaperoned group, do yourself a favor: Prearrange to have a trustworthy resident pick you up from the airport (or train or bus station) and provide transportation to someplace safe and secure. Arriving in a strange country in an exhausted state is stressful enough; having to then haggle with extortionate cab drivers or catch a public bus to a place you've never been can prove overwhelming. After hours in the air, what Helen required most was a comfortable, quiet place to rest her body and reset her internal clock. She would have loved to access a reliable telephone or Internet line to let family and friends back home know that she'd arrived safely. Her reality was quite different. Having arrived solo and without any form of welcome, she was immediately thrust into the vast unknown to reach a distant field site. Her "Oz experience" is all too common:

> The bus from Guatemala to the city of San Salvador was slow and excruciatingly stuffy. We passed the body of a dead man lying unnoticed on the side of the road. The person who was supposed to meet me at the bus station had not turned up. I sat on my luggage in the crowded and dirty station and fought hard to quell the rising panic. (in Scheyvens & Storey, 2003, p. 120)

For others, the passage from airport to field site can be filled with singular delight. As his journal records, India first entered Jonathan, a lanky, blonde-haired undergrad from Orange County, not through his mind but through his senses.

> My taxi ride with windows down was a most memorable introduction to India. I sat in the back and just took in all that was around me: women dressed in brilliantly colored saris, men dressed largely in white, sharing the road with buses, bicycles, trucks, and rickshaws. My cab driver effortlessly zipped through traffic, driving on whatever side of the road he felt like, and using his horn as if it were the greatest noise ever invented. At one point he turned back to me and, with great pride, boasted about being the fastest driver in Delhi. I would have normally just laughed, but in this case I gave him the benefit of the doubt. I hadn't felt such exhilaration in months, maybe years. With an ear-to-ear grin he asks if I want to slow down or if I'm ready to go fast. At that moment I just wanted him to concentrate on the road. But what came out of my mouth was, "I want you to go as fast as you can." His grin grew even wider, and with a bobble of his head, off we went. I recall watching a Hollywood car chase a month or so later and thought to myself, "My cab ride was way more intense than this."

Whether your first hour or two in-country is marked by dread or delight, consider yourself fortunate if soon after arrival you find yourself winding down in a college dorm room or a local family's home. Although your fatigued body probably will crave sleep, try to stay up until 10 or 11 p.m. local time. Secure your luggage and then take a brief walk (as long as it's not in a dangerous area). This is one way to immediately acclimate yourself, not only to a new time zone, but also to your new surroundings. Walking helps to ease the restlessness of trying to sleep in an unfamiliar place. Use these twilight moments to remind yourself why you've left home for another social world. Then try to get a "normal" night's sleep. Ultimately, you'll need to give yourself 48 hours or so to unwind and to prepare for entry into the community.

Settling In

In his allegorical novel *The Castle*, Franz Kafka tells of a wandering surveyor summoned to work in a village controlled by elusive, whimsical leaders in a nearby castle. He struggles to find a way to the castle but soon realizes that no roads lead there. The village's sly and suspicious residents alternately welcome and dismiss him. Despite continuous rebuffs and reversals, the civil servant is determined to decipher the mysterious customs and conventions of this world. He's convinced that there *must* be rules that fit together and structure everyday life. Part of his job is to figure them out and to adopt the expected behaviors. Only by doing so will he be able to win local acceptance and complete the task for which he was sent.

Like Kafka's character, one of the main tasks in our new community is to settle in to a new social environment. The advantage we bring to this undertaking is that we've done it before. We've already passed through hundreds of other life adjustments, big and small, within our homeland. Perhaps our family moved from the country to the city (or vice versa), or we left home to go away to college. At school or work we've probably had to adjust to roommates and workmates whose personal habits, language, ideas, and preferences in music and food were different from our own. If you've ever married or been involved in a serious relationship, the process of entering into another human being's reality shouldn't be entirely foreign to you. These adjustment skills are part of what we bring to this novel cultural setting. It's now time to "unpack" them.

Many foreign-study and service programs assist with the transition process by arranging for a formal orientation to the host campus and community within the first week after arrival. Besides providing basic academic and health-and-safety information, orientation sessions aim to ease students into a strange milieu and, hopefully, minimize their cultural blunders. The underlying assumption is that if we *know* some basic facts about our new circumstances we will *feel* more positively inclined to adapt ourselves to them. There is some truth to this, especially for novice sojourners. But prefield orientation shares the same potential drawback as premarital counseling: It provides answers to questions that are not yet being asked. It's not until we actually get established in the host community and concrete realities begin to hit us that "getting oriented" takes on a whole new feel of immediacy and relevance.

Wandering About

Even with a strong felt need, gaining a foothold in the local community is far from automatic. Physically "being there" is just the first step. Our actual entrance into the community requires that we venture out to observe everyday life, interact with strangers, and slowly absorb an alternative reality. Philip Glazebook writes in *Journey to Kars*, "When you have submitted to looking about you discreetly and to observing with as little prejudice as possible, then you are in a proper state of mind to walk about . . . and learn from what you see" (in Storti, 1998, p. 153).

The link between walking and learning is significant. We humans are pedestrians. And although we're used to covering ground quickly by motorized vehicle, we need a slow-motion mode of transport to truly absorb our surroundings. Space changes utterly when we experience it on foot. We can stop at a place, focus attention on a particular person or object, wonder, and ask questions to discover clues about something we desire to know or understand. World-walker Paul Otteson (1996) attests:

> Walking is a great teacher. Your imagination wanders through the scape as your legs pound out a rhythm. You see detail instead of scenic blur. You meet humans, but not as you rush to find a museum or make a train. You meet them when you're tired and need some water. You earn an openness that's inviting. The effort you exert walking drives a place into memory. When you've walked it, it's yours. You've "been" there. The walk-story is a journey unto itself that you can recall forever after with gladness, longing, and a humble pride. You own a piece of the world, and ownership gives strength. (p. 35)

Some prefer to jog their way into the community. For Maureen McGranaghan (1999), jogging offers not only physical exercise but also exposure to backstreet sounds and smells that would have been screened out by a taxi or sightseeing bus.

> After arriving and settling in, I adjusted quickly to life in Prague, and I took the initiative to explore my surroundings. As a college runner attempting to keep up my training, I worked out different routes, and while I thought, at first, that all the streets twisted and wound back on themselves in a huge labyrinth, I soon discovered loops and made connections. In fact, my running led me to observe the city closely; even while riding a bus or tram, I was often looking out the window and poring over the map trying to put it all together.

Many European cities are more or less accustomed to the presence of solitary foreigners darting through city streets in bright tracksuits or swim trunks. In other areas of the world, the political and cultural climate may not be so supportive. While I was living in India, for example, my daily jogs through the locale surrounding my flat never failed to excite local dogs and children. Both would chase me, the latter yelling *Angrez! Angrez!* ("Foreigner! Foreigner!"). They simply weren't used to someone of my skin color loping around their neighborhood. After triggering these reactions for several weeks, I settled for less conspicuous morning walks.

An alternative to taking the world on foot is to rove city streets or countryside by bicycle. Faster than walking and slower than riding a bus, the bicycle sets us slightly higher than passersby and offers us a combination of self-powered freedom and flexibility unmatched by any other form of transportation. Writing from a small town in China, Ben recounts his delight in going where curiosity beckoned:

> The last three days have been incredible! I have met *so* many people and have just gone out into the community in my free time. I take two-hour bike rides, but the distance I cover might take only 30 minutes. People just stop me, wanting to talk, though I don't speak much Mandarin yet. I spent 30 minutes with a goat herder, one hour with three students sitting in a field, an hour and a half in a family's home (they invited me in, gave me two popsicles, and just talked and laughed with me). I met a man who works shoveling coal into a burner at a factory, and two hay balers who

have told me every day to come back the next day. I met a college student who took me down by the river to his favorite spot to sit and talk. I met a girl in an Internet cafe who looked over my shoulder for one hour as I typed a paper—and she doesn't even read English! I have just been making time to ride my bike places and just see who will stop me to talk.

Whether on foot or bicycle, set out to explore the length and breadth of the surrounding area. Follow the curiosities and questions that naturally surface: What is the immediate vicinity like? What types of vehicles are on the roads? How crowded is it? What kinds of people live here? What types of clothes do they wear? What do they do at different times of the day?

Move through the streets expecting to encounter the unexpected. The genius of slow-moving travel is the way it orchestrates surprise and serendipity. A turn down this street and we discover a favorite eatery. The next day, a right instead of a left and we happen upon an open-air market populated by rural produce sellers. To become familiar with the spaces that people occupy is to learn something important about their lives, even before meeting them personally. Wander along boulevards and waterfronts, through parks and backstreets, between buildings and sidewalk stalls. Exchange glances and greetings with merchandise vendors, store owners, and street children. When you're ready to rest, pop into a local cafe and position yourself with a clear view out to the streets. Then take a few minutes to compose a record of your observations and initial impressions. Kerrie offers us a model in her description of a bustling road adjacent to Delhi University (India):

Walking down Probyn Road, I'm struck by the fact that people are doing every kind of imaginable activity—sleeping, eating, traveling, urinating—at all times of the day, and all in the street! My senses are full and I have only this page to empty them. In one blink of my eyes (to be sure it is not my imagination) there are cycle rickshaw drivers carrying heavy loads of cargo and up to three passengers; litter of all types finding its way to depressions in the street; a man urinating on a wall; another man sleeping on his ice cream stand before opening for business; and a white sky enveloping it all. My ears are filled with the honking of horns, the howling engine of scooters, the bells of rickshaws, and the chirping of birds. The sun is intense enough to feel through the filter of air thick with moisture, and of course

sweat is a constant coolant. For my taste, I try coconut juice sipped from
its own shell after a vendor cuts the top off. And this is a calm road. . . .

Detailed observational notes like these are an important part of cultural discovery. They allow for continuous dialogues—internal and with
community members—related to aspects of local life that confuse,
intrigue, or even offend us. Writing heightens our awareness of what's
around us as it anticipates the many impromptu opportunities we'll have
to probe beneath the surface with residents.

When people ask, "What are you doing here?" simply answer, "I am
here to be a neighbor." Explain that you are there to become a part of a
family and neighborhood, to listen, to follow curiosity, to make friends,
and to live out the "great dream" the best you can during a relatively
brief period of residence.

At the same time, resist the temptation to ask too many questions of
too many people too soon. An extended period of simply "wandering-
with-awareness" enables us to identify aspects of local life that are worthy
of amplification. As William Foote Whyte (1993) learned in his study of
urban young men in the Italian neighborhood of Cornerville in Boston,
"One has to learn when to question and when not to question, as well as
what questions to ask" (p. 78). Our goal at this point in the orientation
phase is simply to sensitize ourselves to the social spaces where local
residents "do life." With each successive foray into the community, the
places and peoples we discover will become more familiar and less
threatening.

Crossing Thresholds

In ancient legends all the way up through Hollywood blockbusters, heroes
of different types pass beyond the veil of the known into the unknown.
Dorothy finds herself in Oz and, in time, steps onto the yellow brick road.
In *The Lord of the Rings*, Frodo crosses out of the Shire into a world totally
foreign to him. In *Star Wars*, Luke leaves his home planet of Tatooine to
confront Darth Vader. Strange and foreboding lands exist at the limits of
the hero's life horizon and cultural competence. They are full of wonder
and promise, but also danger and dread. It is only as the hero-wanderer

advances beyond his or her limits that true "entrance" into another realm
of experience occurs.

Having safely arrived in our host community, we have already passed
the first threshold. Other tests and thresholds await us over the first days
and weeks. Every day something new or different is likely to happen. We
may feel like a child again, learning how to eat, bathe, shop, cross the
street, and communicate in ways that stretch us to the limits of our cultural adaptability. For some of us, this is precisely why we have consciously chosen to cross into stress-producing situations. One student
recently remarked, "I decided on a program in Kathmandu [Nepal] for
the sheer density of the stimuli."

There's a certain wonder, delight, and exhilaration that comes with
having all our senses placed on full alert. Yet we are just as likely to
respond to those stimuli with confusion, desperation, and exhaustion.
Every peak experience in an unfamiliar culture is also, on some level, a
cultural puzzle to solve, a window into a facet of the culture not yet
comprehended. Intercultural experience tends to mingle peaks and val-
leys, with the latter rarely leaving us feeling ecstatic. It's safe to assume,
for example, that you will get lost, swindled, or harassed along your
heroic path—and maybe several times. Other tests and new thresholds
are sure to follow, requiring not just patience and composure but also
new understandings of yourself and the surrounding culture. Three of
these thresholds are virtually inescapable and warrant special attention:
dealing with people who approach you, haggling with vendors, and managing your time.

Dealing With People Who Approach You

As educational travelers, most of us want to build bridges to the local
culture. We wish others to see us as warm, friendly, and generous. Instead
of insulating ourselves from residents, we're eager to enter the culture on
its own terms. So when someone approaches us with special offers (e.g.,
to change money or show us around) or special requests (e.g., to give
money or buy his or her product), often our immediate reflex is to oblige.

Exercising a principled openness to local influences is an essential
threshold to cross-cultural learning. At the same time, we need to use

discernment in dealing with strangers. Many of those we meet in the community will exude an easy friendliness and be genuinely interested in encouraging and helping us. Others are intent on one thing and only one thing: fleecing culturally naive travelers. Especially in third world cities where masses of people teeter on the edge of survival, learning how to tell one type from the other becomes a major challenge. To do so accurately requires contextual awareness that is only built up over time.

Poverty is the breeding ground for con artists and thieves, many of whom possess a sophisticated arsenal of tricks. As pointed out in chapter 4, a favorite target is trusting and unattached foreigners who are clueless about the social landscape. Women are particularly vulnerable to being approached by men on the streets looking either to sell them something or charm them into feigned friendship in the hopes of getting sex. Knowing how to position ourselves in relation to hucksters of all stripes is a critical test—one that we should study hard to pass.

Our options are actually fairly limited. Some travelers simply resign themselves to getting conned or ripped off as the price paid for an outgoing and interactive field experience. Others determine to keep all locals at arm's length, refusing to stop and talk with anybody, anywhere. Between these two poles we must learn to tread a fine line between precaution and paranoia, especially in crowded tourist centers, where hustlers and touts tend to concentrate.

Street beggars are a special case. Many rural-to-urban migrants, finding neither work nor opportunity in the big city, have no recourse but to send their children out to beg for change or hawk petty items at street junctions. Amber writes from Ethiopia: "Addis Ababa is *so overwhelming!* It's swarming with tons of street children, tons of old and disabled people. I constantly get people asking me for money—I mean *all* the time! I just don't know how to handle it." How *do* we handle it? How are we to distinguish between the deserving and undeserving?

Adding to our natural ambivalence is the fact that begging often is big business. In India, as depicted in the 2008 British film *Slumdog Millionaire*, thousands of young children are involved in a veritable "Beggar Mafia." Kidnapped while still infants, they are then disabled, drugged, or denied adequate nourishment before being paired with another maimed beggar to elicit the sympathies of passersby. Knowing this, it's all too easy to become jaded. Amber continues: "When I first got here and saw disabled street children, my heart would break. Not knowing what my response should be, I just followed the example of others: I told the street children to 'go away.' Now I find my heart completely closed off to the dozens of begging children I pass every day."

Begging may be a deeply flawed method of redistributing wealth from the haves to the have-nots of this world. But letting ourselves lapse into callous indifference only injures our moral sensibilities. Whether to give or not to give ultimately must be decided case by case, because much depends on our knowledge of the particular beggar and the larger social context. We simply cannot give to all beggars but neither must we refuse all beggars. Over time, our giving probably will be selective, biased in favor of those who provide some service (like helping us practice the language or find a store). Instead of our "gift" reinforcing the notion that poor folk are simply welfare wards of wealthy Westerners, it can become a legitimate and dignifying form of payment for services rendered.

Haggling With Vendors

Walking through bustling open-air markets or commercial centers, we should also expect to encounter vendors of various local goods and services. Fruits and vegetables, clothes and curios, taxis and tour guides—almost anything you need (or don't need) is there. Yet more often than not, prices, instead of being fixed or stickered, are negotiated between buyers and sellers. Particularly in the developing world, bargaining is a way of life.

As an outsider to this tricky commercial world, remember that having the leisure time and money to travel abroad automatically makes you fantastically rich compared to virtually any street seller, taxi driver, or shopkeeper you encounter. Knowing this, many vendors will inflate the fair price up to 10 times, hoping to extract as much money from foreigners like you as possible. Buyers are expected to be familiar enough with the value of local products and services to figure out the lowest price the seller is willing to take.

The "game" of haggling for a mutually acceptable price officially begins when you see something you want to buy. Stay relaxed but emotionally detached. Any sign of overexcitement or uncertainty instantly gives the seller the upper hand. As with an eBay bid, consider what the item is worth to you and set a maximum price in your mind. Then casually ask the price of the item. When the seller names the price, pause and then offer about *half* of the asking price. If the vendor immediately accepts, you're probably getting ripped off. More than likely, though, he or she will laugh or feign astonishment, telling you that your low-ball offer is ridiculously below their cost. Don't be intimidated by the vendor's reaction. Allow the offer/counteroffer process to play out until the price reaches what you're willing to pay. If your price point isn't reached, tell the seller you're going to shop around. Then leave. If he or she calls you back, another round of haggling begins. If not, chances are, the last price was the seller's best price.

There are some who regard this kind of hard bargaining as exploitative of "barefoot businesspersons" struggling to make a living within failing economies. "If you really want something," a friend once advised me, "you should expect to pay a fair price, not the lowest possible price." Like giving to beggars, the appropriateness of haggling depends on the cultural context. While bargaining is rare in the South Pacific, many Egyptian and Turkish shop owners would be insulted if you were to refuse to haggle over prices. In much of North Africa and Asia, bargaining serves as a social lubricant that creates and sustains relationships.

It also matters what you buy. Some things—like hotel rooms, restaurant meals, and bus fares—often have fixed prices that can't be bargained down. For tourist handicrafts and curios, however, we may actually want to pay top price (and even more). Doing so provides added income to sellers without driving up prices for local residents (who rarely purchase tourist items). On the other hand, paying high prices for basic goods like produce and clothing may actually harm local residents. If local merchants can get premium prices for their goods and services from foreigners, they will be less likely to sell to their neighbors at normal rates.

Managing Your Time

A third threshold to pass during our orientation period concerns time or, more specifically, time management. Having left the ordinary routines of home, most of us will be eager to cross into the field of adventure. Compared to intense Oz-land experiences, "schoolish" activities like attending lectures, reading academic materials, mulling over issues, and writing "reflection" papers appear a dull and dissipating use of time. "Time is limited," we tell ourselves, "and it's best spent meeting new people, seeing new sights, and having fun."

Some of us will be disposed toward experiencing much and analyzing little. We should bear in mind, as previously noted, that many of the encounters we tend to regard as "eye opening" and "life changing" may not take us very far intellectually. I recall interviewing a student who had recently returned from one month of feeding and bathing destitute people at one of Mother Teresa's homes in Kolkata. "I'm forever changed," she told me in a subdued but utterly sincere voice. Clearly, her self-donation on behalf of the suffering had affected her deeply. But when I asked her to explain what social and political conditions had made the need for such a home so great, she replied with puzzlement, "I have no idea." Time invested in developing her emotional mind had not been balanced with time dedicated to probing causes and consequences with her thinking mind.

Even those with more academic and research-oriented goals may have difficulty balancing competing time demands. Any given week on the field may be taken up with language learning, service activity, directed reading, casual interviewing, and report writing. Then there are the inevitable periods of "wasted time" as a result of illness, bad weather, no-show appointments, and late buses. Weeks can go by without adequate physical rest and downtime, especially in intense urban environments where quiet places to relax and "unstring the bow" for an extended period of time are few and far between. Surviving punishing conditions and work schedules requires regular periods of downtime during which we can enjoy a good meal or movie and do some meaningful processing of our experiences. By building natural breaks into our schedule from the beginning, we will be less likely to sideline our studies out of sheer physical and emotional exhaustion later on.

Community Reconnaissance

The thresholds we cross through informal movements and encounters prepare us for the core of our orientation experience: a systematic exploration of a specific, settled place. Every community is manifestly rich in history, character, and internal strength but is also a place that daily struggles toward being a decent, life-giving society. The community reconnaissance guides us in our first steps toward learning how groups of people, embedded within a local ecosystem, learn to do life together. It offers a basic strategy for gathering and developing specific forms of "cultural intelligence" through a series of 10 field exercises.

Whether conducted as a formal part of group training or as a self-directed process, this phase of our orientation is best done with the assistance of a trustworthy guide. If you are living with a host family or serving with a community organization, family members or coworkers may be willing to assist. Otherwise, return to local acquaintances with whom you've initiated casual conversations and try to solicit their help. In Guatemala City, a young man agreed to escort me throughout the city for a week in simple exchange for shared meals. Years later, in the town of Lampeter, Wales, the local postman invited me to accompany him on his morning delivery route to the town's homes and businesses. Both guides proved to be rich sources of local knowledge as we rambled, side by side, through the community. Perhaps more important, they modeled the kind of socially appropriate behavior that saved me from repeated faux pas over the months that followed.

Sometimes all-too-willing guides come looking for us. Areas with a lot of tourist traffic seem to breed a special class of "stranger handlers" who are quite practiced at spotting outsiders, introducing themselves, and offering assistance. Most have picked up English by watching Hollywood films or dealing with foreigners like us and are genuinely likeable, helpful people. Others, however, are disaffected and rather sleazy marginals whose only "business" is to befriend travelers and collect "commissions" for their services. They have nothing to lose and everything to gain, whether money, status, sex, or a way abroad. We do well to avoid them.

The alternative to prearranging a guide is to simply ask for assistance from various residents on an as-needed basis. At this point in our global learning, there's no need to conduct formal interviews with regular informants. Our goal is much more modest and immediate: to learn how to meet survival needs in an unfamiliar setting. Most of the cultural assistance needed to support this goal can be found along the way. Clerks in stores, pedestrians on the street, waitresses in restaurants, local residents waiting at a bus stand—these are suitable helpers. Most will not have expertise on every aspect of the local culture, but they will serve as valuable sources of the specific information we need.

Procedure

1. Coordinate with a community "guide" to complete the 10 Orientation Exercises that follow. You may want to schedule certain blocks of time over several days. If you are working as a team, divide into pairs; groups of three or more tend to overwhelm local conversation partners. Exercises can be split among three or four team pairs.

2. Use your residence as a base for going out, gathering information, and reflective writing. If your residence is not within walking distance of a commercial center, plan on taking a bus to an "epitome district." These are ceremonial places, often in the town center, that express the essence of the larger area by hosting parades, folk festivals, religious carnivals, and the like. They tend to offer a variety of public places—parks, plazas, a central avenue, an outdoor market— that reveal much about the city as a whole and give it a heart.

3. As you progress, collect various field materials (e.g., a local map, currency and coin, menus, agency brochures, bus schedules) that illustrate aspects of community life and can be referenced at later dates. Bring enough cash to change into local currency (both paper money and coins) and buy a map, a newspaper, and lunch. And be sure to carry a handheld pocket notebook and pen or pencil. You'll need them to jot down key information related to each exercise.

4. At the end of each day, convert your jotted notes into an expanded journal entry for each of the exercises. Resist the temptation to think that you can simply commit the information to memory without recording it. In each entry, include as much relevant detail as possible. Label each orientation exercise with the date and a topic title (e.g., "local currency").

A *final note:* As you begin to walk and talk, don't worry too much about getting lost. Carry the phone number and address of "home" with you, and give someone an estimate of the time when you will return. If you find yourself completely disoriented, call home or simply use the opportunity to engage someone in assisting you.

Orientation Exercises

1. *General directions and impressions.* Using a map of your orientation area, find the center point. Read the names of the north–south streets and the east–west streets. Is there a consistent naming or numbering scheme? *Record* the name of the nearest main intersection. From your starting point, begin walking in one direction for several blocks, and then return. Do it again, walking in another direction several blocks and then returning to where you started. Try to get a "feel" for the immediate vicinity—the movements of people, the sounds and smells, and the types of buildings. *Record* your general impressions. Try to identify key landmarks and institutions (e.g., banks, factories, hospitals, schools, markets, department stores) serving the local area. *Record* several of these.

2. *Local currency.* Locate a bank or legal money-changing office. *Record* the current exchange rate. Change your desired amount of money. While still in the office, take a few minutes to study the notes and coins. What different denominations are in circulation? What symbols are represented on the various bills and coins? Ask a clerk or customer to explain the meaning of the symbols. *Record* the denominations, symbols, and meanings.

3. *Personal safety.* Identify one or two informed persons (e.g., a hotel manager, a tourist advisor, a police official) to question about personal safety: How does one best guard against pickpockets and bag snatchers? What should one carry or not carry on oneself? What streets or city sections should be avoided? What special precautions should be taken by a woman walking alone or in a small group? Are there certain times of the day when it is unsafe to move about? *Record* their responses.

4. *Food services.* (a) Notice the kinds of places where local residents buy grocery items. Is there a local open-air market with assorted stalls? Small, neighborhood general stores? Modern supermarkets? Discuss the different types of stores with your guide or a temporary helper. What stores are most popular with different kinds of people? What differences are there in the varieties and prices of merchandise? *Record* what you learn. (b) Obtain information about three different kinds of eateries frequented by locals (not

tourists), ranging from a street stall to a full-service restaurant. Find out the times they open and close. Walk into each eatery. While in the eateries, examine their respective menus and their bathrooms. (Ask for a take-home menu, if available.) *Record* the names of five similar drink and food items from each eatery and compare their prices. Then observe the customers in each place. What can you infer from their dress, behavior (both verbal and nonverbal), and grooming habits? *Record* how particular restaurants seem to cater to different customers. (c) Select one of the surveyed restaurants to take a lunch break. Study the menu. Consult the waitress or waiter and your dictionary in deciding what to order. Relax, and enjoy your meal.

5. *Local history.* (a) During your lunch break in the restaurant, try to identify a bilingual customer or restaurant worker to engage in conversation. (You may also find this person at an Internet cafe, market, or bus stand.) Casually introduce yourself and ask several questions about the area: How long have you lived in X? How has X changed since you first knew it? What is causing the changes? What do you like most about living here? What do you like least? *Record* his or her responses. (b) Find a bookstore selling English-language materials. Ask the store clerk for help in locating and recommending books describing the city's local history. (Also check for language-learning materials, a local newspaper published in English, a detailed city map, a scheduling calendar indicating national holidays, and a durable notebook for journaling.) *Record* the title(s) of books on local history. Before you leave, purchase an area/city map, a calendar, and a daily or weekly English-language newspaper.[1]

6. *Current affairs.* Find a relaxed setting (perhaps a park) to spread out the newspaper you bought. Thumb through the various sections of the paper, noting the subjects of various articles. Select two to three articles that investigate matters of local or national concern. Read the articles. Then identify an adult in the setting you feel comfortable initiating a conversation with. Approach this person, introduce yourself as a newcomer, and invite him or her to offer an opinion about the subject of one of the articles. *Record*

the name of the newspaper, the titles of the articles, and a short summary of the issue or event that you read and discussed.

7. *Social etiquette.* Find out what is customary behavior in the following areas: (a) *In a restaurant,* how do you politely attract the attention of a waiter? If a *social or business event* is scheduled to begin at 11 a.m., when should you arrive? Can an invitation be refused without causing offense? When invited to a *home or office,* what are some routine courtesies you should observe? Are you expected to eat all foods and to drink the local beverages? What is the appropriate response when an *unknown person* (e.g., a beggar) asks for money, food, or help? (b) When are you expected to bring a gift? What kinds of gifts and for what occasions? When gifts are exchanged, is it impolite to open the gift in the presence of the giver? (c) How do people greet and take leave of each other? What words and gestures are used? Are there differences based on age, gender, or social status? When entering a room, does one greet everyone, only females or males, no one, or only the first person who greets you? (d) Are there special ways of showing respect to certain persons (e.g., bowing, lowering head, or standing)? Are there customs affecting the way one sits or where one sits? (e) Are there particular facial expressions or gestures that are considered rude? What are considered "personal" questions? *Record* this information.

8. *Romantic relationships.* Romance is defined differently from one culture to another. Foreigners may either find themselves the object of someone else's interest or unwittingly communicate interest in another person who then responds. Pose the following questions with a same-sex guide or helper who knows the culture well and with whom you share good rapport: (a) What rules govern "romantic" relationships in this country? Is it appropriate for husbands and wives to touch, embrace, or kiss in public? How does a man show he is interested in a woman (or another man)? How does a woman show she is interested in a man (or another woman)? How should a woman show she is not interested in a man who is interested in her? (b) How do you know when a relationship is becoming something more than just a friendship? What

are some common signs that the other person is taking the relationship much more seriously? Do unmarried women and men date? If so, do they date in groups? Do they need a chaperone? In what types of social activities do young women and men participate together? What is the norm regarding touching and kissing in public? Are private sexual liaisons tolerated? What do men/women do to signal that they want to pull back or cool down a relationship? *Record* the information.

9. **Public transit.** (a) What modes of public transportation are evident on the streets (e.g., bicycle, bus, donkey cart, rickshaw, motorbike, private automobile, taxi)? *Record* the names locals use to refer to them. (b) Identify the bus stand nearest to your residence. How is it marked? Inquire of someone waiting for a bus: Where are the buses going? How are the buses marked? Where can you catch a bus to X (a destination of interest to you)? How much is the fare? Do you pay the driver, a bus runner, or place money into a box? Does the bus require exact change? *Record* the information. (c) Take a taxi with a host family member or experienced friend to the central market or local shopping area. How do you signal for a cruising taxi to stop, or do you have to look for one at a designated queue? How do you know how much the fare will be? Is it negotiated or clearly indicated on a meter? Where should riders sit? Are there any restrictions on the number of passengers allowed? Do drivers typically engage the riders in conversation? *Record* the information.

10. **Dos and don'ts.** This final exercise follows naturally from the previous conversation on the attitudes held by community residents toward foreigners. With a local resident, discuss how someone of your nationality, gender, religion, and socioeconomic status can be sensitive to local customs and expectations. (a) What behaviors (e.g., ways of talking, walking, eating, dressing, socializing) would convey respect for different sectors of the local society? What common courtesies and formalities do local people appreciate? Which behaviors tend to annoy, confuse, or offend? (Probe for gestures, language use, dress styles, mannerisms, social interactions, and food likes and dislikes.) *Record* several insights that can help you adapt to the local culture. (b) In order to guide the conversation

on a range of dos and don'ts, ask your helper to comment on how the community would treat each of the behaviors listed in Table 7.1 if exhibited by a foreigner of your gender and age. Check (✓) the most applicable box.

Regions Beyond

Once we have completed these tasks and found our bearings, our first steps to becoming an accepted presence in the community are over. We have learned our way around and struck up conversations with local residents. We have executed a variety of "survival" tasks and become a perceptive observer through the keeping of a field journal. Potential perils have been faced and key thresholds crossed. Having eased our way into the immediate area, we can now look forward to exploring regions beyond.

Even as individuals cannot be understood apart from the social and physical environments that shape them, it is also impossible to understand a single community outside of its larger regional context. Villages and towns are inextricably bound to the land and systems of urban centers, and vice versa. Megacities like Beijing, China, and Sao Paulo, Brazil, excavate the surrounding countryside for building materials, divert water from neighboring agricultural lands, and provide daily labor for thousands of rural migrants. In Los Angeles, Latino newcomers sell flowers and fruit at traffic lights of multilaned boulevards and freeway off-ramps. In Dhaka, Bangladesh, the cycle and auto rickshaws are decorated with colorful country—not city—scenes. These images speak of a *regional* reality—the countryside in the cities and the cities in the countryside—that follows the global interpenetration of the Third World in the First World, and the First World in the Third World.

In the weeks ahead, budget several days to thread through various points of the surrounding region. For these excursions, bus travel replaces foot or pedal power (unless you're an avid cyclist). Virtually everywhere in the world, be it an urban metropolis or a rural province, there is a network of bus routes that connect you to points beyond. Although notorious for their *lack* of comfort and speed, buses provide an unequaled exposure to regional life in its relentless motion.

Table 7.1: Cultural Dos and Don'ts

	Customary	Allowed	Frowned Upon	Criminal
Spitting in public				
Whistling in public				
Cursing in public				
Giving money to beggars				
Combing hair in public				
Wearing sunglasses indoors in public places				
Walking barefoot in public				
Laughing aloud in public				
Littering				
Haggling in the marketplace				
Taking photographs of people without their permission				
Taking photos of airports and train or bus stations				
Tipping waiters and waitresses at restaurants and hotels				
Making eye contact				
Speaking loudly in public				
Tipping taxicab drivers				
Wearing visible tattoo marks				
Men wearing dreadlocks or braided hair				
Wearing body piercings				
Men walking in public without a shirt				
Women smoking in public				
Women wearing sleeveless blouses and shorts in public				
Women wearing bikinis				
Men and women swimming together in public pools				

Table 7.1: (Continued)

	Customary	Allowed	Frowned Upon	Criminal
Young men and women hugging in public				
Sitting with legs crossed in the presence of elders				
Blowing one's nose in public				
Addressing people by their family name/surname				
Removing one's shoes when entering a private home				
Presenting a gift with the left hand				
Touching or patting someone's head/hair				
Placing one's leg(s) on the table or chair				
Counting money into someone's palm				
Using an iPod in public places (buses, parks, etc.)				
Using "thumbs up" sign to indicate "OK"				

Adapted from *Do's and Taboos Around the World: A Guide to International Behavior* (p. XXX), by Roger Axtell & John Healy, 1993, New York: Wiley & Sons.

First there's the view outward to the city streets, sidewalks, buildings, parks, cafes, and storefronts. "Through the window," Maryada notes during her morning commute into Brussels for language school, "I see a man with shaving cream on his chin and a group of women chatting over coffee on the patio of a cafe. I watch a youngster buying foot-long sausages in the *boucherie* and special cheeses from the *fromagerie*. The doors to the shops with shoes in the window are being opened and a line has already formed in the *boulangerie* for fresh baked bread or sweet croissants." Bus riding allows us to feel the flow of geography and comprehend the seamless interface among local people, daily business, and material culture.

Then there are the bus riders themselves, a veritable "community on wheels" inviting us into direct contact and conversation. Effective global learning requires a certain public vulnerability, and on the bus we must rely on another's driving ability, another's time table and directions, another's civility. Melissa's bus-riding experience in Oaxaca, Mexico, suggests only some of the surprises that await us:

> Around midday the bus becomes a crammed roller coaster barreling down the highways, sliding by other vehicles in near-miss maneuvers, and refusing to slow down for pedestrians crossing the streets. In the morning it's common for vendors to step aboard and walk up and down the aisles hawking their goods. If we're lucky an occasional street musician will belt out popular songs to the captive audience, hoping to earn a day's wage. The bus is my constant reminder that I'm in another country where a different set of rules applies.

Conclusion

Getting oriented to an unknown community and regional culture requires considerable motivation and initiative, matched only by its potential rewards. With greater awareness of and sensitivity to the physical geography, patterns of social interaction, and norms of behavior (i.e., what is permitted and what is not), we can expect to participate more fully and effectively in the life of the place where we have been set down. In the months that follow, expect to uncover even more of the community's social organization. Different groups of people inhabit different formal and voluntary organizations—families and religious associations, schools and pubs, factories and issue-based coalitions—and each features webs of relationships that give the place its distinctive character. Most of us will, during our term of residence, find ourselves occupying one or more of these networks. Our defining task will be to move from being a suspected outsider to a functioning, accepted member of a human economy where neighbors cherish and watch over what they have in common. Expect the orientation period to reveal only the first steps toward this end. In addition to generating basic survival-type information needed to navigate the local culture and landscape, it serves to "orient" our mind and heart *toward* the community—honoring its history and traditions, sharing its aspirations and sorrows, and ultimately, finding common ground to contribute to its future.

Bon voyage!

FOR REFLECTION AND DISCUSSION

1. Why is it important to devote the first days (if not weeks) in-country to settling in, wandering about, and gaining a "foothold" in the local community?

2. What emotions (e.g., anticipation and enthusiasm or fear and dread) surface as you contemplate completing the 10 Orientation Exercises with the help of a local guide? What do you *think* about what you feel? That is, what do your emotional responses tell you about *you*: your travel motivations, the perceived "fit" between your personality and the new cultural setting, your preferred learning styles, and so on?

Note

1. Neighborhood libraries and community centers can also be valuable sources of information on local history and current affairs. Librarians, in particular, are invaluable guides to books, newspapers, newsletters, periodicals, and maps that paint a picture of the place and its people over time. They can also identify local clubs, sports teams, and community associations that would welcome you as a temporary guest.

Suggested Resources

Axtell, R. (1997). *Gestures: The do's and taboos of body language around the world.* New York: Wiley & Sons.

Culture Shock! Guides. Portland, OR: Graphic Arts Centre Publishing.
Entertaining crash courses in the customs and etiquette of dozens of countries, filled with real-life insights.

Culture Smart! Guides. London: Kuperard.

   A concise, commonsense guide to the quirks, customs, and common courtesies of various countries.

Darrow, K., & Palmquist, B. (1987). *Transcultural study guide* (2nd ed.). Stanford, CA: Volunteers in Asia.

Faul, S. (1999). *The xenophobe's guide to the Americans.* London: Oval Books.

Hess, J. D. (1994). *The whole world guide to culture learning.* Yarmouth, ME: Intercultural Press.

Kohls, L. R. (2001). *Survival kit for overseas living* (4th ed.). Yarmouth, ME: Intercultural Press.

Kwikpoint International Point-to-Picture Translator (passport size). Available online at http://www.kwikpoint.com

   Laminated, pocket-size foldout card with a visual vocabulary of 600 universally recognized symbols for communicating in any language, by just pointing to your needs.

McRum, M. (2007). *Going Dutch in Beijing.* New York: Henry Holt.

Mole, J. (2003). *Mind your manners.* Boston: Nicholas Brealey.

Paige, R. M., Cohen, A. D., Kappler, B., Chi, J. C., & Lassegard, J. (2002). *Maximizing study abroad: A student's guide to strategies for language and culture learning and use.* University of Minnesota: Center for Advanced Research on Language Acquisition.

Storti, C., & Bennhold-Samaan, L. (1997). *Culture matters: The Peace Corps cross-cultural workbook.* Washington, DC: Peace Corps Information Collection and Exchange.

References

Axtell, R., & Healy, J. (1993). *Do's and taboos around the world: A guide to international behavior.* New York: Wiley & Sons.

McGranaghan, M. (1999, Spring). Walking an opossum: My trip to the Czech Republic. *Newsletter of the Institute for International Education.*

Otteson, P. (1996). *The world awaits.* Santa Fe, NM: John Muir.

Scheyvens, R., & Storey, D. (Eds.). (2003). *Development fieldwork: A practical guide.* Thousand Oaks, CA: Sage.

Storti, C. (1998). *Figuring foreigners out.* Boston: Intercultural Press.

Whyte, W. F. (1993). *Street corner society* (4th ed.). Chicago: University of Chicago Press.

THE JOURNEY HOME

*The whole object of travel is not to set foot on foreign land; it is
at last to set foot on one's own country as a foreign land.*
—G. K. CHESTERTON

I T'S ONLY NATURAL to view the achievements associated with the
weeks and months spent in a foreign community as defining our "success" as global learners. After all, didn't we have some of the most memorable experiences of our life? Didn't we succeed in becoming an accepted
presence in a new household or university community? Join residents in
efforts to improve local life? Hone our global awareness and, perhaps,
our cross-cultural research skills? And come to perceive ourselves and the
world from an altered perspective?

Each of these triumphs contributes an intellectual and emotional
intensity that is often absent from ordinary life. Many of us speak of
"never feeling more alive" than when we were immersed in and surren-
dered to conditions that stretched and inspired us. Even if our circumstances included bouts of protracted sickness and acute loneliness, we
carry a profound sense of having somehow "grown up" through what we
experienced.

Returning home is supposed to signal a welcomed end to the force of
life "in the field." Home is where familiarity dominates, whether it's the
people, the language, the foods, or the routines of everyday life. It's where
we don't have to think before we act, where we don't have to struggle to
"adjust." That's the theory, anyway. And that theory plays out quite well
for many (maybe most) sojourners who encounter no great difficulty in

taking up at home where they left off prior to departure. But depending on factors specific to our background, personality, host country, and sponsoring program, the reality may be quite different. Coming home can actually take as much getting used to as going abroad ever did, *and maybe more.* Whereas we anticipate having to adapt ourselves to differences abroad, we don't expect the same as we set foot back on native soil.

In this chapter, try to imagine your return, not so much as the final curtain of an epic journey but as its final act. Months of living away from home have served up a variety of once-in-a-lifetime encounters, along with exposure to people and ideas from different parts of the world. Particularly if we spent an extended period of time in one place, we will have established an intimate bond with certain social spaces and personal relationships. Leaving, then, is far from a benign or incidental part of our performance. The journey home is in many ways the capstone, the finale, of our global-learning experience.

Our temptation is otherwise to "close" these experiences prematurely by swapping a few stories and sharing a few photos before moving on to graduation or our next life challenge. The alternative to winding down and leaving behind is to allow our reentry to offer us a rare opportunity to take some of the most potentially transformative moments of our life and consider what they might mean for the future. Negotiating between and across two cultural worlds requires an investment of time and intentionality. But in the end it allows us, like Joseph Campbell's (1968) mythical hero, to "come back from this mysterious adventure with the power to bestow boons on his fellow man" (p. 30).

"You Can't Go Home Again"

The experience of cross-cultural living and learning is often bittersweet. One day we imagine spending the rest of our lives in our new home away from home. The next day we find ourselves anxiously counting the days until we board the plane and return to "normal." If circumstances become truly unbearable, we tell ourselves, there is always the option of exiting prematurely. This pocket prerogative keeps us from ever being *totally* separated and isolated from our place of origin: We can always go home again. This is also what distinguishes the common traveler from the true exile. Travelers, as members of a global elite class, enjoy the security of a return ticket. Exiles have no such defense; most are compelled to leave home for survival's sake, with no immediate hope of returning.

In another sense, as novelist Thomas Wolfe once put it, "You *can't* go home again." That's because you're probably a different person than when you left. Having struggled to overcome so many "dragons," both within and without, you now look at yourself and your natal culture differently. Your hometown hasn't moved, and your network of family and friends is still intact—but both *feel* different, almost like a foreign land. It's not just the faster pace of life and the sheer size of things like automobiles, houses, and shopping malls. Nor is it all the new gadgets and trendy clothes that have been introduced since you left. These and other features of home can certainly be disorienting, especially at first. But you eventually come to recognize them as familiar aspects of the culture in which you were born and bred.

No, the thing that keeps you from automatically reverting to your former lifestyle is *you*. To the extent that certain basic assumptions about the world have been challenged through our cross-cultural environment, we may find ourselves painfully out of joint with life back home. This displaced feeling is commonly referred to as "reentry shock" or "reverse culture shock." Although unexpected, it's typically not sudden or once and for all. Instead, it has its own roller-coaster cycle of emotional highs and lows that can begin months before one physically returns home.

This was the case for Bethy as she prepared to leave Oaxaca, Mexico. In her journal she describes the personal struggle she felt between missing home and putting down deeper roots in the host culture.

> Saturated by the experiences of the past three months, I realize that I no longer look with those same eyes. It's in these monotonous moments of recognized blindness that I acknowledge my truth: Half of me feels so at home and comfortable here that life has lost its surprises, while the other half of me already has my bags packed to go home.

Mixed emotions are a natural part of our attempt to narrow the cultural distance between our hosts and ourselves. Even after months of patient, focused attention to differences, we, like Bethy, must acknowledge that, however deeply we have seen, we have only scratched the surface. There are worlds within worlds yet to discover. The minor adjustments that our hosts and we make toward each other cannot hope to offset the weight of our respective cultural heritages. Culture runs too deep. Our limbo state of being marginal to the culture prevails until either we are accepted as a full-fledged member of the host group or we depart.

Caroline was nearing the end of a five-month global-learning term in Kampala, Uganda, the only blonde-haired, blue-eyed woman for miles around. She had immersed herself as much as possible in the local culture. Taking up residence with a large extended family, she quickly learned to adapt to a shared room, a repetitive diet of beans and cassava, gawking crowds, the sticky heat, and no electricity. A more different way of life from what she was accustomed to in south Orange County, California, could hardly be imagined.

Although she had no desire to "go native" and stay, a certain sadness marked Caroline's preparations for the journey home. The relentless emotional and physical demands would soon be a memory. But she also knew how impossible it would be to ever re-create back home the same sense of personal achievement—that feeling of having "passed through the fire" and prevailed. She also would need to bid farewell to friends and family members who had sustained her and to whom she'd become emotionally attached. This grief would be tinged with guilt as she recognized that her economic privilege enabled her to do what her hosts could not—leave.

Her time of departure finally arrived. With a good-bye party and one last round of photos, Caroline brought the Uganda chapter of her life to a close. Boarding the plane in Kampala for Los Angeles, she could hardly contain the anticipation of being joined again with loved ones. After a grueling 20-hour flight, the plane finally landed on native soil. Caroline cleared customs, collected her baggage, and made her way out to the reception area, anxiously awaiting her reunion.

> When my plane landed, all I could think of was grabbing my luggage and seeing my family. I was exhausted, but the excitement kept me going. I remember walking out of baggage claim and they were all standing there with balloons and flowers. But more than anything, I rejoiced in seeing their smiling faces. I had mentally prepared myself for this moment for a whole month.

Returnees sometimes speak of this as the "honeymoon" phase of their return. Countless hugs and kisses, flower bouquets, and fresh-baked cookies welcome us home. Everyone is eager to hear about our trip. We bask in the attention, along with the many amenities we missed while away: meals at favorite restaurants; Starbucks lattes; long, hot showers; thick green lawns; a washer and a dryer; a bedroom of our own; the latest movies in Dolby stereo; and cruising with friends. Again, Caroline recalls:

> The first day I was back I spoke with some close friends and even went out to lunch with one. I relished the freedom of driving my car and using my time to do whatever I wanted. I no longer stood out. Everything was once again familiar: the ringing of the phone, the drone of cars, the call to dinner over the intercom—it was everything I was looking forward to returning to, and it felt so good.

This phase of blissful indulgence tends to last about a week, if that long. The euphoria then begins to wear off and home begins to feel so comfortable, so convenient, so clean, and oh so . . . *boring.* Compared to life abroad, the pace can seem oppressive, the people wasteful, the food tasteless, the culture colorless. The campus may feel no better, like an artificial "bubble" of exclusive cliques, surface conversation, and seemingly irrelevant courses.

Efforts to reconcile the mundane culture of home with mountaintop experiences in distant lands can prove physically and emotionally exhausting. It can also be painfully frustrating. That's because we don't see home the same way as before. People around us talk about the latest thingamajig, pop star, or blockbuster film, but we find ourselves largely uninterested. Others appear self-absorbed and superficial, while images and insights from abroad keep replaying in our mind. The last thing we want is to let those experiences be swept way in a whirlwind of sedating activity.

Our homecoming also tends to exaggerate the bias we felt on leaving, whether for or against our home culture. One of my relatives, on returning from every overseas trip, habitually kisses the ground while declaring how thankful she is to "live in the greatest country on earth." In this case, idealized images she might hold of her homeland effectively filter out negative aspects while reinforcing the positive. This "self-fulfilling prophecy" also works in reverse: Disenchantment at home predisposes us to enthusiasms abroad. Who hasn't known those whose world travels abroad were largely fueled by the urge to be liberated from the most disagreeable aspects of their family and everyday life? Paul Fussell (1987) explains:

> Why is travel so exciting? Partly because it triggers the thrill of escape, from the conscription of the daily, the job, the boss, the parents. "A great part of the pleasure of travel," says Freud, "lies in the fulfilment of . . . early wishes to escape the family and especially the father." The escape is also from the traveller's domestic identity, and among strangers a new sense of selfhood can be tried on, like a costume. (p. 13)

In that travel provides at least temporary escape from inherited traditions and personal identity, it can be seen as an act of rebellion, a means of separating oneself from the dominant influences of kith and kin in order to define and assert an identity of our own. I travel; therefore, I am.

Somewhere Over the Rainbow?

The attitude of most returnees to home, however, is neither total love nor total loathing. More often, we find ourselves in a mental state described by Bruce LaBrack (1996) as "a kind of split loyalty manifesting itself in attempts to validate and integrate both cultural worlds while having ambivalent feelings about aspects of both" (p. 7). The feeling of simultaneously being "in two minds" often highlights an underappreciated truth: that "home" isn't just a physical space we inhabit but a lifestyle we construct. It's a cherished set of values, relationships, places, and rituals that we learn to assemble *wherever* we are. "No one *goes home*," explains Craig Storti (1990). "Rather we return to our native country and, in due course, we *create a new home*" (p. 100). Just as we had to construct a home in our host culture, we must now learn to reconstruct a new home in our home culture.

This can be an exacting task. In Caroline's case, withdrawal, excessive sleeping, and irritability came to mark her homecoming.

> After the excitement of seeing everyone wore off, I found myself always being tired. The jet lag had not worn off, and I did not care to fix it. I

would go to bed sometimes at 7 p.m. and wake up at 4 a.m. Waking up this early always left me to think about getting up early in Uganda, but it wasn't the same. The sun doesn't shine as brightly here. When I see a child being disrespectful to his mother, I impulsively want to do something about it. Driving was also very strange. For five months I was used to swerving around cars that were going too slow, or beeping cars to move out of the way. There were no real rules of the road. But now there is this structure and organization to everything, and it is starting to frustrate me.

Close friends and family members, even the ones we'd expect would be interested in every detail of our journey, often display a polite disinterest in our storytelling. Some are too busy with their own lives to spare time for our tales. They quickly shuffle through photos with only occasional requests for elaboration. Others might interpret our vivid accounts of life abroad as a subtle judgment of their "boring" existence (especially if we begin every other sentence with "When I was in . . ."). Most simply find it difficult to enter into our field experience and maintain attention for anything longer than a quick summary. Caroline recalls:

> My biggest frustration was that it seemed that old friends just didn't care about me. I had only one good conversation about my trip. Most just asked me about my experience out of politeness. "So, how was Uganda?" I got tired of responding, "Oh, my trip was great!" when really that wasn't the whole truth. But all they wanted was a simple one- or two-line answer. Here I'd thought I was missing out on so much when I was gone. These reunions made me realize I was different.

The longer we've been away, and the more we've allowed realities abroad to affect us, the more likely we will feel like a stranger at home. Often it's a combination of signals—from polite disinterest to petty quarrels—that tell us, and those closest to us, that *something has changed.* We're not the same person who we were when we left. But then again, neither are they. While we were away, everyone else's life *also* moved on, albeit probably in different directions. When we come back together after months apart, the relationships may have grown closer or farther apart. Either way, they've changed. This is why we can't return home again. The people and place identified with home may still be there, but what we bring to them—and them to us—has moved.

Bringing the World Home

Making sense out of what we bring home lies at the center of educational travel. As Aldous Huxley once said, "Experience is not what happens to a man; it is what a person does with what happens to him" (1932, Introduction). We have doubtless met many new and fascinating people, been awed by what we've seen (both tragic and beautiful), and been stretched to our physical and emotional limits. The question is, *So what?* What does it all mean? How have we actually grown as a result, and what will we do with those changes now? If reentry is simply about readjusting ourselves to a former consciousness and lifestyle, what's the point of global learning in the first place?

At one point of his life, playwright W. Somerset Maugham voyaged to the Far East in search of personal renewal. He would later report, "I went looking for adventure and romance, and so I found them . . . but I found also something I had never expected. I found a new self." The greatest gift of travel was not in the places visited and the people met; it was in the transformed person he had become as a result of both. Maugham reminds us of how easy it is to return home with treasured memories but without significant shifts in the way we view the world, others, or ourselves. Distance and difference are merely fused into an aimless aesthetic experience. The result: a traveled passport and address book but an untraveled consciousness.

Chapter 6 described some of the factors—whether within us, within the host culture, or within the sponsoring program—that can influence the outcome of our travels. To that list we add yet another consideration: how we position ourselves back home. Although reentry styles are highly personalized, Théoret, Adler, Kealey, and Hawes (1979) suggest there is a continuum of three dominant patterns.

At one end of the continuum are the "reverting returnees"—those who, after returning home, distance themselves from their foreign experience and uncritically resume their predeparture lifestyle. Certain realities abroad may have provoked them, at least momentarily, to look within and question some firmly established perspectives and behaviors. But once they're back, the native soil of prior habits and peer "group think" prove too hard for new insights or commitments to take root.

At the other end are the "alienated returnees." Instead of simply reverting to the person they were before they left, alienated returnees find themselves either rejecting their home culture altogether or waging a single-handed campaign to change it in unrealistic ways. According to Janet Bennett (1993), their sense of alienation stems from the perception of themselves "as so unique they may be incapable of envisioning a peer group with whom they can relate" (p. 115). This helps to explain why those returning from intense cross-cultural ventures are often seen "huddling" together. Feeling between cultures and without a permanent "home," they find a psychological and emotional resting place in the company of those with whom they've shared common experience.

The third reentry style, and the one with the greatest potential for personal change, is the "integrative returnee." When asked the inevitable question, "How was your trip?" their reply moves the conversation beyond a mere travelogue of what they saw and heard and felt. They also speak of new world understandings and self-discoveries—and how both are being synthesized into a revised identity and lifestyle. In common with their reverting and alienated counterparts, integrative returnees may be acutely aware of the incongruity between their foreign experience and the regular routines of home. The difference is they refuse to either automatically revert to old ways or get stuck in an alienated mode of framing their home culture as all bad and their host culture as all good. They opt for something infinitely more educative: to allow the real dissonance they feel to awaken a courageous questioning of their essential self.

"I Didn't Expect That"

To use the bewilderment that commonly attends our journey home to educational advantage, we must first learn to put it in a proper cultural context. Fairly common, even predictable, situations back home may catch us by surprise and arouse intense anxiety. Why is this? Why do I feel so exhausted? Why does there seem to be so much excess and waste? And why do so many appear apathetic and narrow in their perspectives? Exploring answers to questions like these initiates a process of cultural analysis that, in turn, can lead us to take informed action in relation to troublesome conditions and behaviors. Attempts to actively resolve new annoyances and violated expectations are what lead us, consciously or unconsciously, into new perspectives and practices.

1. *I didn't expect to feel so physically and emotionally drained.* Cross-cultural study and service can be terribly draining. Many of the physical effects—like jet lag and lethargy, body lice and amoebas—may actually not be felt until after returning home. Consider breaking up your return in stages, stopping at one or two places en route to home. Then honor your travels by paying attention to your body and soul when you finally arrive. Schedule several days of rest—and a thorough medical checkup. Then try not to overschedule your days. Leave space for daily walks, solitude, and personal reflection as opportunities to sort out what is going on around you and how you are reacting to it. Recognize your emotional vulnerability and avoid making major life decisions until you are a bit more grounded.

2. *I didn't expect to feel so "foreign" back home.* Our world back home will appear changed in proportion to how much *we* have changed through our journeys. If you find yourself feeling somewhat out of step with others around you, consider that this is the experience of exiles the world over. In fact, you might try thinking of yourself as a newly arrived immigrant beginning to know the place for the first time. Take the same interest in familiars at home as you did in exotics abroad—what they're thinking about and hoping for. Travel often serves to awaken us to parts of our native world that we hardly recognized before. Explore these new realms through the pages of a journal or in conversation with a good friend or program advisor. Above all, appreciate that displacement and foreignness, though at times quite painful, is often the basis for deep personal change. Recall the ideal expressed by Hugh of Saint Victor in the 12th century: "Those who find their homeland sweet are still tender beginners; those to whom every soil is as their native one are already strong; but those who are perfect are the ones to whom the entire world is as a foreign land."

3. *I didn't expect to feel so bored back home.* There are few things as constantly stretching and stimulating as cross-cultural living. Back home we might expect that "fully alive" feeling to continue, only to find that our family and campus can't match it. As a result, we may feel restless

and bored, even depressed. This helps explain why some returnees cling to certain features of their life abroad; doing so prolongs the intensity of the foreign experience. In most cases, the antidote to feelings of "flatness" will not be to book a return trip immediately, but to involve oneself more deeply at home. Ask yourself: How might I use—or continue to develop—my cultural insights, my foreign language skills, and my passion for a better world? Frustration and boredom often come from feeling there is no way to apply what we've learned in the home environment. The final section of this chapter lists a number of potential outlets, both on campus and in the local community. Consider each of them with care. Remember: it is often in the restless minds of those not quite "at home" in familiar surroundings that the driving force for culture change is most luminously revealed.

4. *I didn't expect to feel so critical toward my own country, and toward some of my friends and family.* Travel from one culture to another often results in a measure of estrangement from our own. Interacting with those whose identities and perspectives have been shaped by other cultural systems can push us to reconsider, often in disturbing ways, the views we hold of our own native land. Citizens of other nations may be quite critical, for example, of a western narrative of world history or of unsolicited intrusions into their political and economic life. Others will tend to see certain sides of reality that we, from our cultural standpoints, might either wish to deny or remain oblivious to. None of us are born critical of our homeland; to the contrary, our natural impulse is to doggedly defend it against perceived attack. It's only when new experiences or perspectives act to unsettle deep-seated certainties that we begin to probe the ways those core assumptions have been fixed in our consciousness. The fruit of this reflection can be a more enlightened and nuanced view of the good and the bad, the laudable and the shameful, both in our self and in our society.

5. *I didn't expect others to show such a lack of interest in hearing about my experiences.* One thing you can count on upon returning home: No one will be as interested in hearing your travel tales as you will be in sharing them. Once they've heard the highlights, most are ready for you to be your "old self" again. It's easy to interpret this as a personal rejection. However, it simply points to the fact that those without the same or

a similar experience *can't* relate except on a superficial level. The situation may be compounded by a shocking level of ignorance about the world, largely the result of shallow and, often, distorted images supplied by the mass media. "When you come back from the Third World to the West," Noam Chomsky (2002) writes in *The Common Good*, "you're struck by the narrowing of thought and understanding, the limited nature of legitimate discussion, the separation of people from each other. It's startling how stultifying it feels, since our opportunities are so vastly greater here" (p. 154). It isn't that people just don't care. They may need to be approached in the right way. Build realistic expectations. Prepare in advance to respond to surface questions, rehearsing distilled versions of your stories. Then, don't just *tell* them—*show* them by sharing photographs and artifacts, playing music, and preparing your favorite dishes. Above all, remember to save the best for yourself. "I swear I see what is better than to tell the best," wrote Walt Whitman, "It is always to leave the best untold."

6. *I didn't expect to have such a difficult time explaining how my experiences affected me.* Even with sympathetic listeners—those who invite you to share your inner journey in glowing detail—you may find it difficult to do so in a coherent manner. The "show-and-tell" of your trip is over, and you still haven't been able to communicate precisely how or why you feel a certain way. That's okay. Personal changes need time to incubate, to advance from isolated feelings to integrated understandings. Refrain from immediately trying to "sell" friends and family on new revelations acquired abroad. When given the chance, express gratitudes rather than platitudes. Especially resist the tendency to compare the best of the host culture with the worst aspects back home. Every culture has a mix of good and bad elements. When you're too critical of home or too lavish in praise of things foreign, you run the risk of losing your audience, as such remarks are usually laced with subtle judgments. Be as good a listener as a talker, attuned to ways of better understanding and acting on your experience. Realize that, in the end, explaining one's personal transformation is not nearly as important as living it.

7. *I didn't expect people to misunderstand me or see some of the "wrong" changes in me.* Some friends or family members may focus on superficial changes in your behavior or beliefs and seem put off by them. Why

doesn't Julia want to go shopping at the mall? Why won't Jason eat meat anymore? They may also be unprepared for some of the deeper changes that you're struggling to sort out. Monitor yourself, and try to be aware of the reactions of those around you, especially during the first few weeks. Some of those closest to you may fear that you've "gone native," rashly assimilating ideas and values from abroad that repudiate the habits of home. Others may be clueless as to the changed or expanded dimensions of your personality. The last thing an integrative returnee wants to hear on returning is, "You haven't changed at all!" Expect that most of the positive changes in your life will not be immediately obvious to others. They are likely to appear as "covert competencies," those novel and spontaneous responses to everyday situations that emerge, unannounced, over time from new ways of viewing one's self and the world (LaBrack, 1995).

8. *I didn't expect to feel so "homesick" for some of the people, places, and experiences in my host culture.* Just as you probably missed home for a time after arriving at your program site, it's just as normal to experience some longing for the people and places that you grew accustomed to, even if only for a few months. What we found most evocative abroad may be what we most hunger for now at home: a slower pace, the quaintness of local life, being the center of attention. Back home we're just "one of the crowd," quietly holding on to fragments of past experience. Activate your memory. Complete your travel journal or sketches. Organize photos, postcards, leaves, clippings, and other items gathered from your journey into an original collage or "memory box." Maintain phone or e-mail contact with your host family, internship staff, and foreign friends. Then follow your homesick feelings into your hometown. Visit ethnic restaurants, religious services, and performing-arts venues where treasured features of your host culture have taken root in local soil. Consider how you might weave another language, cuisine, and set of cultural traditions into the fabric of your life at home.

9. *I didn't expect to feel clueless as to any next steps to take—that is, how to really grow from my experiences.* New experiences don't automatically change us. They must be contemplated in relation to a horizon—a distant vision—that gives ultimate meaning to our actions. Unfortunately, the pace and pressures of "life in the fast lane" can easily frustrate attempts toward integration. When this happens, life-changing experiences get

compartmentalized. Like souvenirs or photo albums kept in a shoebox, only occasionally do they get taken out and looked at. Especially if you've been immersed in extreme circumstances, chances are you'll return home with more questions than answers. Lack of closure surrounding complex and disturbing issues—like infectious disease, the status of women, and political corruption—can actually stimulate deeper learning, provided you are intentional about pursuing them. Seek understanding. Take time to educate yourself about the root causes of pressing problems, either through personal study or a well-structured reentry course. Doing so will help you to develop a more unified mental framework for organizing and integrating your learning.

10. *I didn't expect to feel so in between cultures, not sure what the "new me" should be.* Psychologist Peter Adler (1975) once commented that the intercultural experience begins with "an encounter of another culture and evolves into the encounter with the self" (p. 18). As returnees we often complain of identity confusion, of not being sure who we are or should be. For months we've attempted to accommodate the ways of a foreign culture. Now, some of the things we've always taken for granted may seem unimaginable luxuries—like 20-minute showers and $20 restaurant meals. Because people tend to act in ways that are consistent with their conceptions of self, what are we to do when our identity is no longer rooted in just one set of cultural realities?

The most common response is to reduce the internal bind by simply readopting old definitions of self. But there is an alternative. We can choose to struggle through that bind toward a transformation of our life.

The Ambivalence of Home

In *Return to Laughter*, anthropologist Elenore Bowen (1964) documents the long and winding journey of self-scrutiny that adaptation to a radically different culture entails. She concludes that, in the end, "it's not enough to be true to oneself. The self may be bad and need to be changed, or it may change unawares into something strange and new. I had changed" (p. 290). The metamorphosis begins within us but it potentially extends well beyond us—to our family, peer group, and the broader society in which we were born and bred.

Once we return home, reconciling the new with the old takes on a special urgency that only intensifies the greater the degree of cultural dissimilarity that needs to be renegotiated. An art major setting out solo to learn the intricate process of batik in an Indonesian village is likely to return home in a much different state of mind than her counterpart who spent a semester partying in Prague with 25 other co-nationals. Among other things, we'd expect the art student to return home with a renewed appreciation for the many consumer choices, political freedoms, and opportunities for self-advancement that she may have previously taken for granted.

At the same time, she may also find herself painfully out of step with certain aspects of "home" that she now regards with some disdain: long, bumper-to-bumper commutes; 50-hour workweeks spent in a sterile cubicle; and the ubiquitous nighttime ritual of being "amused to death" in front of a television or computer screen. Having inhabited an alternative way of life for several months, these normal features of modern urban culture are suddenly called into question. Scenes from her Indonesian journey continue to replay in her mind: the relative absence of motorized vehicles, terraced paddy fields on gently sloping hills, handmade furniture and clothes, and age-old traditional stories retold for hours on end. What is she to do with these images, and with any wisdom they might evoke?

Having made a deep emotional investment in another culture, we can't be expected to simply "blend" back home. I've known travelers who, on return, wanted to immediately divorce their car, kill their television, and stop consuming anything that wasn't either free or fair-traded. For my part, after two years living in an Indian village, I couldn't bring myself to "waste" a fresh paper towel from a restaurant dispenser to dry my hands. Instead, I rummaged the trash bin for one half-used.

Not that all of those returning from high-immersion programs are so conflicted. Many manage to keep their recent experience alive by revisiting people and places through photo albums or travel journals. Others don national garb, adopt the habit of removing their shoes upon entering a home, and decorate their room with indigenous artifacts. Attempts like these to preserve prized parts of the host culture in our consciousness often confuse well-meaning parents and friends. It looks to them that we're simply trying to avoid or deny the inevitable process of "fitting in" back home. But what appears to others as mild neuroses may actually signify a profoundly personal project: to reconstruct a style of life that transcends the "maddening" aspects of home. Christofi and Thompson (2007) report on Susan, a study-abroad student recently returned from Cyprus:

> I had this almost panicky feeling at the pit of my stomach, like someone was grabbing my gut. . . . I had this kind of feeling deep down that I'd made a mistake and "Oh my God, what do I do now?" . . . And then there's my parents who are excited that I'm there, and they're happy that I'm there, and it's so hard to say to them, "Um, you know, I really don't like it here." (p. 57)

Susan's deep ambivalence toward "home" reminds me of British psychiatrist R. D. Laing's (Laing & Esterson, 1964) contention that those who suffer a psychological breakdown (and are often labeled "mad" or "schizophrenic" by society) may actually be taking the first step toward a cultural breakthrough. Their refusal to surrender to prefabricated identities and lifestyles becomes an incipient assertion of true sanity.

Of course, what is "mad" and "sane" is always defined within a particular cultural context. How, we might ask, can we be certain as to who, really, has become mad—us or our home society? Questions like this occupied the life of Algerian philosopher Albert Camus. He once described his birth as taking place "halfway between poverty and the sun"—never completely removed from the struggle and insecurity of his poor childhood in north Africa, though ever reminded of the nearness of life-giving beauty by the Mediterranean basin where he resided. In Camus' mind, despair about life and love of life were experientially fused. Many of us can bear witness to the same confounding mixture of sadness and brightness, tragedy and triumph in the places we've lived. Ironically, the bitter injustices we observe are often what energize passionate intellectual journeys into realities "we can't explain, or explain away" (Iyer, 2004, p. 7). Near his life's end, Camus himself would write, "I feel humility in my heart of hearts only in the presence of the poorest lives and the greatest adventures of the mind. Between the two is a society I find ludicrous" (1968, p. 7).

Far from being a sign of maladjustment and failed perception, then, the "unfinished business" that commands our consciousness should be seen as the doorway to transformative learning. "I know in my own case," admits Iyer (2004), "that a trip has really been successful if I come back sounding strange even to myself; if, in some sense, I never come back at all, but remain up at night unsettled by what I've seen" (p. 8). In the end, to "never come back at all" is to allow the comfortable and protected life of home to play against the backdrop of those we've known who are sick, insecure, mistreated. Instead of shutting out the unsettling images and memories, we choose to widen our circle of concern, to feel the burden, and to allow it to affect our choices.

Thriving at the Margins

Under the streets of London, in the "tube" stations, a recorded voice repeats three words every time a train or subway pulls into the terminal: "Mind the gap!" The warning refers to the hazardous space between the station platform and the train door that can imperil unaware commuters. As homecomers, we face a gap no less precarious. We can allow our state of cultural in-between-ness to lead us into either painful isolation or positive integration.

On the one hand, we bear the imprint of our home culture: its language, traditions, social roles, and systems of belief. Coping with the demands of life back home requires that we rely on the codes and conventions of this inherited way of life, much of which we hold dear. On the other hand, we are pressed to come to terms not only with what we've grown to respect and value in our host culture, but also with certain elements in our home culture that have been called into question. Long ago, Everett Stonequist (1937) described in *The Marginal Man* our predicament as "poised in psychological uncertainty between two social worlds, reflecting in [our] soul the discords and harmonies, repulsions and attractions of these worlds" (p. 8). How does one bear the burden of an identity continuously "under construction" within spaces where one never feels completely "at home"?

The strain of living on the margins of two or more cultures has long been acknowledged by saints and sociologists alike.[1] Marginal figures feel themselves to be outside the chatty world of most other natives, and can even suffer estrangement from former intimates. They are, in Edward Said's (1994) words, "beset with half-involvements and half-detachments" (p. 36). But marginality can be as much a creative force as a social burden. Relative to others in their cultural milieu, marginal characters often possess a wider horizon, a keener awareness, and a more critical outlook.

Instead of simply thinking how one is *supposed to* think, and doing what one is *supposed to* do, marginal persons exhibit a restless curiosity to question *why*. Why, for instance, are so many people—rural peasants and urban pieceworkers, street vendors and rag pickers, sex workers and street kids—left homeless in the new global economy? And why, when we dare ask that question, do so many people blithely respond, "That's just the way it is"? For marginals, pat answers rarely suffice. They know, especially with the weight of firsthand experience, that the contrasts between the richest and the poorest segments of humanity are not predetermined and irreversible "facts of life." Rather, they are contingent realities that resulted, to a large extent, from real choices made by real persons throughout history.

Those who dare to live at the margins make a unique contribution to cultural renewal by challenging what is "obvious" and "natural" to others from a broader, more comparative perspective. But this special, culture-shaping vocation cannot be realized alone. Changes in personal identity and social perspective require the support of peers and role models. Unless there is a critical mass of others with similar experiences and questions, it's only a matter of time until much of our field experience will become dormant. We, too, will either regress into the old (as the "reverting returnee") or surrender to a sense of cynical powerlessness (as the "alienated returnee").

Our challenge, as *integrative* returnees, is to think and act in ways that enrich and enlighten both others and ourselves. Not only must we be able to alternate between cultural frames of reference; we must also learn to appropriately apply new values to novel situations. A first step in this direction is to resist the temptation to see our global learning as only a private benefit and not also a public good. Begin to ask, What can I do to *continue* my journey in ways that serve the commonweal?

Hidden Within the Linings

Legend has it that when Marco Polo and his father rode into Venice after 24 years in Asia, they were not even recognized because of their tattered garments. To prove that they were indeed the Polos, they dramatically ripped open the linings of their ragged coats. Out spilled jade, diamonds, and precious gems collected from their far-flung travels. What about you? What "precious gems" are sewn within the linings of *your* experience? How might what's been gifted to you come to gift others through intelligent, meaningful actions expressed on campus, in the community, and in your personal life? This chapter closes with eight ideas.

1. *Help internationalize your campus.* Colleges and universities are increasingly trying to reengineer themselves, both intellectually and institutionally, to deal with new and portentous global realities (Altbach & Knight, 2007). In the enterprise commonly known as "internationalization," perhaps one of the most underutilized resources are foreign students and study-abroad returnees—those who are learning to perceive, think, and value "outside the box" of their national and cultural heritage. Rather than wait for a formal invitation to share your "precious gems," seize the opportunities placed in front of you. At lunchtime, purposely seek out those from other cultures to "break bread" with. Consider writing an article for the campus newspaper that addresses a global issue of particular interest to you. Offer to discuss the struggles and achievements of your journey with those enrolled in a special prefield orientation or cross-cultural training class. Reciprocate the hospitality shown to you as a foreigner by becoming a "cultural mentor" for an international student, perhaps from your host country. And talk to your major advisor about a special project that follows up on critical questions related to your international experience; independent study courses exist in virtually every major.

2. *Rediscover "place" in your local community.* Journeys *across the globe* ultimately prepare—and impel—us to see *around the block* with new eyes. Every domestic community offers us opportunities to cross borders of difference and join others in their daily struggles for better health care, housing, group relations, or education. In doing so, we position ourselves

not only to apply what has been learned abroad, but to also discover strands of beauty and truth within next-door nations that can be woven into a richer, more world-wise personal character. Following graduation, some study-abroad returnees find other like-minded souls to put down roots with as an "intentional household," mingling their collective lives with residents of a marginal community. Others organize a "Traveler's Tales" series that they take to middle schools and senior-citizen centers. All of us have special talents and know-how that can advance the common good in partnership with local organizations. Whether through an after-school program, at a migrant center or a women's shelter, or in one of hundreds of other local groups, opportunities abound to serve side by side with those who model local responses to global problems.

3. *Cultivate primal joys.* Take time to recall the people you met abroad whose lives expressed the things worth loving in this world: local rootedness, a foundational faith, manual work, interdependent relations, artistic expression, compassionate service, and reverence for the natural world. Remind yourself of how these primal pleasures were able to flourish without relentless media distractions and diversionary entertainments (such as expensive vacations, recreational shopping, and clubbing). Look for ways to intentionally integrate these values and virtues into your daily routines and interactions. Find a small, faith-centered "village" where ordinary folk experience conviviality and community. Create things you love that also contribute something meaningful to the world. Plant a garden. Prepare a meal from scratch. Start a bedtime ritual of reading or meditation. Help to create an "alternative path" that is mindful, purposeful, and joy filled.

4. *Discern vocation.* Novelist Frederick Buechner (1973) reminds us that true vocation is that place "where your deep gladness and the world's deep hunger meet" (p. 95). Altruistic forms of travel enable us to engage with the world's deep hunger, even as they help us to recognize the types of experiences that make us truly come alive. Sorting out personal passions and life pathways often takes years of patient experimentation with assorted life projects and encounters. The act of homecoming is just one of many points in our life journey where we are primed to actively reflect on the world, to clarify our deepest values and aspirations, and to contemplate ways to connect our happiness with the happiness of others.

5. *Embrace a sustainable lifestyle.* One of the potential benefits of educational travel, particularly in resource-poor areas, is the opportunity to try on ways of life with relatively low environmental impacts. Some of us have lived with families that used very little electricity, washed clothes by hand, bathed with a bucket of water, and ate food that was locally grown. Will we allow the daily lifestyle adjustments we made abroad to impact the way we live our lives back home? Before venturing an immediate response, consider that most of us are wealthy enough—relative to the cost of water, electricity, fuel, and food—that our consumption is largely constrained not by financial capacity, but by our habitualized appetites. In other words we can afford *not* to adjust our lifestyles.

We also know that short-lived deprivations are rarely enough to prompt a thorough reexamination of the culture of consumption etched within our psyche and behavior. The best chance for deep and enduring change is to allow those we lived with and were loved by to continue to shape us. Some of us will have entered so empathetically into the world of our hosts that we now find ourselves a divided person—at once irreversibly tied to the world of privilege *and* emotionally related to the feelings and experiences of others in radically different social and economic circumstances. Certain questions may continue to vex us: How do I now relate to those I left behind—ones who can only dream of the opportunities and options I take for granted? Is it hypocritical to have nice things and also want to act justly toward the materially poor? How can I keep from acquiescing to a style of life that is "normal" for me but damages both the earth and distant neighbors? Difficult questions like these can actually be the labor pains of a more "sustainable" life—one that contributes to a more humane and environmentally sound world community, present and future. But in order to actually bring that life to birth, we must move from *sympathy* as mere emotional closeness to *solidarity*—a full commitment of the will to the well-being of earth and human others. This may require that we push the "reset" button on some ingrained habits.

6. *Reduce junk-food consumption.* One of the best ways to reduce our collective impact on the earth is to reduce our consumption of junk food. Throughout the affluent West, but also in much of the third world, processed foods loaded with refined sugar, white flour, saturated fat, and salt

are contributing to skyrocketing rates of obesity, heart disease, and type 2 diabetes. "For the first time in history," writes Jane Lorimer, "the poor are fat and the rich are thin" (2006, p. 26). The earth also suffers under an industrialized food-production system in which two thirds of the earth's available agricultural land—including some of the world's most biologically diverse regions—is dedicated to raising animals and their feed crops to satisfy the global demand for a meat-rich diet. In the process, unsustainable amounts of petroleum and water are being used. By just reducing junk-food consumption we could have a dramatic impact on packaging-waste, land use, and fuel consumption, not to mention our health and cheerfulness. Experiment with buying good, local, and unpackaged produce from a farmers market. Then consult *Diet for a Small Planet* by Frances Moore Lappe for guidance in preparing flavorful meals that are low in fat, high in fiber, and enable us to live lightly on the land.

7. *Ride a bicycle.* Bicycles outnumber cars on our planet by two to one, providing mobility for low-income people, with minimal environmental impact and small investment demands. It is, hands down, the world's most efficient conveyance, using less energy per passenger-mile than any other form of transportation, and with negligible operating costs. No wonder western cities are increasingly turning to bicycles for police patrols and messenger services. Bicycles provide a flexible means of personal transportation while also reducing congestion, pollution, and traffic-related stress. And bicycle commuters consistently report being happier, more alert, and more productive than average.

For a growing number, the bicycle also signifies a convivial "movement" for change—one that is nonhierarchical, anticonsumerist, artistic, intensely local, and technologically self-sufficient. "The bicycle is the vehicle of a new mentality," says James McGurn, author and cyclist. "It quietly challenges a system of values which condones dependency, wastage, inequality of mobility and daily carnage [and] provides little scope for self-aggrandisement, consumerism or big-business profit" (1987, p. 193). No doubt this is some of what inspired British author H. G. Wells to remark, "When I see an adult on a bicycle, I do not despair for the future of the human race."

8. *Discover the joy of less.* Whoever it was who suggested "the greatest wealth is to live content with less" no doubt found himself or herself at

odds with the heart of urban industrial society: natural resource exploitation, endless commodity production, and conspicuous consumption. The "modern way of life," for all its perceived benefits, fails to deliver on its promise of deep meaning and fulfillment in life.[2] When generalized to the rest of the world, the demands of a fossil-fuel-based, automobile-centered, throwaway economy clearly surpass the earth's regenerative capacity (Brown, 2009; McKibben, 2007). And, contrary to popular perception, the environmental costs of our turbocharged lifestyle won't be ameliorated simply through the "breakthrough" technologies that enable us to continue living ever larger—except now with plug-in hybrid cars, Energy Star–rated appliances, and larger recycling bins. To move civilization onto an environmentally sustainable path, our fundamental ways of thinking and consuming must change. In short, we need to discover the joy of less by embracing an ethic of *enough*.

For many of us, "enough" is a deeply subversive idea. Against the grain of the broader culture, it calls us to act on the uniquely human capacity for *self-restraint*. It turns out that one of the best things the well off can do to practice meaningful solidarity with the working poor is to live simply and share resources—to use no more than our "fair share" of the earth's nonrenewable resources. We already know what to do: Adopt an uncluttered lifestyle. Give away or sell clothes, books, and other items that are seldom used and could be used productively by others. Then buy only those products that are durable, functional, and nonpolluting in their manufacture and use. Radically reduce fossil-fuel consumption by downsizing house size and putting tight restrictions on auto and air travel. Install low-flow showerheads with a shutoff button (allowing you to turn off the water when soaping). Substitute ceiling fans for air conditioners, and clotheslines for dryers. Resist brand names, and learn to use clothes and other things until they actually wear out. Take the money saved and invest it in community projects that strengthen collective assets (e.g., education, water, medical supplies) without fostering dependency. Dedicate one day each week to personal renewal, without shopping or watching movies. Take it one step further and undertake a 24-hour e-media "fast": no television, computers, cell phones, video games, or iPods from one sunrise to the next. During this time, get in touch with how a hyperreal world of instant messages and downloads, along with nonstop entertainment, acts to distract our attention and numb our ability to think about the world as it really is. Small acts like these, one day at a time, by millions of people can help reverse the pervasive logic of "more" that leads to the exploitation of persons and the destruction of nature.

"But can the habits ingrained in my old self really change?" you ask. Try to think of a habit as a stream that always seeks the shortest route downward (gravity permitting), cutting into even the deepest rock over time. Doing anything consistently enough cuts a deep gorge into our psyche. This is why it is so difficult for people to get off junk food or shorten their showers after years of habit formation. To change a deep-rooted habit, you must take steps to *divert the stream*—that is, to consciously form a new habit. By making a conscious change in behavior, you begin to dig a new channel in your psyche. New neural pathways are created in the brain, making it easier to initiate that action the next time, and the next.

Conclusion

We have now come full circle—from predeparture decisions concerning where, why, and how we will journey, to finally being reintegrated into our families, colleges, and communities. Travel abroad, especially when structured to achieve college-level educational goals, can signal an important transition from youth to adulthood. Anthropologist Victor Turner (1975) spoke of such rites of passage as "liminality," a state of being "neither here nor there . . . betwixt and between the positions assigned and arrayed by law, custom, convention, and ceremony" (p. 95). The experience of being "neither here nor there," though unsettling, provides unlimited possibilities for constructing a consciousness that transcends a single identity or parochial loyalty. We may ultimately find it impossible to *not* be at home *somewhere*. At the same time, we need not begrudge our temporary sense of rootlessness. Consider the insight of exile Theodor Adorno that "it is part of morality not to be at home in one's home" (in E. Said, 1990, p. 365). Despite the perils and conflicts, being suspended between two cultures confers the rare ability to reframe our own sense of "home" by understanding the ways others imagine it. The long, slow, and hard work of acquiring cross-cultural understanding ultimately finds its payoff in our ability to think and live from a hybrid consciousness, and then to use this special aptitude to make a positive difference in the world.

FOR REFLECTION AND DISCUSSION

1. Having now returned to your native land, where do you find yourself emotionally and psychologically in relation to "home": more deeply invested (i.e., patriotic), more disinvested (i.e., dissident), or more dislocated and rootless (i.e., nomadic)? What do you *want* and *need* "home" to be?
2. How do you feel about the prospect of uncritically resuming your predeparture lifestyle to the point that it becomes "home" again, and the relationships and insights from your foreign experience fade?

Notes

1. Various concepts have sought to capture the condition of being physically present in, but not psychologically committed to, any one cultural system, rendering one able to combine elements from two or more cultures without negative consequences to group distinctiveness or individual identity. These terms include the apostle Paul's *sojourners and exiles* (I Peter 2:11), Robert Park's *marginal man*, Georg Simmel's *stranger*, Thorstein Veblen's *social marginality* and *intellectual iconoclasm*, W. E. B. DuBois's *double consciousness*, Thurgood Marshall's *double vision*, Victor Turner's *liminality*, Edward Said's *exiles*, Jane Bennett's *constructive marginals*, and David Hollinger's *postethnic perspective*.

2. "Hedonics" (happiness) researchers like Daniel Kahneman (*Well-Being*), Jonathan Haidt (*The Happiness Hypothesis*), Eric Weiner (*The Geography of Bliss*), Dan Gilbert (*Stumbling on Happiness*), Martin Seligman (*Authentic Happiness*), Greg Easterbrook (*The Progress Paradox*), Alan Durning (*How Much Is Enough?*), Richard Lyard (*Happiness*), and Mihaly Csikszentmihalyi (*Flow*) reach a similar conclusion: For truly happy people, "standard of living" does not neatly equate with "quality of life." Up to about $10,000 per capita income, money

consistently buys happiness. Past that point the correlation evaporates: More money and more stuff fail to deepen individual satisfaction and life fulfillment.

References

Adler, P. (1975). The transitional experience: An alternative view of culture shock. *Journal of Humanistic Psychology, 15,* 13–23.

Altbach, P., & Knight, J. The internationalization of higher education: motivations and realities. (2007). *Journal of Studies in International Education, 11(3–4), 290–305.*

Bennett, J. (1993). *Cultural marginality: Identity issues in intercultural training.* In M. Paige (Ed.), *Education for the intercultural experience* (pp. 109–135). Yarmouth, ME: Intercultural Press.

Bowen, E. S. (1964). *Return to laughter: An anthropological novel.* New York: Anchor Books.

Brown, L. (2009). *Plan B 4.0: Mobilizing to save civilization.* New York: W.W. Norton & Company.

Buechner, F. (1973). *Wishful thinking.* New York: Harper & Row.

Campbell, J. (1968). *The hero with a thousand faces.* Princeton, NJ: Princeton University Press.

Camus, A. (1968). *Lyrical and critical essays.* New York: Vintage Books.

Chomsky, N. (2002). *The common good.* Boston: Odonian Press.

Christofi, V., & Thompson, C. (2007). You cannot go home again: A phenomenological investigation of returning to the sojourn country after studying abroad. *Journal of Counseling & Development, 85*(1), 53–63.

Fussell, P. (1987). *Norton book of travel.* New York: W.W. Norton.

Huxley, A. (1932). *Texts and pretexts: An anthology of commentaries.* London: Chatto and Windus.

Iyer, P. (2004). *Sun after dark: Flights into the foreign.* New York: Knopf.

LaBrack, B. (1995). Uncovering "hidden skills" after study abroad. *Educational Perspectives, 29*(1), 9–13.

LaBrack, B. (1996, November 11). *The dual ethnocentric: Why study abroad may not lead to internationalism.* Paper presented at the 49th International Conference of the Council on International Educational Exchange, Monterey, CA.

Laing, R. D., & Esterson, A. (1964). *Sanity, madness and the family.* London: Penguin Books.

Lorimer, J. (2006, November). Fast food, obesity and ill health: The urgent need to shift from chemical-based to real foods. *Positive Health, 129,* 26–32.

McGurn, J. (1987). *On your bicycle: An illustrated history of cycling*. New York: Facts on File Publications.

McKibben, B. (2007). *Deep economy: The wealth of communities and the durable future*. New York: Holt.

Said, E. (1990). Reflections on exile. In R. Ferguson, M. Gever, T. Minh-ha, & C. West (Eds.), *Out there: Marginalization and contemporary cultures* (pp. 357–366). Cambridge, MA: MIT Press.

Said, E. W. (1994). *Representations of the intellectual: The 1993 Reith lectures*. New York: Vintage.

Stonequist, E. (1937). *The marginal man: A study of personality and culture conflict*. New York: Russell & Russell.

Storti, C. (1990). *The art of crossing cultures*. Yarmouth, ME: Intercultural Press.

Théoret, R., Adler, N., Kealey, D., & Hawes, F. (1979). *Re-entry: A guide for returning home*. Hull, Quebec: Canadian International Development Agency.

Turner, V. (1975). *Dramas, fields, and metaphors: Symbolic action in human society*. Ithaca, NY: Cornell University Press.

INDEX

social, 87–89
spiritual, 92–94
and travel, 71–96
misunderstandings, on return, 214–215
money, 116–117
  orientation on, 193
money belt, 113, 116
  packing, 120
moral purpose, 43
Morris, Jan, xii
Moyo, Dambisa, 23
muggings, 110–111
Mumford, Lewis, 50

Nash, James, 90
neck wallet, 113, 116
  packing, 120
New Global Citizens, 30
non-western, term, 12
Norberg-Hodge, Helena, 86
North. *See* First World
Nouwen, Henri, 64–65
nutrition, poverty and, 18

Oberg, Kalvero, 176n1
O'Grady, Ron, 76
Omidyar, Pam and Pierre, 29
online searches, precautions with, 132–133
organizing principle, need for, 43–44
orientation, 178–203
  arrival tips, 179–181
  exercises for, 193–197
  formal, 181–182
  resources for, 202
  settling in, 181–182
Osborne, Lawrence, 2
other, attitudes toward, 56–59
Otteson, Paul, 182

packing, 119–125
Page, Larry, 29
Palmer, Parker, 54
paradox. *See* culture shock
passports, 106–107
Paul Simon Study Abroad Foundation Act, 28
Pavese, Cesare, 55–56
pepper spray, 123

personal traits, and cultural adaptation, 168–170, 169*t*
phrasebook, 123–124
phrase search, 134
plug adaptor, 124
politics, research on, 137
Potts, Rolf, 86–87
poverty, 15–17
  approaches to, 28–32, 31*f*
  aspects of, 31
  connections with, 62–63
  global consensus on, 29
  new, 21–24
  and travel, 76–77, 82–84
power of attorney, 119
power relations, 34
  analysis of, 87–89
  questioning, 59–63
  values and, 48
preparation, 97–126
  for health risks, 107–109
  importance of, 98
  mental, 98, 127–150
  personal details, checklist for, 117–119
primal joys, cultivation of, 222
programs, type of, 99–101
Putnam, Robert, 9–10

query, 144
questions, postponing, 185

Rabinow, Paul, 130
Ray, Paul, 47
receipts, and insurance, 109
reconnaissance. *See* exploration
records, 142
recovery, in transformation, 161–163
redemption story, 46–49, 53
reentry shock, 204–208
  analysis of, 211–216
regions, 135, 136*t*
religion
  research on, 137
  and story, 45
research, electronic, 131–149
responsibility, 14–39
  Havel on, 37